THE BRM GUIDE TO BUILDING YOUR FIRST MODEL RAILWAY

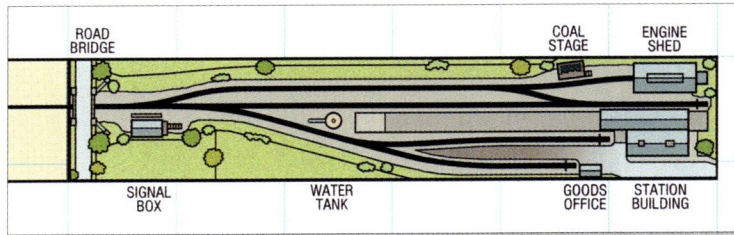

Welcome to the **BRM** *Guide To Building Your First Model Railway*. Inside this publication we'll be taking you step-by-step through the creation of a modest model railway layout we've called 'Edgeworth'.

When you look at layouts in magazines or at exhibitions you see the culmination of many, many hours of work. Those models aren't built by supermen, they are just people who have plugged away at their hobby. Mistakes have been made, bodges covered up and an awful lot of fun had along the way.

Unlike most similar guides, I'm working through a single project from start to finish. Construction involves picking up all the skills you would need for a much larger model - but using my own layout building experience, I'm going to make the case for starting small.

For simplicity, we're keeping things as simple as possible but if you want to do something different, we'll try and suggest alternatives to our methods where possible. If you want to discuss the layout and make your own suggestions, over on our forum **RMweb** too there is a thread for the layout where I'll try to answer your questions.

Starting from scratch, 'Edgeworth' should take around 12 to 18 months modelling time. By the end of this most people will have a model to be proud of and if they fancy it, something to display at a model railway exhibition. Even if you aren't a show-off like me, the finished article ought to be presentable when displayed at home, but I bet you can't resist proudly showing it to visitors, and why not!

You'll also be able to see other project layouts in the Practical **BRM** areas at exhibitions, so if you want to come along and waggle a point motor or prod at the plywood, be our guest. The main thing is to give it a go and find out just how enjoyable layout building can be.

Phil Parker

BRM Modelmaker & Writer

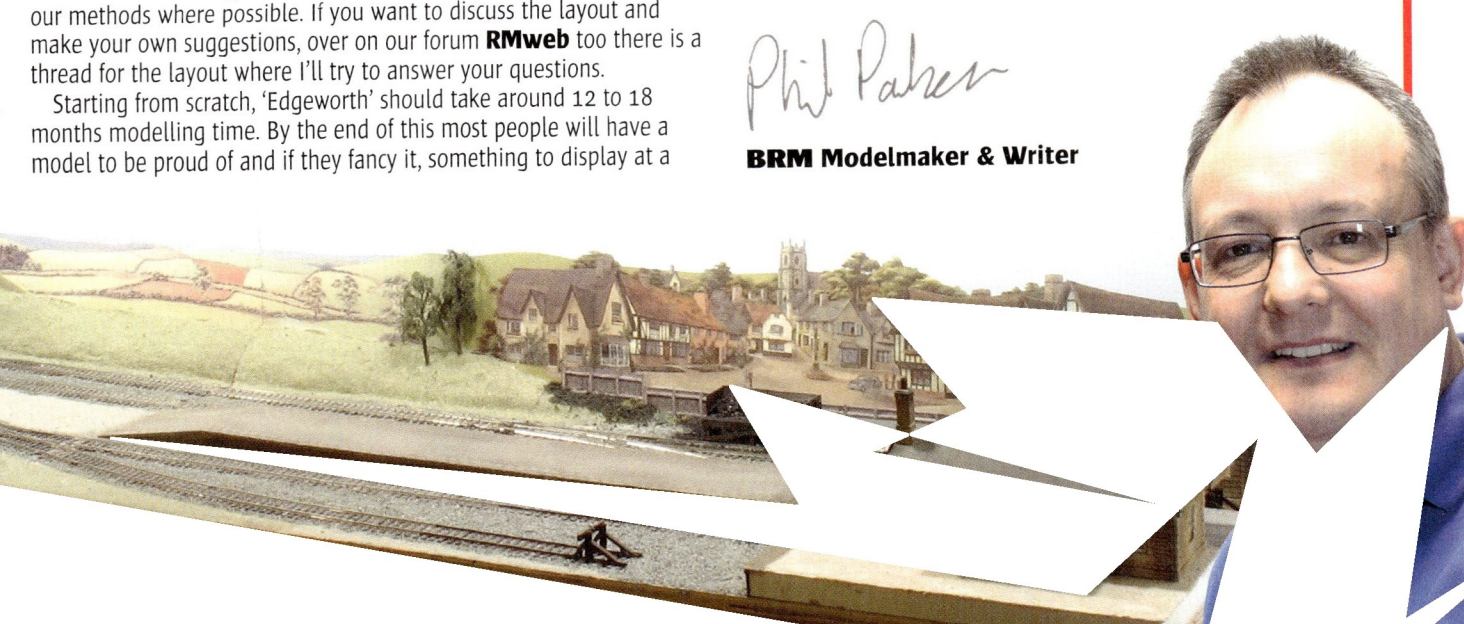

Lifetime Guarantee & Controller Types

Choose Your Controller for Life...

We have been producing Model Railway Controllers for 40 years. Our analogue controllers have stood the test of time, and so has our **lifetime guarantee**:

"We undertake to replace, free of charge, any parts found defective within the lifetime of the unit providing that the item has not been tampered with."

What's the difference between the controller types?

Our **Mains Powered Cased Controllers** come complete with transformer, and can just be plugged in, connected to the track, and away you go. **Panel Mounted Controllers** require a separate transformer, and also need to be mounted onto a control panel to be used effectively.

We also produce various controllers with **Feedback** and **Simulation**, two effects controlled by the controller itself. **Feedback** senses the load on the circuit and helps maintain the locomotive at a steady speed up and down gradients. **Feedback** controllers are not suitable for use with locomotives with coreless motors. **Simulation** (also known as Inertia) allows a train to accelerate, coast, and be braked to a standstill, by use of a regulator and a brake.

Mains Powered Cased Controllers

GMC-COMBI Single Track Controller/Transformer
Most Suited for HO/OO/N Scale Layouts

Fantastic for small layouts or beginners upgrading a starter set, the Combi has both a 12V DC output to run one track, and a 16V AC output for accessories.

BEST FOR Beginners

GMC-D Twin Track Controller
Most Suited to HO/OO/N Scale Layouts

Our best selling controller. Runs a two track railway with minimum of fuss. The D Controller has two 12V DC track outputs, as well as a 16V AC output for accessories.

BEST FOR Twin Tracks

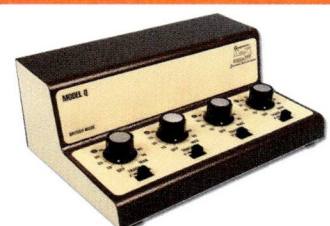

GMC-Q Four Track Controller
Most Suited to OO/HO/N Scale Layouts

The best selling four track mains powered controller available today. It offers impressive value for money with its four 12V DC track outputs, and two each of 16V AC and 12V DC outputs for accessories.

BEST FOR Four Tracks

Panel Mounted Controllers

GMC-100 Single Track Panel Controller
Most Suited to OO/HO/N/Z Scale Layouts

Some experienced modellers may wish to incorporate their controller into a panel they have made to control their layout. The Model 100 Controller has a single 12V DC output.

BEST FOR Control Panels

GMC-U Single Track Controller with Simulation
Most Suited to OO/HO/N/Z Scale Layouts

With the brake knob controlling the 12V DC track output, this controller allows you greater realism when running locomotives.

BEST FOR Realistic Running

Hand Held Controllers

GMC-W Single Track Walkabout Single Track Controller
Most Suited to OO/HO/N/Z Scale Layouts

Fitted with 1.5m of cable, this controller allows you the freedom to move around your layout while still controlling your layout. it has a single 21V DC track output.

BEST FOR Flexibility

PRICES

Full details of our Analogue Controller range can be found in the Gaugemaster Full Catalogue.

It also contains details of our Digital Controllers, Scenics, Point Control, Electrics and much more in the Gaugemaster range.

It also contains selected items from many of the other brands that we stock.

Code	Description	Price
GM353	Gaugemaster Full Catalogue	£3.95
GM354	Gaugemaster 2015 New Items Leaflet	FREE

Cased Controllers

Code	Description	Price
GMC-COMBI	Single Track Controller/Transformer	£39.95
GMC-100M	Single Track Controller	£84.95
GMC-100MO	Single Track Controller for O Scale	£84.95
GMC-10LGB	Single Track Controller for G Scale	£99.95
GMC-10LGB5F	Single Track Controller for G Scale with Fan	£169.95
GMC-P	Single Track Controller with Simulation	£99.95
GMC-D	Twin Track Controller	£94.95
GMC-DF	Twin Track Controller with Feedback	£99.95
GMC-DS	Twin Track Controller with Simulation	£164.95
GMC-TS	Three Track Controller with Simulation	£174.95

Panel Mounted Controllers (Orange text shows transformer required)

Code	Description	Price
GMC-100	Single Track Controller (GMC-T1/M1)	£34.95
GMC-100.O	Single Track Controller for O Scale (GMC-T2/M2)	£54.95
GMC-U	Single Track Controller with Simulation (GMC-T1/M1/WM1)	£44.95
GMC-UF	Single Track Controller with Feedback (GMC-T1/M1/WM1)	£39.95
GMC-UO	Single Track Controller with Simulation for O (GMC-T2/M2)	£59.95
GMC-UD	Twin Track Controller (GMC-T1/M1/WM1)	£54.95
GMC-UDF	Twin Track Controller with Feedback (GMC-T1/M1/WM1)	£59.95
GMC-UDS	Twin Track Controller with Simulation (GMC-T1/M1/WM1)	£69.95
GMC-UTS	Three Track Controller with Simulation (GMC-T1/M1/WM1)	£79.95
GMC-UQ	Four Track Controller (GMC-T1/M1/WM1)	£84.95

Walkabout and Hand Held Controllers
(All GMC-T1/M1/WM1)

Code	Description	Price
GMC-W	Single Track Walkabout Controller	£39.95
GMC-WS	Single Track Walkabout Controller with Simulation	£55.95
GMC-HH	Single Track Handheld Controller with Feedback	£39.95

Transformers

Code	Description	Price
GMC-M1	Cased Transformer 16V AC	£49.95
GMC-M2	Cased Transformer 18V AC 2.5V	£54.95
GMC-M3	Cased Transformer 24V AC	£54.95
GMC-M4	Cased Transformer 12V AC	£54.95
GMC-T1	Open Transformer 2x 16V AC 1a	£24.95
GMC-T2	Open Transformer 18V AC 2.5a	£24.95
GMC-T3	Open Transformer 24V AC	£24.95
GMC-T4	Open Transformer 2x 12V AC 1a	£24.95
GMC-WM1	Wall Mounted Transformer 16V or 12V DC 1.1a	£19.95

Did you know...

If you don't have a handy accessory output from a controller, the **GMC-WM1** Wall Mounted Transformer can be used on its own to power accessories such as point motors and lights from the 16V output. Just plug it in and connect it up!

THE BRM GUIDE TO BUILDING YOUR FIRST MODEL RAILWAY

CONTENTS

24 Introducing... **EDGEWORTH**
Here's a rundown of the layout that we're going to build throughout this guide.

36 HOW TO **WIRE THE LAYOUT**
Adding electricity to power locomotives and accessories isn't as complicated as it may appear. We guide you through wiring a simple layout.

82 THE BRM GUIDE TO BUILDING YOUR FIRST MODEL RAILWAY — HOW TO... **SCRATCH-BUILD A GOODS OFFICE**
This Goods Office is a great introduction to scratch-building and the perfect way to model on the cheap.

06 **THE WONDERFUL WORLD OF MODEL RAILWAYS**
Anyone can enjoy Railway Modelling, as *Phil Parker* explains.

10 **SCALES AND GAUGES**
Phil Parker explains how to decide what scale will work best for you. Decisions, decisions...

12 **PROTOTYPE INSPIRATION: STATIONS**
It's good practice to base various aspects on prototype locations. Here are a few stations I've collected for future projects.

22 **TRACKPLANS**
Layouts come in all shapes and sizes to suit locations. Here are a few to get you started.

28 **BASEBOARDS**
A solid base makes for a better layout. *Phil Parker* looks at the best options out there.

32 **LAYING TRACK**
Here are a few top tips to ensure that you lay your track correctly for smooth running.

42 **BALLASTING TRACK**
With track now down, we can turn our attention to ballasting and making track look more realistic.

44 **BACKSCENES**
A good quality backscene will add a large degree of realism to your layout. Here are the basics.

52 **PLATFORMS**
'Edgeworth' needs a platform. This is a guide on how we made ours the easy way.

54 **ROADS AND PAVEMENTS**
Roads can play an important part in defining model railways. Here are some from other layouts.

56 **ROAD VEHICLES**
Motor vehicles would have been scarce in the 1930s, but they're essential for layouts post 1940s.

68 **METCALFE GOODS SHED**
Here's a quick guide to building your very first card kit. Give it a go – you can't go wrong.

72 **STONE-BUILT ENGINE SHED**
It's time to build a home for your locomotives. Here's a simple solution using a Ratio plastic kit.

74 **STATION BUILDING**
Have you travelled by train to Glastonbury Festival? If so, you might recognise this station.

88 **HEDGES AND FENCES**
Here's our simple, step-by-step guide to building fencing for layouts.

90 **FIELDS AND UNDERGROWTH**
It's time for 'Edgeworth' to go all green as we model fields and undergrowth.

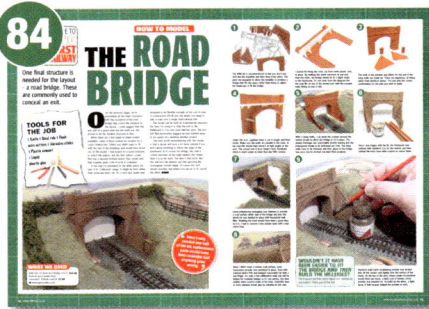

84 HOW TO MODEL **THE ROAD BRIDGE**

42 HOW TO **BALLAST TRACK**
With the track laid, on it moves to ballasting. Here's our simple guide to giving your track a more realistic look.

48 HOW TO MODEL **HILLSIDES & RETAINING WALLS**
It's time to start landscaping the layout. Follow this guide to make your lightweight hillsides with detailed retaining walls.

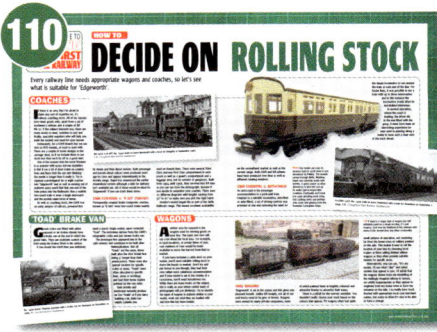

110 HOW TO **DECIDE ON ROLLING STOCK**
Every railway line needs appropriate wagons and coaches, so let's see what is suitable for 'Edgeworth'.

THE BRM GUIDE TO BUILDING YOUR FIRST MODEL RAILWAY

THE WONDE
MODEL

Anyone can enjoy railway modelling, as **Phil Parker** explains.

If your views are influenced by popular television drama then you're probably thinking of a slightly weird, middle-aged loner sitting in his loft wearing a tired and dirty cardigan. He's muttering to himself and fiddling with a huge train set with *Mallard* thrashing around next to an HST. If that drama is a 'whodunnit?', then the police will soon burst in and arrest them for some terrible crime.

While this hackneyed description might apply to a few people in our hobby - hopefully without the criminal bit - in reality modellers can be found in all walks of life. You'll find all ages, sexes and abilities represented, bound together by a common interest. I once sat in a pub after an exhibition with a group including two lawyers, a theatre manager, a physics professor, bus driver, local councillor and bishop - beat that for an eclectic mix!

All this is possible because of the incredible variety of subjects railway modelling encompasses. The enthusiast will turn their hand to a variety of skills when building a layout. For a start there's the planning. What sort of model do you want to build? Where will it live? Do you aspire to showing the model at exhibitions? Perhaps running nights with a group of friends operating a complicated system appeals more. Do you have access to a suitable room to leave the model set up or will it need to be built in stages with other work being carried out away from the model?

Next there's the subject to consider. Great Western branchline or up-to-date modern main line? Perhaps there's a station you remember fondly from years ago that would be pleasant to re-create in miniature? I usually find that a single

RFUL WORLD OF RAILWAYS

Gilbert Barnatt's 'Peterborough North' is the result of years of detailed research to ensure the trains, timetables, buildings and environment are authentic. ANDY YORK

photograph can inspire me regardless of how far back in history it comes from.

For many people, the desire to run a particular company's locomotives or rolling stock will guide their decision. It's not unheard of for a layout to be built around a single locomotive, the entire scene being created to give it somewhere to run.

Either way, for an accurate model, some research will be required and this can range from detailed work in a public record office to a day out with the family on a preserved railway line, snapping a few photographs along with the way.

If the modern day scene appeals then simply looking out of the window while taking a train journey might do the job but for those interested in eras that have passed into history, there's a surprising amount left to see in the present day. Many dockside warehouses are now fashionable apartments, but look carefully and there's plenty of evidence of their past life - something that can be said for many buildings.

Research can be so enjoyable it becomes a hobby in its own right, but for most of us it soon becomes time to leave the library and start work.

That usually means building some baseboards, requiring a modest level of carpentry skill. We aren't talking about fine furniture making but DIY-level woodwork. In later chapters, we'll look at the simplest way of assembling a suitable base for the model.

The next stage is tracklaying and wiring, two more aspects of the hobby that can form major interests. Some modellers see dealing with electricity as a step to get over with as quickly as possible, others enjoy time with soldering irons and switches. Be careful though because if

N gauge is particularly suited to modelling the modern railway scene with its long fixed formation passenger and freight trains. This is Glenrothes MRC's 'Blackwood Junction'.
NIGEL BURKIN

your fellow modellers find out you like wiring, you'll be called upon to provide help and could end up like one chap I met recently who has wired 20 complicated layouts for other people!

With everything working it's time to start on the more traditional model-making areas - scenery, buildings and rolling stock. Yet more skills to acquire, but ones that are fun and can be practised without too much worry. Sometimes you need to return to your childhood and relish the messiness that accompanies slopping plaster over a hillside and covering it with flock or static grass!

As well as being deeply satisfying, skills involving close-up work can be good for a modeller's health. Those who work with older people report that a hobby or interest, especially a creative one such as railway modelling, keeps minds active far better than passive activities such as watching television.

Railway modelling is, of course, a very creative activity. While there are many technical skills to be picked up, the modeller also needs a dose of artistic talent. Not necessarily the ability to paint a fine picture, but an appreciation of something looking 'right'. A layout should be pleasing to the eye, be it a bucolic country scene or gritty slice of urban life. There's no way to teach this but simply looking at real life and then at a model will help. You quickly pick up when something doesn't work, and then you find the ability to sort it out.

The need to pick up skills is the main hurdle to many who wish to build a layout. As a beginner everything looks difficult and you wonder how you'll manage. After all, very few of us have a background that saw any practical skills come our way through either education or work. However, this is the case in all walks of life.

Boiling an egg is the first step in learning to cook, a far more useful skill than building a railway. Learning to drive is another good example - how many of us stalled cars in our early days because the gear lever and clutch seemed impossible to manage? A similar number to those who now operate these same controls without thinking I suspect.

Just remember a couple of important points. Firstly, this isn't brain surgery. If you make a mistake with your modelling, the chances are no-one gets hurt. Maybe a model doesn't turn out as well as you might like, but then that's the way the world works. We all learn more by making mistakes than getting things right. The people who know this more than anyone are those 'expert' modellers you see at exhibitions and in the pages of magazines. I always say that a lot of the skill involved in this hobby isn't getting things right first time, but hiding the rectified bodges afterwards.

Modelling isn't necessarily a solitary process. While our 'typical' modeller mentioned previously might spend his time shut away in his loft, railway modelling can be a tremendously social activity.

In the UK alone, over 500 model railway exhibitions are held every year. Unless you live in a very remote part of the country, this means there will be several occasions each year where a modest journey will bring you in to contact with other enthusiasts. From village halls to the largest exhibition centres (see left), you'll find examples of every skill level on display along with people who will be only too happy to chat and explain how they carried out the various tasks required to produce a model. Alongside the exhibits will be traders, eager to lighten your wallet while providing the

Choosing an interesting and achievable subject for your layout is one of the most exciting parts of the process.
ANDY YORK

important supplies needed to advance any model.

Most of these exhibitions are organised by local model railway clubs and you'll normally find a group of people who share the same hobby and will welcome with open arms anyone with similar interests. To those who don't share an interest, a hobby can appear to be a strange way to spend time. Club members don't come with these issues, although you'll probably find railway company loyalties run strong with some of them.

Club membership gives access to a huge pool of information. If you have a problem, the chances are someone will already have encountered it and can explain how they solved it. Most clubs are pretty relaxed and over a cup of tea the railway-based banter will be fun even if it doesn't get any modelling done.

Don't feel you need to be an expert to join a club either. All levels of ability are welcome. If a member is making baseboards, someone willing to hold the end of a piece of wood being cut is more valuable than anything. A willingness to 'muck in' with aspects of a club will soon see new arrivals welcomed in to the fold.

In return, as well as the pool of information available, other opportunities will present themselves. My early trips out to shows operating layouts came this way. Several members were exhibiting layouts and needed extra operators occasionally. This saw me visiting events around the country and meeting even more modellers, including many of the famous names you read in print today.

Another advantage is the chance to become part of a team building a layout too large to consider at home. If scale-length express trains are your interest, club layouts might be the only chance you have to give your stock a good run. Even if you have the space, sharing the work with other people speeds progress and even allows you to specialise in an aspect that appeals to you more than others. If you really hate wiring for example, you'll probably be able to leave this to the club 'sparks' as he might not enjoy making buildings or working on the scenery as much as you do.

In addition to physical clubs, there are many groups and associations for specific interests such as individual railway companies or scales. These used to revolve around an in-house magazine or newsletter, but now often taken advantage of the internet to offer discussion forums and online information sheets to members.

Beyond this are virtual communities such as **RMweb** where thousands of enthusiasts meet up online to chat about the hobby. Many share the results of their efforts on the forum or in their own blogs, usually to the acclaim of other members who can appreciate the efforts and modelling.

The point is that this hobby can be anything you want it to be. From building a perfect scale recreation of a mainline station to a more impressionistic approach of a similar scene, or perhaps getting out in the garden with some live steam, even simply pinning track down to a board and watching the trains go by, there's something in railway modelling for everyone. Just remember, it's a hobby and should be relaxing.

Enjoy it. **BRM**

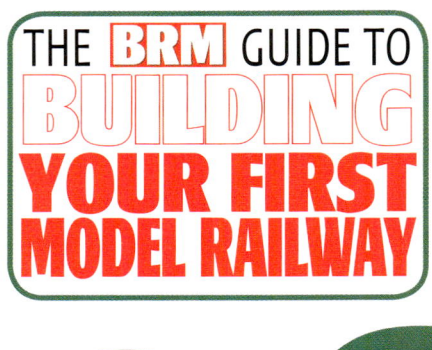

THE BRM GUIDE TO BUILDING YOUR FIRST MODEL RAILWAY

SCALES & GAUGES

Phil Parker explains how to decide what size of trains will be best for you.

One of the earliest decisions any modeller makes is which scale to work in. To a beginner the choice can be confusing with a myriad of options from the tiniest T Gauge to model engineering scales large enough to ride behind.

To make matters easier, we'll stick to the most popular in the UK, which happen to be the ones with the widest manufacturer support.

O GAUGE
7mm:1ft scale, Track gauge 32mm
The largest of the popular scales, O gauge was the most common scale for railway modelling until the 1940s. Then, as houses became smaller, people found it harder to fit a reasonable layout in and moved to smaller scales. In recent years, it has seen a revival as with more RTR items appearing. It's possible to build a small shunting layout in a normal room but if you want to operate long trains, it's probably better to join a model railway club.
Specialist Society - The Gauge O Guild
W www.gaugeoguild.com

OO GAUGE
4mm:1ft scale, Track gauge 16.5mm
By far the most popular scale in the UK with around 80% of the market. The history of scale is convoluted but has resulted in 1:76 scale models running on 1:87 scale (16.5mm gauge) track. This compromise doesn't satisfy everyone but it's been around too long for the manufacturers to change. There's very little you can't buy in the scale offering the modeller the widest choice of prototypes to model without resorting to kit-building, and making it perfect for the beginner.
Specialist Society - The Double O Gauge Association
W www.doubleogauge.com

OO is by far the most popular scale in the UK. It doesn't suit everyone, but is perfect for beginners.

Wisbech & Upwell tramway locomotives in (from left to right) O gauge, OO, 3mm scale and N gauge, showing some of the wide variety of sizes available to modellers.

Every scale/gauge has its advantages and disadvantages, it's just a case of finding out what suits your interests and requirements.

WHAT'S THE DIFFERENCE BETWEEN SCALE AND GAUGE?

Scale defines how large the models are compared to the real thing. Thus in a 4mm:1ft (1:76) scale model, every foot in length or height on the prototype is represented by 4mm on the model. A 6' tall man will be 24mm tall on the layout.

Gauge refers to the distance between the rails. For various historical reasons this isn't normally an accurate scaling down of real life on British N and OO models. OO gauge track for example scales out at 4' 1" wide - 7" narrower than it should be. Some modellers use 4mm scale but wider, more authentic track gauges (18mm or 18.83mm) to more accurately represent the prototype.

Modellers tend to treat the terms as interchangeable and most will understand if you say you are working in 'OO scale' even though it's not strictly correct.

TT GAUGE/3mm SCALE
3mm:1ft, scale, Track gauge 12mm

Introduced in 1957 by Tri-ang, TT stands for 'Table Top' indicating you could build a layout in an even smaller space than OO. Sadly, sales were not good enough for the scale to survive commercially once N gauge appeared on the market. However, there are modellers who still work in the scale and have developed kits to supplement RTR stock that is only available secondhand.

Specialist Society
The 3mm Society
W www.3mmsociety.org.uk

N GAUGE
2mm:1ft scale, Track gauge 9mm

The smallest popular British scale and supported by two major manufacturers as well as many cottage industries. In recent years, the quality and range of models has improved immensely. For the space-starved or those who prefer to model a grand vista, it's the scale of choice.

Specialist Society – The N Gauge Society
W www.ngaugesociety.com

SO, HOW DO YOU DECIDE?

Firstly, have a good look at models in all the scales; ideally at an exhibition but if not, in magazines and online. If possible, chat to people working in each scale too.

The two main factors will probably be space and how confident you are as a modeller. Most people start by buying locomotives and rolling stock ready-to-run (RTR). This suggests either OO or N where the range of available items is greater. Should you prefer O gauge then you are going to find yourself making kits for many items. For many this is the appeal as your layout will look different to everyone else's but building it will take longer. As far as space goes, well if your plan won't fit the room using a large scale, you need a smaller one. Either that or change the plan.

It's often said that as modellers age and can't see the detail in smaller scales, they should move up to O gauge, however this isn't entirely true. While the bigger models are easier to see, they tend to have more detail which is just as small as the detail on the smaller models.

We've built 'Edgeworth' in OO as it's the most popular scale in the UK, there is a wealth of items ready to be used including many years of high-quality secondhand stock. Don't let this worry you though as we've heard of several modellers building the same layout in N gauge and all the techniques you'll find in this guide will work well in both.

THE BRM GUIDE TO BUILDING YOUR FIRST MODEL RAILWAY

PROTOTYPE

BEAMISH 1985

The North of England Open Air Museum at Beamish includes a station brought piece-by-piece from its original locations. The main building is from Rowley on the Stanhope & Tyne Railway, the signalbox from Carr House, the goods shed from Alnwick and the coal drops from West Boldon.

KYLE OF LOCHALSH 2008

Most books on Scottish railways usually include a photograph or two of this station. The main buildings haven't changed, but the track is much simpler than in steam days. The area to the right used to be sidings serving fishing boats at the quayside.

A Caledonian Railway 'Jumbo' under a Great Western water tower? It can only be a preserved line, in this case the Severn Valley Railway. If you wish to run locomotives from lots of different companies, then modelling a preserved railway is an excellent idea.

CRIANLARICH STATION 1997

Several West Highland Line stations in Scotland share similar architecture with island platforms, wooden shelters and signalboxes. The log traffic seen on the left is typical for the area, as is the terrible weather that can strike at any time!

ARLEY 2008

Many preserved railways go to extraordinary lengths to re-create stations as they would have been in the past. Modern commercial and safety considerations can mean changes have had to be made. While Arley is a very typical Great Western Station, were the platform edges painted white before the war? It would be worth checking old photographs to be sure.

INSPIRATION

When you come to build your model railway, it's good practice to base various aspects on prototype locations. Here are a few stations I've collected for future projects.

BEWDLEY 2011

WYE 1994

The platform shelter at Wye in Kent isn't very different from Hornby's R510 Platform Shelter - a model that's been in the range since the 1980s. On the opposite platform there is a more imposing brick-built main building and at one end of the site, a level crossing. During the Second World War there were extensive sidings, but these disappeared under housing years ago.

www.model-railways-live.co.uk

THE BRM GUIDE TO BUILDING YOUR FIRST MODEL RAILWAY

5 RULES For Building a First Layout

For those about to embark on their first layout, or anyone else building a model railway, here are five useful rules to remember…

1: Keep It Small
Don't make it over the top

On a small layout, no job takes very long. I remember a friend building his layout in a sizeable shed announcing, "I'll be spending the next year ballasting." Spreading ballast is one of those jobs that has to be done but it's well down my list of fun things to do.

If your model is modest, the dull bits won't take very long. More importantly, if it's your first effort, you'll learn what works and what doesn't so any future layouts will be much quicker to build.

Finding a home for your small layout will be much easier than a larger one and the costs will be lower too. If anything goes wrong (and it will) it won't matter so much. You'll see the results faster as well.

2: Get Running
Keep yourself interested

Get something working as soon as you can.

We all love playing trains. For many it's what the hobby is all about, so try to get the project to a stage where you can move a locomotive around. A couple of leads attached to the track with crocodile clips will do, you don't have to finish the wiring.

As well as maintaining your interest, there is a serious purpose. Track should be tested before the scenic work progresses too far. You won't find out that a curve is too tight or there is a wagon-derailing lump on the main line if you don't run plenty of trains early on.

3: Go For It
Practice Makes Perfect

Planning your masterpiece is fun but don't let it stop you getting started. Every one of the layouts you see in a magazine started with someone cutting the first bit of wood.

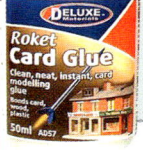

4: Learn As You Go
We all make mistakes

'The man who never made a mistake, never made anything' as the saying goes. He certainly never built a model railway layout. I've cut wood too short, laid track in the wrong place, fixed bracing where a point motor needs to be fitted, the list goes on. Getting it wrong is part of the learning process. The trick is to fix the problem or at least not tell anyone about it!

5: Enjoy It!
It's a hobby, not a chore.

THE HISTORY OF... MY LAYOUTS

We learn more from our mistakes than by getting things right. My layout building history is a bit chequered, but each one taught me something. I've dug through my photo albums to bring you a potted history of my model railways.

THE CAWOOD, WISTOW & SELBY LIGHT RAILWAY

In the early-1980s, my father Brian and I joined the Leamington & Warwick Model Railway Society. Coming into contact with serious railway modellers who took their layouts to exhibitions, we decided that this looked like fun so chose a prototype for our first efforts and got stuck in.

Built on chipboard topped baseboards braced with softwood, construction was as conventional as could be for the time. To save money we made the track using PCB components from SMP (now available from Marcway) which after a lot of tweaking, worked pretty well. It looked a lot better then the track you could buy too - Peco Code 75 finescale trackwork was way off in the future.

The model gained two feet in length after its first show when we found the terminus station, Cawood, was too cramped as built. Rolling stock was largely ready-to-run and based on what we had rather than what was appropriate.

> Built on chipboard topped baseboards was as conventional as could be for the time.

The layout at its second show, the local club event in Leamington Spa theatre. Sadly, the band advertised on the noticeboard has outlived our model.

An ex-GWR railcar used to operate because I had one and it looked nice. Even if I had been able to afford the correct Sentinel steam railcar in kit form, my skills weren't up to putting it together.

The wagons were built from a wide variety of sources. Spratt & Winkle couplings were very popular at the time (all the club layouts used them) and so we fitted them too. Our model represented a real branch line in Yorkshire. Thanks to a book with plans of all the main buildings, the stations aren't too inaccurate, at least as far as the structures go. Fortunately, the line featured identical stations and goods sheds, so my Dad made two of each using cardboard and Superquick brickpaper.

A NEW HOME

After three shows, the layout was consigned to the shed and eventually dismantled, apart from Wistow station which still survives. The problem was that we couldn't put the model up in its entirety at home. This meant that it didn't get run so we weren't able to fix any snags before it appeared in front of the public. As raw beginners, we needed a lot of snagging time!

Along the way I learnt how to make wagon kits run well and discovered that cheap flock powder fades very quickly. Woodland Scenics material looked expensive at the time, but at least it stayed green instead of turning yellow.

Oh, and if you insist on building a model based on a prototype, expect to find someone who knows about it when you take the layout out to an exhibition. At our first show, before the public had entered the building, a friend looked at the model and said, "Blimey. Cawood station." He used to drive by it every day on his way to work!

FACT FILE
- **SIZE** 20' 0" x 2' 0"
- **SCALE/GAUGE** 4mm:1ft (OO)
- **FIRST EXHIBITION** 1985

Wistow station. In real life, like most country stations built on cheap land, it's quite long at over $\frac{1}{4}$ mile. We built it on a 4' baseboard, had it been to scale the model would have taken over the whole layout.

THE BRM GUIDE TO BUILDING YOUR FIRST MODEL RAILWAY

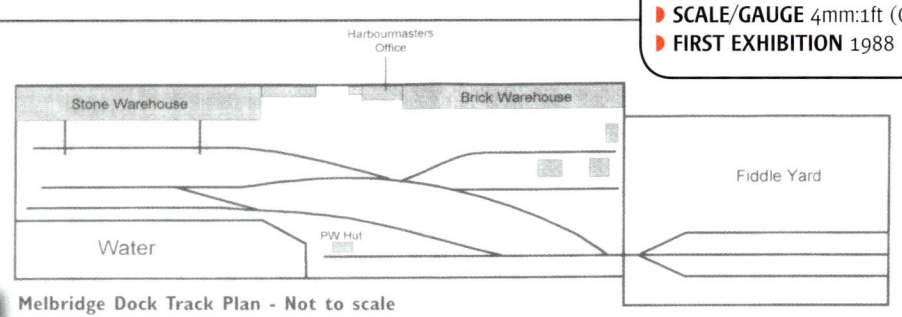

FACT FILE
- SIZE 9' 0" x 2' 0"
- SCALE/GAUGE 4mm:1ft (OO)
- FIRST EXHIBITION 1988

MELBRIDGE DOCK

For our next layout something more modest was in order; if it wasn't successful on the exhibition circuit, at least we'd have something to play with at home. This forced us to limit the length to 9', small enough to go up in a spare bedroom.

Since everyone seemed to be building rural branch lines we also thought that an industrial setting would be a bit different. I don't recall how we ended up building a dockside, but it probably had something to do with including a 'Clyde Puffer' since they are such fantastic boats. The trackplan is actually a GWR station with the platforms replaced with water. It fitted the baseboard and offered lots of shunting possibilities.

This was our first plywood baseboard and has certainly stood the test of time. The scenic section is only 18" wide, allowing for 6" at the back so the control panel could be built-in to reduce the need for plugs and sockets. There's also plenty of space for mugs of tea.

Not everything worked out immediately. Plans for a double slip were foiled because the Peco point motors couldn't move the blades - a pair of Y-points was used instead. Our fiddle yard incorporated a Peco Code

Our first outing with Melbridge Dock in 1988.

MELBRIDGE TOWN

FACT FILE
- SIZE 18' 0" x 6' 0"
- SCALE/GAUGE 4mm:1ft (OO)
- FIRST EXHIBITION 1996

Emboldened by the success of 'Melbridge Dock', we decided to have a go at something larger. With one layout touring the circuit, surely we ought to be able to build a much larger model and receive even more acclaim?

The plan was based on a Nottingham station and offered both passenger and freight workings. Halfway along the boards were some transfer sidings which we imagined would be where trains for the docks would be shunted. Along the back would run a working tramway that would turn in front of a high-level station. The fiddleyard would be a traverser to allow a regular procession of trains to entertain the public.

What followed was a lesson in not learning from both successes and mistakes. The plywood baseboards were cut by hand with mixed results. A panel was built into the back, but this meant it was 18' long. We'd allowed a year and a half before the first show, about nine months too little as it turned out. The curved ends were built in a weekend at the railway clubrooms while one of the club layouts was at a show - we didn't have the space to erect it at home.

Even when we did appear in public, the fiddleyard didn't work properly (it never did), there was no lighting rig, the wiring was ropey and all we could do was run trains around the circuit and hope no-one noticed. A list of improvements was drawn up, but these were sidelined in favour of working on the Dock in time for the **BRM** Doncaster show later in the year.

One of the few overall views of the layout, this one at the Derby exhibition.

The plan was based on a Nottingham station and offered both passenger and freight working.

TOO MANY PROBLEMS!

By the time we looked at our list, it was obvious that things weren't good. Every job seemed enormous. I'd

Our first layout in a magazine! From February 1997 **BRM** we have this portrait taken by Tony Wright in the days when a shoot involved around eight pictures taken on a medium format film camera.

Weymouth Harbourmaster's office is based on a plan in a 1960s magazine. It's amazing how many people have kept the same plan tucked away to build it one day. My model is made from cardboard, covered with Slater's embossed Plastikard brickwork.

100 three-way point that the Romford-wheeled stock didn't like much so this was replaced with a home made version to match the rest of the track. This worked a perfectly, far better than we had expected when looking at the plan in the kit.

TRANSPORTATION

The layout broke down into sections for transport in the family car, a Mk 1 Ford Fiesta. Our little layout went down very well with the public, so we started to travel around with it quite a bit. As I was becoming more proficient at locomotive kitbuilding, we added a display case for locomotives out of use over the fiddleyard as well as information panels along the front. This made the whole thing too big for the car and forced us to hire a van, making us less popular with exhibition managers.

Despite a 6' long scenic section, there was still a lot of modelling to do. The warehouses dominate the background and are scratchbuilt from Daler board covered with plastic card. Most of the other buildings are made the same way, mostly based on photographs we took or spotted in books. There is an awful lot of detail in a small area, which pleases exhibition visitors.

It's still on the circuit, we rarely put the layout up at home since we spend enough time operating it for the public. Appearances are rarer nowadays but still fun. Even after over 100 shows, we haven't got bored with operation and I still enjoy making models to run on it.

> The trackplan is actually a GWR station with the platforms replaced with water.

Small layouts can be packed full of detail such as this hut, scratchbuilt from plastic sheet. The chair and grindstone are from Cooper Craft. Remains of a bonfire were inspired by a similar scene spotted in real life but always catch visitors' eyes as it's a simple thing to model.

Some of the modelling was OK, my scratchbuilt signalbox was based on a plan. Behind it you can see the exit to the dockyard in the middle of the massive retaining wall.

As with our previous layout, the trackwork was built from SMP components and was one of the best things about the model.

built over 20' of retaining wall. The town section looked OK as we'd found some nice American kits for the buildings, but the idea of making many feet more of it for the tramways wasn't appealing.

Basically, this was too big a project for two people, especially when the model couldn't be set up all the time. Work had to be concentrated into bursts of activities. Unable to test the model properly it wasn't possible to sort out any problems, especially with the electrics.

In the end we decided to sell the thing to try and recover the cost of the materials. At the second and last show we did a deal and handed the model over to a new owner with a shed big enough to make use of it.

After a re-wiring, new fiddleyard and some alterations to the buildings, the model did appear at a couple of shows and worked as we'd always envisaged it. I still have most of the wagon kits I bought for it awaiting to be built though.

THE BRM GUIDE TO BUILDING YOUR FIRST MODEL RAILWAY

FACT FILE
- SIZE 8' 0" x 1' 0"
- SCALE/GAUGE 4mm:1ft (OO)
- FIRST EXHIBITION 1998

THE HELLINGLY HOSPITAL RAILWAY

After the 'Melbridge Town' problems, a return to small layouts was very much in order. I also wanted to build a model that could be transported in the back of my VW Beetle.

Initially inspired by a really nice drawing of the line's electric locomotive on the cover of Peter Harding's history of the line, a prototype only a mile and a quarter long seemed easy to compress into a small space. All the interesting trackwork was within the hospital site anyway.

A prominent water tower and the locomotive shed were essential features and fortunately well-photographed. More to the point, this was a very private line, hardly seen by the public so no-one was going to know if I got anything wrong were they?

The baseboards were made from 6mm plywood cut by a local wood yard. The plan was to be able to set the model up as quickly as possible. We'd been using loose pin hinges since 'Melbridge Dock', but for the first time these weren't supplemented with bolts.

SO FAR, SO GOOD

'Mk 1' was completed with very few traumas, apart from the overhead wire. Assuming I could simply copy tramway modellers methods I left this a bit late and then found making it work to be a lot harder than anticipated. It seems that keeping a trolley pole with a 2mm diameter wheel running along a wire is challenging, tramway modellers often use pantographs which are a lot easier. In the end we cheated and modelled the line in 1900 when the contractors were still building it. Their steam locomotives could do the bulk of the operation with electric power reduced to guest appearances when conditions were appropriate.

I ended up building the model twice as when I measured the space in the car, I hadn't allowed for it to squeeze between the door pillars so it was 4" too long. The opportunity was taken to shorten it, but make the board wider. The new proportions improved the display with more room for details. I reused the buildings, which speeded the work up a lot. The 6mm ply was a mistake as the boards have always been a bit wobbly.

Modelling a prototype is enjoyable, especially all the research. It turned out that all sorts of people from all over the country really did know the line. The first appearance in Derby saw us under scrutiny from a lady who had worked at the hospital, whose mother had been the head cook and had a sister who still worked there!

> **Baseboards were made from 6mm plywood cut by a local woodyard.**

The scenic section might be tiny at only 3' long, but there was still lots of modelling required. Here the electric locomotive (Roxey Mouldings kit) and tramcar (scratchbuilt) face each other by the weighbridge hut with the rest of the hospital in the background.

Looking the other way we see countryside: the line ran through manicured gardens until it reached the main site. A contractor's locomotive hauls a pre-Grouping wagon back towards the main line connection.

MICRO LAYOUTS

THE MELBRIDGE BOX COMPANY

FACT FILE
- SIZE 70cm x 30cm
- SCALE/GAUGE 4mm:1ft (OO)

There's no need to build a full-sized model railway to try things out. Micro-layouts are becoming much more popular. These are little more than operating dioramas but still provide a huge amount of fun to build.

The entire model packs into a pair of box files. All the buildings have removable tops to allow the lid to close and the MDF extension goes in the fiddle yard box.

18 www.RMweb.co.uk

FLOCKBURGH

It's a good idea when modelling in a new scale to try things out in a small way. With ever more high-quality RTR models appearing, it was proving harder to stand out in a show. After all, if most of the locomotives I'd spent hours building could be bought off the shelf, why bother?

A growing collection of Tri-ang TT models had lead to us joining the 3mm Society and discovering the possibilities of the smaller scale. Ballachulish on the west coast of Scotland looked like an appealing prototype, but before jumping in, a smaller test layout seemed wise.

Taking a Cyril Freezer plan as a basis, we built the model on 9mm plywood. This was supported by a slot-together leg system that works well once we remember how to put it together! The track uses PCB components from the 3mm Society.

Fortunately we had learnt our lesson and the layout could be erected in its entirety at home. Had this not been the case, the model would have been on a bonfire as making the rolling stock operate properly stretched our skills to the absolute limit. Finescale 3mm is far more demanding than conventional OO, requiring accurate chassis building, an appreciation of the importance of gauge-widening and some nifty tricks with basic components.

Modelling in 3mm finescale is far more demanding than conventional OO.

Our first outing was the Warley NEC show; perhaps not the ideal event at which to début a layout. As it turned out, the hours of tinkering, fettling and bad language saved the day and the model worked pretty well.

For the first couple of years, the trackwork finished at the edge of the baseboard, but when Cyril Freezer saw us, he suggested that we should extend the model a little to show why it stopped where it did. After some consideration, we made an 18" square board which bolted on the end, including a harbour and chapel that halted the progress of the line and the model looks a lot better.

FACT FILE
- **SIZE** 10' 6" x 1' 6"
- **SCALE/GAUGE** 3mm:1ft (14.2mm)
- **FIRST EXHIBITION** 2004

'Flockburgh' under construction in all its plywood goodness. Always envisaged as an exhibition layout, the lighting rig was built before the scenery rather than the more traditional last-minute job just before a show.

The entire layout. It's still a little light on detail but in this scale, everything has to be made so the process takes a lot longer than in OO. Another good reason for building small.

MELBRIDGE PARVA

Charged with running a 'Model in a Box File' competition for the Double O Gauge Association, I thought I'd better prove that it really was possible to build an operating layout in a conventional box file. As it was I needed two - one for the scenic section and another for the fiddleyard.

Trackwork consists of a pair of points forming a Z-shaped plan between the yard and extension board. While not the most exciting model to operate, the fun was in constructing the buildings and overcoming the challenge of creating a model railway that could be packed up into the box files.

Much of the modelling is the same as I've used on 'normal' layouts. The buildings are Daler board covered with Slater's Plastikard or modified kits. Static grass fibres at the ends of the siding make it look suitably run-down.

'Melbridge Parva' fits in a plastic box with the fiddle yard held in the roof with Velcro. The whole thing would fit in the luggage rack of a train for transport.

FACT FILE
- **SIZE** 71cm x 18cm
- **SCALE/GAUGE** 4mm:1ft (OO)

Another challenge layout. This time I was presented with a 'Really Useful Box Company' 71cm plastic box by someone who wanted to see me build a layout in it.

A plywood baseboard top was framed with thick softwood. There wasn't space to use Peco point motors, so I had to try the SEEP version instead.

The buildings were scratchbuilt apart from a much-modified and detailed Airfix locomoive shed at the front.

The height of this building determined the thickness of the baseboard as I had to be able to close the lid without squashing the roof.

The trackplan is very simple and again, not particularly interesting to operate, however it will work. There are uncoupling magnets for Spratt & Winkle couplings. A control panel plugs in the back and I can run any of my rolling stock used on other layouts.

As a test track, it's very handy when I'm building a locomotive kit. Running a chassis up and down a length of track doesn't test it nearly as much as using it on a layout with pointwork. Being tiny and living in a plastic box means it can be stored in a corner, ready for use at a moments notice.

www.model-railways-live.co.uk

THE BRM GUIDE TO BUILDING YOUR FIRST MODEL RAILWAY

BOOKS & TOOLS FOR LAYOUT DESIGN

There's plenty of help out there if you're just getting started. Here are a few ideas for finding inspiration and information.

There's no need to jump in at the deep end when designing a layout. A whole collection of planning aids is available to the budding modeller. For a start, magazines such as **BRM** publish detailed trackplans for the layouts featured in their pages every month. Have a good look at any plan that appeals to you. It might be that it will be ideal although you'll probably wish to personalise it a little with a few alterations to suit your requirements.

Watch out for the overall size of layouts, especially at exhibitions. In a large hall, quite substantial models can look smaller than you think. As a basic rule of thumb for a first layout, if it's longer than your outstretched arms then you might want to think again. On the other hand, this might be the point at which you decide to join the local model railway club and become involved in a larger team with access to space big enough for the dream model.

Don't imagine that you can work straight from an Ordinance Survey map for a real railway either. Very few locations will fit into the sort of space modellers have without some compression.

BOOKS

It's impossible to list every book on layout design in these pages. As long as people have been building model railways, others have been drawing up plans to guide them. As you'll see on the next page, the plan we're working to comes from a booklet first published in 1958!

One starting point is to look at the manufacturers own efforts. Years ago these were in the Hornby trackplans book, or for older readers, the same thing produced by Tri-ang. We all looked through these to drool over the final plans with four-track main lines, half-a-dozen stations and every operating feature on sale. Then realism kicked in and we realised that we couldn't afford either the money or space for anything other than the first three suggestions.

Nowadays, there are books of plans for all tastes from micro-layouts to adventurous plans

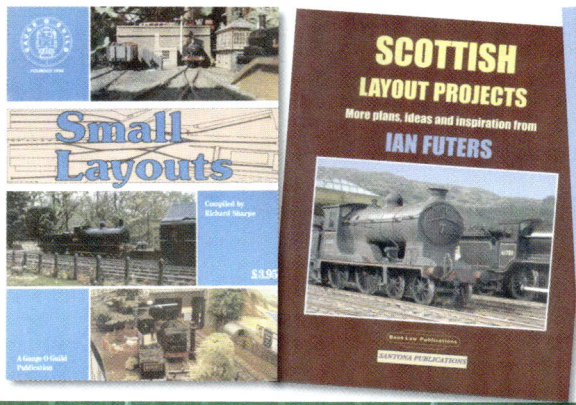

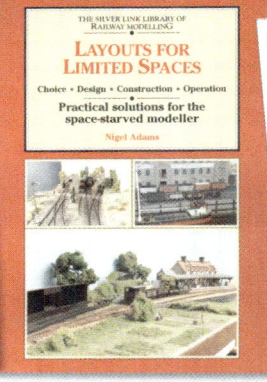
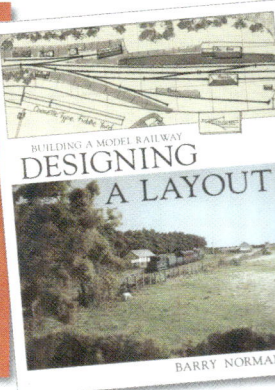

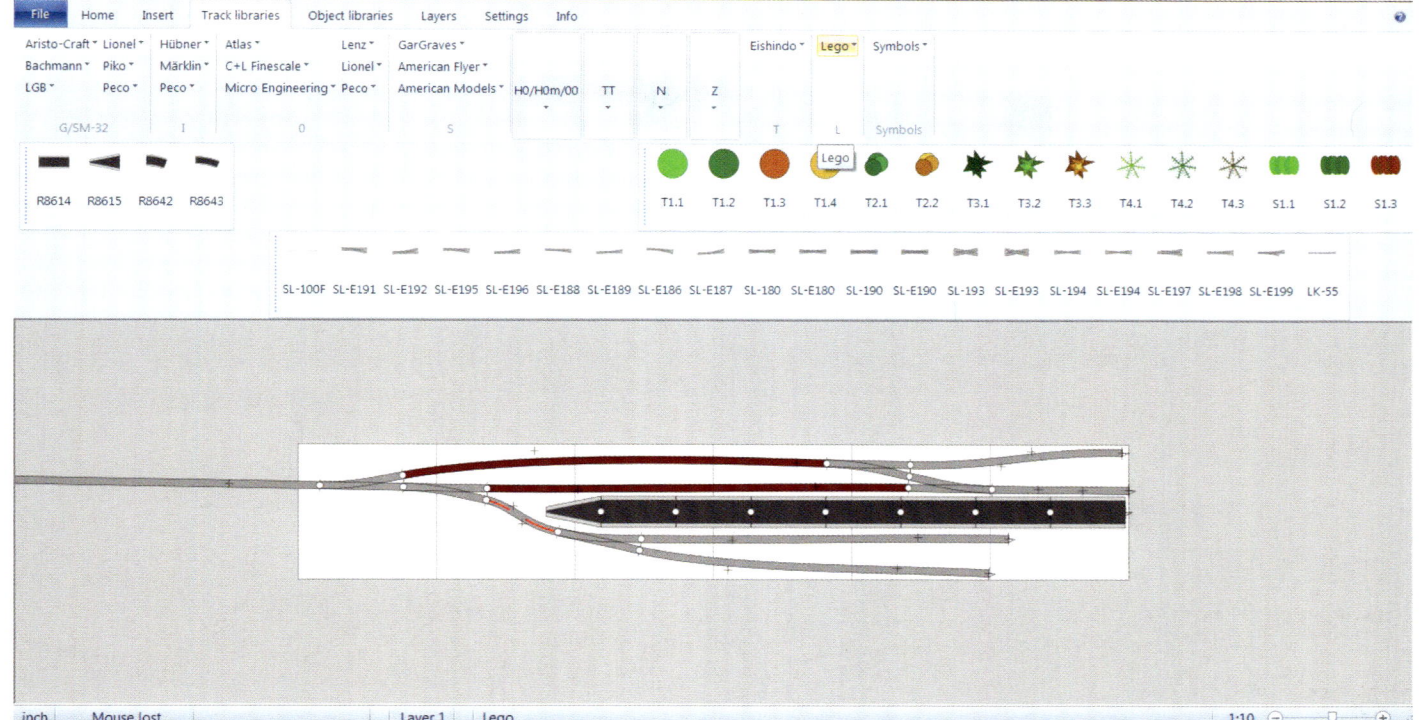

aimed at group efforts. Beginners might be advised to be careful with overly clever micro-layout plans as these often require the construction of a traverser or sector plate to replace some points. While this isn't especially difficult, it's harder than laying conventional points - I'd avoid them for your first effort.

Building layouts in small spaces is a popular theme and here you can find descriptions of models that others have actually built. That way you can be confident that the plan really will fit in the space it claims and hopefully will provide an entertaining layout at the end of the work. Look out for plans that include details of the scenic features - that way you can work out what will be required in the way of kits and other non-trackwork items.

TOOLS

Personally, I've never been any good at working trackplans out with a pencil and paper. Keeping things to scale defeats me and I end up with too much track in too small a space. Nowadays there are tools to help the modeller dream up the perfect layout and as an aid to daydreaming and serious planning, they're invaluable.

COMPUTER SOFTWARE

The options for designing your layout on a screen are many and varied. Using track and scenery libraries, you place components on the virtual baseboard and gradually build up plans that can look very much like the illustrative track plans seen in magazines (see above).

At the simplest end of the market are programs like Hornby Track-Master or AnyRail. Ideal for beginners and intermediate modellers, they aren't difficult to learn how to use. Playing with track on-screen has the advantage that you don't have to worry about space or cost. If you produce a plan that suits your purposes, a shopping list of track required can be produced.

For really serious modellers, Templot offers the ability to design any type of trackwork. While considerably more complex than other programs, there is very little in the way of limitations.

A sizeable online community can offer support and advice as you learn the process. For those building their own track, full-sized plans can be printed ready to stick to the baseboard.

> **Useful Websites**
> AnyRail software - www.anyrail.com
> Templot - www.templot.com

HORNBY TRACK PLANNING TEMPLATES

Hornby's R619 track planning set consists of quarter-scale plastic miniatures of the company's sectional track system that link together like a jigsaw. Although currently out of production, it's still easy to acquire on the secondhand market.

To use, simply draw a quarter-sized version of the space available for the layout and then spend many happy hours shuffling the bits around to build your model. Some useful additions would be lengths of strip wood scaled to match wagons, coaches and locomotives. These can then be tested in loops and sidings.

Taking matters further, how about sticking the finished 'layout' to a board with double-sided tape and modelling the model scenery and buildings? Nothing particularly detailed would be needed, just some rough shapes, but that way you'd be able to see how the finished model will look long before cutting a length of wood or buying any trackwork. Any alterations to the overall picture are simple at that stage.

FULL SIZE POINT PLANS

If you're using Peco track, the company provides free full-sized plans for its trackwork in gauges N to 1. These can be downloaded from the Technical Bureau website and printed at home.

After this, all the modeller has to do is cut the points out and lay them in the space available. Traditionally, the advice is to use a roll of lining paper from a DIY store in place of your baseboard. Mark out the space available and shuffle the paper points around until you're happy.

Even if you've used another method for planning, there is a huge benefit to be gained by using this method as a final check. It's easy to try real rolling stock on it. You experience your model full size and if working on the real baseboards, it's possible to spot those points sitting over under-board bracing that'll be difficult to fit motors to.

A refinement of this method is to have a couple of flexi-track lengths available. These are bent to provide the running tracks and along with the points, allow the builder to look along the track to ensure that all of the track curves are even. **BRM**

> **Useful Website**
> Peco Technical Bureau: www.peco-uk.com

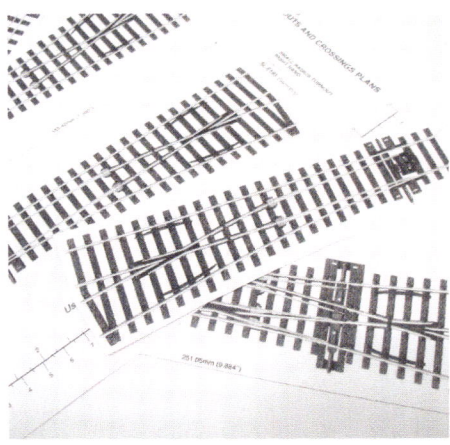

THE BRM GUIDE TO BUILDING YOUR FIRST MODEL RAILWAY

TRACK

CLECKLEWYKE

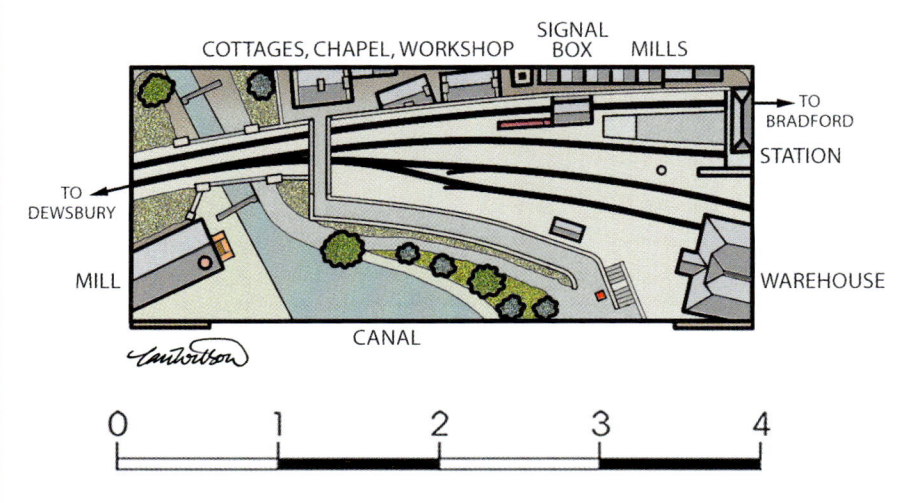

COTTAGES, CHAPEL, WORKSHOP — SIGNAL BOX — MILLS — TO BRADFORD — STATION — TO DEWSBURY — MILL — CANAL — WAREHOUSE

0 1 2 3 4

CRIPPLE CORNER

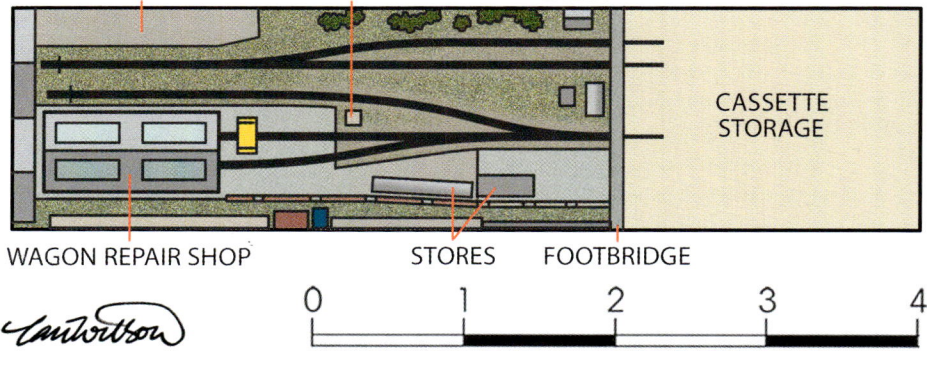

TRAILER PARK — LIGHT TOWER — SHUNTERS CABIN — CASSETTE STORAGE — WAGON REPAIR SHOP — STORES — FOOTBRIDGE

0 1 2 3 4

PLANS

Layouts come in all shapes and sizes to suit their location. Here are a few from the pages of **BRM** to get you rolling.

SHEPHERDS BUSH

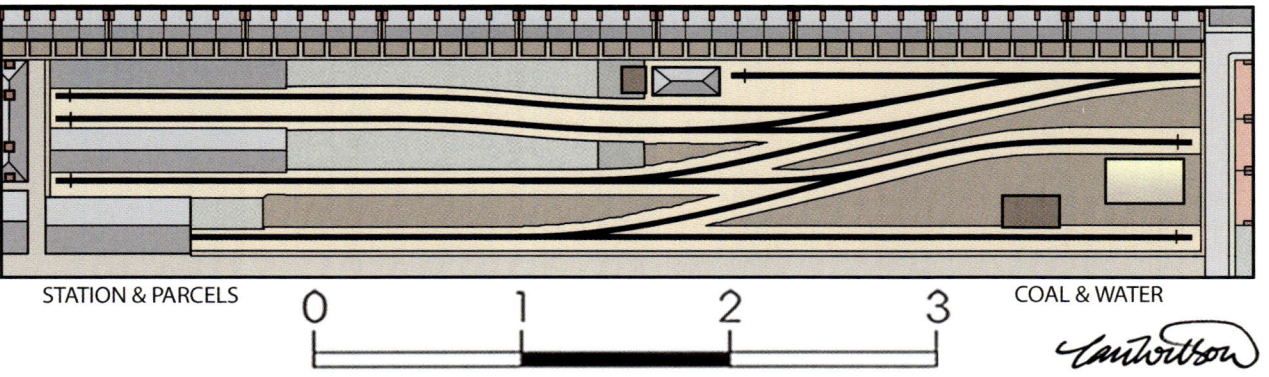

LOW RELIEF TERRACED HOUSING — SIGNAL BOX

STATION & PARCELS — 0 1 2 3 — COAL & WATER

ARDLUI

0 1 2 3 4 5 6

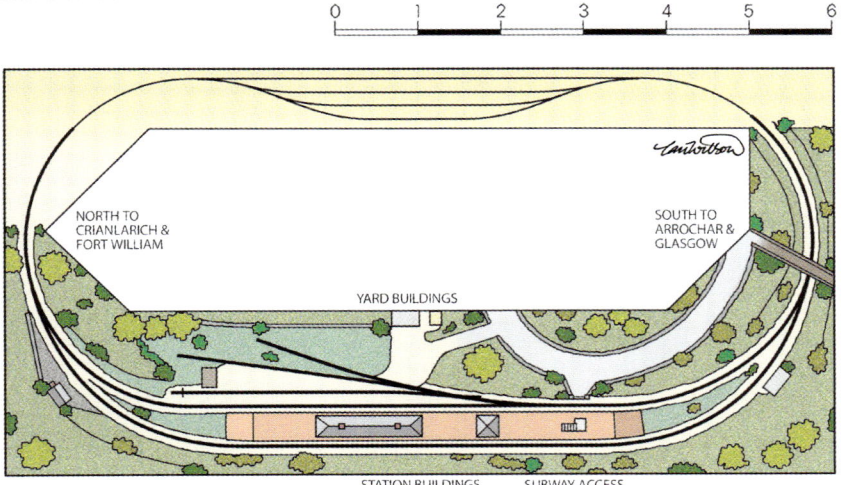

NORTH TO CRIANLARICH & FORT WILLIAM

SOUTH TO ARROCHAR & GLASGOW

YARD BUILDINGS

STATION BUILDINGS   SUBWAY ACCESS

www.model-railways-live.co.uk

THE BRM GUIDE TO BUILDING YOUR FIRST MODEL RAILWAY

Introducing... EDGEWO

Here's a rundown of the layout that we're going to build throughout this guide.

So, the time has come to get started. **BRM** asked me to come up with a layout suitable for beginners to build. Not a train set, but a real model railway, the sort of thing you see at exhibitions and in magazines. Rome wasn't built in a day and a lot of the layouts you see in the press have taken years to come to fruition. What we needed was a layout that could be built reasonably quickly.

Overall size is the first consideration. As my experience proved, if you can't put the layout up at home, you don't make progress on it. Since most of us don't have a huge amount of space to dedicate to the hobby, I'm assuming that something no more than nine feet long will work. We're working in OO, N-gaugers could get away with less space or just stretch the plan to fit the room available.

We're going to use Peco Code 75 trackwork throughout. All modern rolling stock will be perfectly happy on this and it looks more appropriate for a branch line than the more substantial Code 100.

SIZE MATTERS
Since the space available isn't huge, we'll use short radius points. This is a compromise since medium or large radius would look better, but I want to fit a station on the model with space for sidings. Again, if you have more space, use longer points.

Our plan began life in 1958. Cyril Freezer produced the classic *60 Plans for Small Railways* which includes a number for small spaces. We've adapted it a little from his original so the baseboard is 14" wide instead of 12". Mind you, our platforms are wider than the rather narrow ones he designed.

LOCATION
The plan is generic, you could build it to be anywhere in the country. Personally, I've never

GWR locomotives and rolling stock are readily available in model form. These are all from the Hornby range - 14xx 0-4-2T (top right), 61xx 'Large Prairie' (below), and Collett 'B-Set' coach (bottom). A 45xx 'Small Prairie' and 57xx pannier tank are available from Bachmann Branch-Line with a 4-4-0 'Dukedog' and 64xx pannier released recently.

THE REAL THING...
The real Edgeworth is a village between Stroud, Cirencester and Cheltenham in Gloucestershire. No railway ever ran there but several lines were reasonably close making it a plausible 'might have been'.

built a Great Western Railway branch line, so that's what we're doing. With the Severn Valley and Gloucestershire-Warwickshire railways near my home, prototype inspiration is close at hand. The GWR has always enjoyed a large following with railway modellers too.

Years ago GWR branch lines were a bit of a cliché and for that reason all but disappeared from public exhibitions. There are many advantages to the GW, not least some of the short trains they ran. For passenger services we are looking at a 14XX 0-4-2T

and an autocoach or perhaps a 'Flying Banana' diesel railcar. Larger trains can be handled by a 'Prairie' and 'B set' coaches (which always ran in pairs). None of these is any great length and short trains make the layout look larger than it is.

Goods workings demand a Pannier Tank. In fact, most Great Western layouts require at least one of these charismatic little locomotives as they appeared all over the system.

For our buildings, we'll be making use of the Ratio range of plastic kits. Easy to assemble, all the major

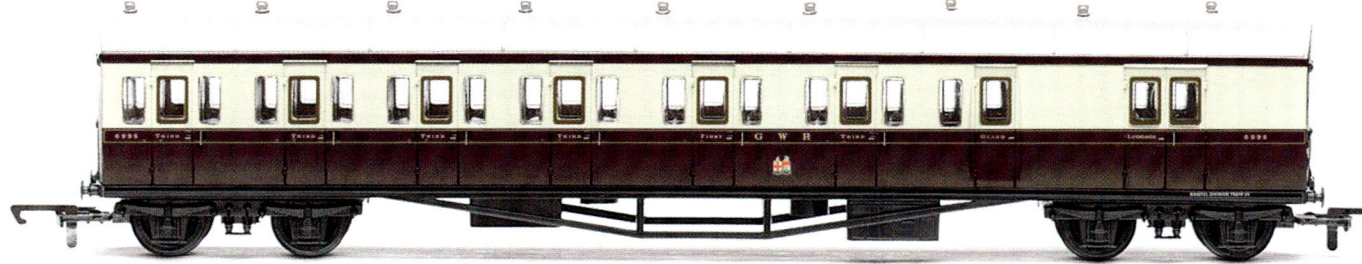

structures can be obtained off the shelf. While ready-built resin buildings might be quicker to use, we want plenty of entertaining modelling on the layout. This is a hobby, not a race to the finish.

At one end of the layout, track heads off to the hidden fiddleyard representing the rest of the system. If you are operating at home then a single point will hold one train ready to be brought on to the layout while another is in the station. We'll assume that the line works 'one engine in steam' to keep things simple.

To cover the entrance, the line will pass out under a road overbridge. This provides the opportunity to build a hill and make use of various scenic techniques to add some nature.

Once all this is complete, there will still be plenty of detail to be added to bring the scene alive. Road transport and people will be required along with all the detritus of life cluttering up the odd corners of our model.

While 'Edgeworth' would make an excellent home-based layout, we're taking it out on the road so you can have a good look and tell me where I went wrong. To do this, we'll need some legs to support it and lights so everyone can see what they are doing.

A model railway is never really finished so I'm sure we'll keep tinkering with the model for some time to come. For the moment though, let's get started with the baseboards, track and wiring. **BRM**

TRACKPLAN

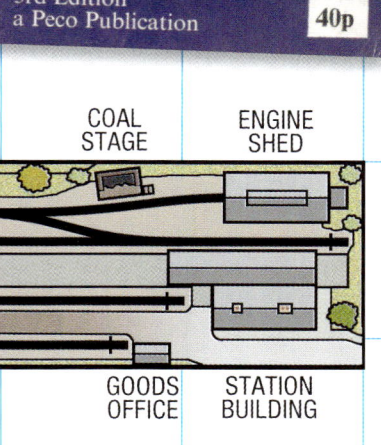

www.model-railways-live.co.uk 25

THE BRM GUIDE TO BUILDING YOUR FIRST MODEL RAILWAY

EDGEW<!-- cut off -->

THE PLAN

Every layout construction ought to start with a 'plan of attack'. Here's how we foresee the construction of ours.

ROAD BRIDGE

Bringing the track on to the scenic section of a layout requires it to pass through some sort of visual break to hide the fiddleyard. My initial plan called for a tunnel, the classic model railway feature for this task, but as several people pointed out, this didn't occur very often in real life. Therefore we'll take the track out under a road bridge. There won't be enough space for a full width road but as long as the bridge face is visible, our imagination will do the rest.

Turn to page 84 for a step-by-step guide to building it.

German military strategist Helmuth von Moltke the Elder summed up building a model railway layout when he said, "No plan survives contact with the enemy."

We have an excellent plan drawn by Ian Wilson, based on the plans I sketched out. My first reaction on seeing the full colour version was, "That looks great. I look forward to building it."

SIGNALBOX

Our signalbox is based on the preserved example at Highley on the Severn Valley Railway. This is partly because it is a really attractive signal box but mostly because Ratio produce a kit to make construction of what can be a complex building an awful lot easier.

Turn to page 78 to see how it's done.

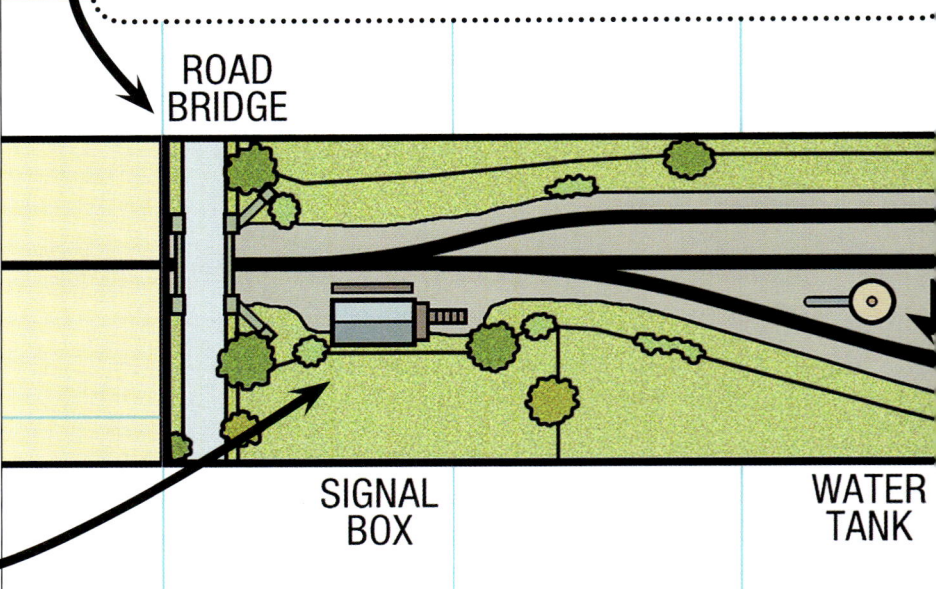

ROAD BRIDGE

SIGNAL BOX

WATER TANK

Having said that, along the way some of the details have been tweaked slightly. Once you start work things don't always fit exactly how you expect. More importantly, sometimes when working with things in three dimensions, you'll spot a more pleasing arrangement. If this happens, it's daft to adhere rigidly to a plan, you'll always regret it later.

Now, this is a layout suitable for a beginner but it's described as building your first layout so there will be plenty of construction. For this reason, most of the buildings are plastic kits rather than ready-to-use resin models. As well as providing the chance to get your hands dirty and make the layout personal to you, it means you'll be able to follow what we've done in years to come. The kits have been around for years whereas the resin models are often limited editions that disappear after one production run. Mind you, if you do find a resin model that you prefer to the kit, go for it. At the end of the day it's your model railway.

> **No plan survives contact with the enemy.**

ORTH

IN WHAT PERIOD WILL 'EDGEWORTH' BE SET?
I've chosen the 1930s GWR 'heyday' when the company was at its height. We'll be careful to try and tailor details to match this period. There won't be any modern cars for example. Trains will be properly cleaned, infrastructure looked after and gentlemen will wear hats.

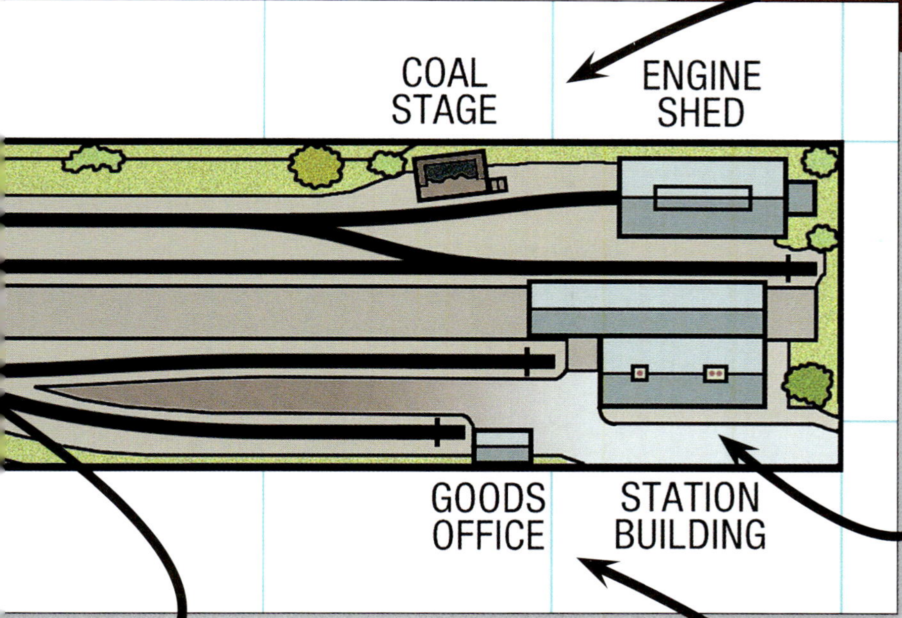

LOCOMOTIVE SHED AND COAL STAGE

Small locomotive sheds are another model railway cliché, but they existed in real life so we can justify one at the end of our branch line. Steam locomotives require quite a bit of regular servicing so at the very least there have to be facilities for coaling and watering.

A small locomotive such as a pannier tank would be out-stationed here to work the first train in the morning. Heavier maintenance would take place at a larger depot or works so all we need is stabling, coal and water facilities.

Turn to page 72 and page 98 for more.

STATION BUILDING

While 'Edgeworth' might not generate large amounts of passenger traffic, the station would still be reasonably impressive. In the period modelled it would be staffed by a stationmaster and a couple of porters, a far cry from today's rationalised railway.

Our model uses the Ratio kit for Castle Cary station. Admittedly this is a through main line station and we're modelling a branch terminus, but who's to say that there wasn't a plan for the line to go beyond here?

Turn to page 74 to discover how to do it.

WATER TOWER

The GWR loved to standardise and so we must have a conical water tower at the end of the platform. This is the only RTR building as Hornby produces a really nice example. Of course we'll be weathering it before use, so it won't be straight out of the box. If you prefer a kit, try Ratio 528 which provides a near-identical plastic version.

GOODS OFFICE

Goods working involved an awful lot of paperwork and the office, however humble, is where it all took place. This isn't salubrious, little more than a posh shed, but these sort of small buildings add a huge amount to the character of a model.

www.model-railways-live.co.uk 27

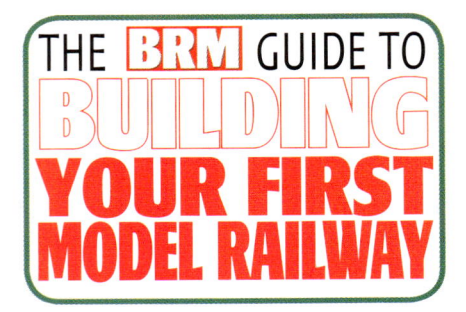

THE BRM GUIDE TO BUILDING YOUR FIRST MODEL RAILWAY

HOW TO BUILD...
BASEB

A solid base will ultimately lead to a better layout and fewer frustrating problems. **Phil Parker** looks at the options.

Build a good set of baseboards and the rest of the layout will be easy. It's a simple truth no matter how much fun you have constructing scenery or buildings; if the baseboards have cavernous gaps between them or the trackbed sags, you'll always wish you'd put more time in earlier.

This is all fine but what happens if you aren't any good at woodwork? Is your only option buying in the services of a professional baseboard company?

Not in my experience. I'm rubbish at woodwork but have found various ways to cheat so I still produce an acceptable result. To be honest, I'm so happy with the methods I used 25 years ago, I've not seen fit to experiment further.

As I showed earlier, 'Melbridge Dock' was built using 9mm plywood.

Each board is 3' long and nothing more than a top with 6" deep beams around the bottom. There's no cross-bracing underneath to get in the way of the point motors and we didn't even varnish the wood. Despite over 100 shows, many thousands of miles on the road and storage in less than ideal conditions, the layout still works as well as it did when we built it. It's light enough to be lifted in and out of a car by one person too.

Here, I saved some wood and weight by opting for a 4" rather than 6" beam. To date this has been strong enough but I wouldn't go any shallower. Do think about your point motors at this stage, if you are going to use large units such as Tortoise point machines, make sure they don't stick out of the bottom of the layout.

Rather than bolt the baseboards together, we used loose pin hinges attached to the sides. These are available from DIY stores. There's no need to try and remove the pins from normal hinges to make them, the real things have large heads on the pins that are easy to grab with pliers. As well as holding the boards together, they take care of track alignment so there's no need to fiddle with bolts when setting the layout up, just pop the pins in and go for a cup of tea. This works well in OO, O and even finescale 3mm scale so we're confident it will be fine for almost anyone.

SHOPPING LIST
- ✓ 9mm plywood
- ✓ 30mm panel pins
- ✓ Loose pin hinges

TOOLS FOR THE JOB
- Pin hammer
- Square
- Drill
- Padsaw
- PVA Glue

OARDS

I'm rubbish at woodwork but have found various ways to cheat so I still produce an acceptable result

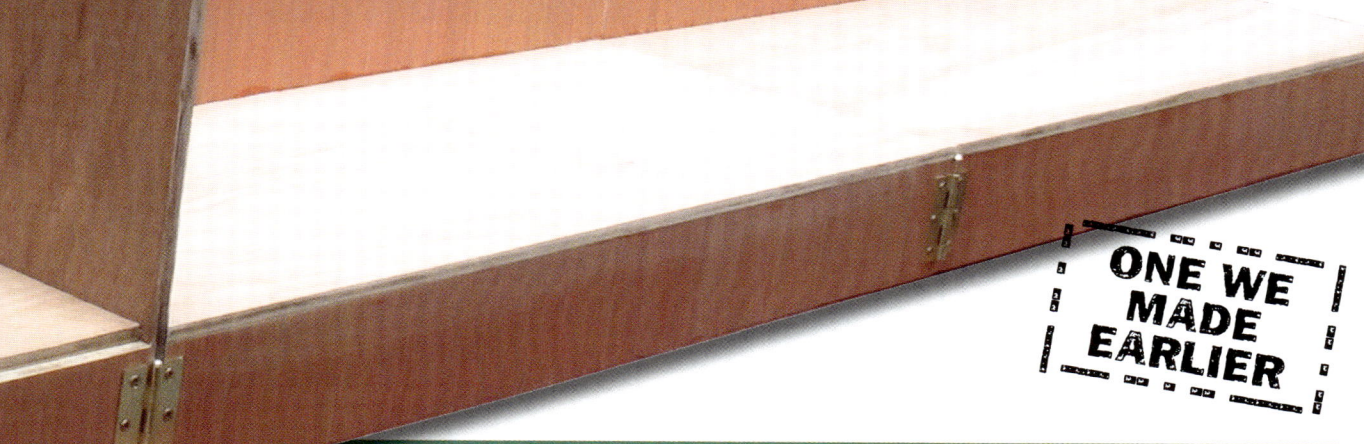

ONE WE MADE EARLIER

CUTTING WOOD

Being hopeless at woodwork, I prefer to get the plywood cut for me. My local hardware store offers the service but so do many wood yards and even superstores such as B&Q. The 'Melbridge' boards were cut when 'Do It All' did it many years ago. After this I just have to glue and pin the bits together to produce a sturdy set of baseboards.

Above After half an hour watching someone else work, I left with a baseboard kit in the boot of the car. Laid out you can see the boards and backs at the top. In the middle is the end piece at the fiddleyard end and either side of this, the beams that run around the bottom.

Left Cutting wood accurately is a lot easier if you have the proper equipment. I don't, but I buy my wood from a shop that does and is happy to do the work if I take in a cutting list and don't turn up on a busy Saturday. To find someone similar in your area, try local hardware shops and wood yards. Larger branches of B&Q also offer the same service.

www.model-railways-live.co.uk

THE BRM GUIDE TO BUILDING YOUR FIRST MODEL RAILWAY

STEP-BY-STEP GUIDE ▶

1

A couple of parts had to be modified because I'd calculated it wrong and we also needed to cut some softwood for the fiddleyard. A mitre cutting tool like this costs less than £25 and is invaluable when accuracy is required. Once you have one, you'll wonder how you ever managed without it.

2

To fix the top to the side beams, we used 30mm pins and PVA glue. While nailing through the plywood isn't hard, starting the pins in the top before bringing the parts together made life easier.

3

Whilst the pre-cut wooden parts make building a square baseboard easier, it's worth keeping a carpenters' square handy to check that the sides are at right angles to the baseboard tops.

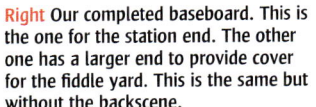

Right Our completed baseboard. This is the one for the station end. The other one has a larger end to provide cover for the fiddle yard. This is the same but without the backscene.

WHAT ABOUT USING CHIPBOARD OR MDF?

Both materials are heavy and hard. Nailing into either is difficult compared to plywood. When cutting MDF you should also wear a dust mask as the dust can be dangerous if breathed in.

MDF is a reasonably stable if used indoors for a permanent layout. It can be very useful for backscenes too, especially as an easy-to-curve version is available. Both will need bracing if used for a baseboard top and normally this is carried out with softwood, which can warp as it dries out. Check the wood by looking along the length of it if you try this.

4 Loose pin hinges, available from a DIY store, are screwed either side of the boards to hold them together. Removing the pins releases the boards for transport.

5 A hole has to be made to allow the track through to the fiddleyard. We drilled some holes and then used a padsaw to join them up into a big enough opening for a coach to pass though with about 3cm space all round. If you have a tunnel mouth handy, draw around the inside of this. Scenery will cover any untidy workmanship later.

WHAT IS SUNDEALA?

Sundeala is a fibreboard that used to be recommended for baseboard tops. The main advantage claimed for it is the ease with which track pins can be pushed in. As we'll see in the tracklaying section, this isn't really a problem with plywood.

If you do prefer Sundeala, it needs to be very well braced. The company recommends support every 40cm. Any less and it can sag over time leaving you with a switchback track. Of course a lot depends on where the layout lives - you'll have more problems in a damp atmosphere for example.

I KEEP HITTING MY THUMB WITH THE HAMMER!

Solution: 'Nail Gripper' is available from most DIY stores for £3. The rubber tool grips the nail in slots around the edge.

If you want to save a few quid or just don't have the gripper to hand, push the nail through some cardboard and use this to hold it in place while you start it.

THE COST?
For the wood, glue, nails and hinges - £73.67

Thank you to...
▶ Torry's Hardware, 30-34 West Street, Warwick for letting us take photographs of the wood cutting.
▶ Leamington & Warwick MRS for allowing me to assemble the boards in their clubroom where there was space to take the photographs.

THE BRM GUIDE TO BUILDING YOUR FIRST MODEL RAILWAY

HOW TO... LAY GOOD TRACK

Now you're ready to lay track. Whilst this is relatively simple, it's vital you follow our advice to ensure the smooth running of your trains!

TOOLS FOR THE JOB

- Pliers
- Straight Tracksetta
- 1mm drill in a pin vice
- Small hammer
- Xuron cutter

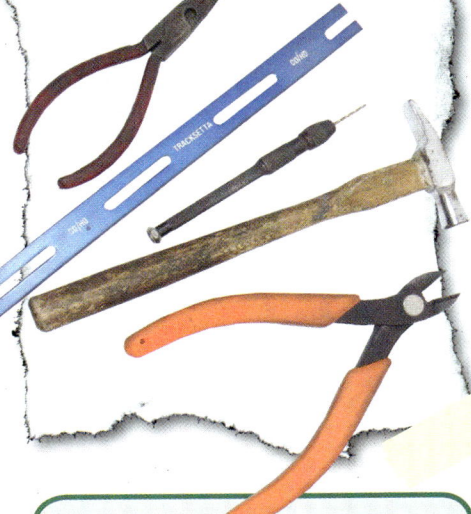

Laying track is simple isn't it? Just nail it to the baseboard and get the trains running.

For the most part, that isn't that far from the truth. Don't throw it down and expect perfect running, but invest a bit of time and care in the job and it's not difficult. On 'Edgeworth', we are using Peco points and flexible track. This is slightly harder to use than sectional track, but as the name implies, you can be more flexible with your design.

We are fixing the track directly to the baseboard without any form of underlay. Some prefer to put a layer of cork down first to reduce the noise but with modern ready-to-run stock, this really isn't a problem. The trouble with any underlay is that once you cover it with ballast held in place with glue, the sound-deadening effects are lost anyway. None of my layouts use any sound deadening and exhibition visitors often complement me on the quietness of my trains.

The other reason to lay cork first is where there should be a ballast hump - the track sitting on a deep bed of stones - but this isn't the case in a station area giving us another reason not to bother.

Work starts by drawing a line from the centre of the tunnel along the board. This provides the position for two of the points, all we have to do is join them up with track. As long as this track doesn't have any lumps in it and there are no kinks in the rail, we should be OK when it's time to run trains.

TRACK PINS

Lots of different types of track pin are available. The main difference is the thickness of the shaft. Thicker pins are a lot easier to use as they don't bend when you hit them with a hammer - which is why we used them. The thinner pins aren't quite so obvious in finished trackwork so if you feel confident, go ahead and give them a go.

In addition to holding track in place, the pins make excellent door knobs for model buildings. Always buy more than you need as you'll always find a use for them.

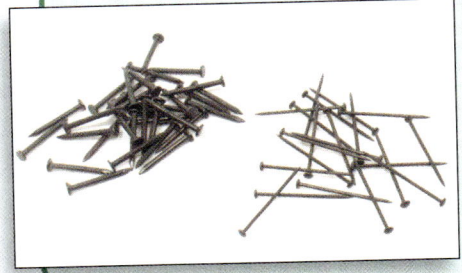

MARKING OUT

① Don't forget to allow for the width of platforms between tracks in a station. We used the surface from one of the kits lined up against the main track to position the line into the bay.

FIXING DOWN TRACKWORK AND POINTWORK

To pin our track in place, we need holes in the sleepers. On sectional track and pointwork these are moulded in place but the flexi-track requires drilling. You'll need a small drill bit, slightly larger than the thickness of the pin and a small hammer.

2 Put the pin in the sleeper hole and then gently tap it down with a small hammer. It's really important not to hit the rails as it is possible to dent them. Using a hammer with a head narrower then the track gauge helps but if you want to be sure, once the nail is started, hold a nail punch or an old bolt on the head of the pin and hit the end of this. Do not force the pin in hard, we need to keep the track in place, if the sleeper bends, pull the nail back out a bit with some small pliers.

3 We laid the track in place on the board and drilled it in situ. People worry about forcing the pins into the plywood. It's not that hard but can be made even easier if once you've drilled through the sleeper you carry on turning the bit a couple of times to break the surface of the baseboard.

4 Points are pinned in place just like normal track. The sleepers have holes but it's worth running a drill through and breaking the surface of the baseboard. It is crucial not to pin the sleepers too hard as you can distort the point, leading to derailments.

Before laying the point, there is another consideration. How will it be operated? We're fitting Peco motors under the baseboard, so a slot needs to be cut for the wire that pokes through. My method is a bit rough and ready. A series of 3mm holes are drilled where the tiebar

will be. The drill is gently waggled side-to-side to join them up and then I tidy the hole up with a small, coarse file.

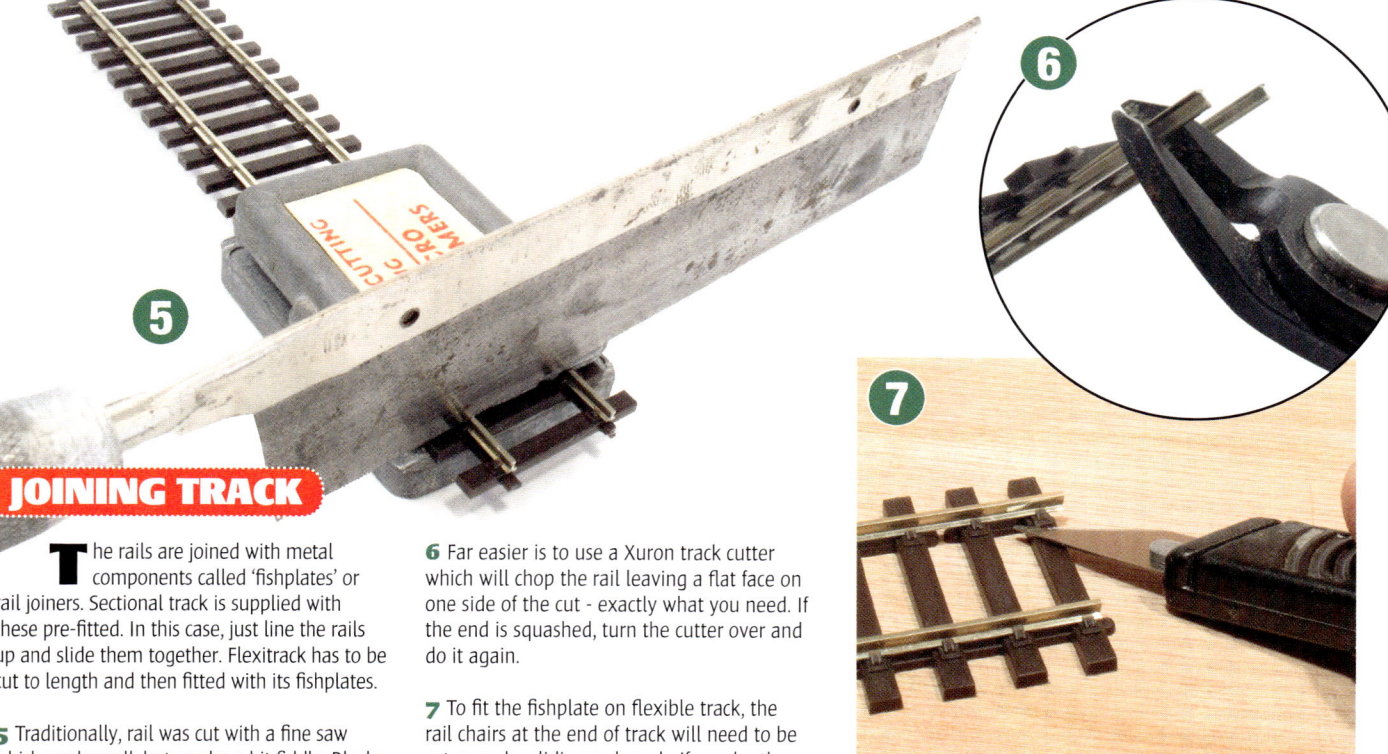

JOINING TRACK

The rails are joined with metal components called 'fishplates' or rail joiners. Sectional track is supplied with these pre-fitted. In this case, just line the rails up and slide them together. Flexitrack has to be cut to length and then fitted with its fishplates.

5 Traditionally, rail was cut with a fine saw which works well, but can be a bit fiddly. Blocks to help hold the rails are available and this helps a little.

6 Far easier is to use a Xuron track cutter which will chop the rail leaving a flat face on one side of the cut - exactly what you need. If the end is squashed, turn the cutter over and do it again.

7 To fit the fishplate on flexible track, the rail chairs at the end of track will need to be cut away by sliding a sharp knife under the rail. Practice this on a bit of scrap track first to increase your confidence.

THE BRM GUIDE TO BUILDING YOUR FIRST MODEL RAILWAY

Save Your Spare Sleepers!
Old sleepers are often seen beside the track on real railways so don't bin any leftovers from tracklaying, just cut away the web between the, paint brown and glue in place as part of the scenery.

8 Normal fishplates allow electricity to flow along them. Sometimes we don't want this (see the wiring detail on page 34 for why) so we used plastic insulating fishplates instead. These work in the same way as the metal version although they are a bit bulkier. You might need to trim the sleepers or even the fishplate a little for a good fit.

9 If the tracks being joined are in a straight line, a Tracksetta tool is useful to ensure you pin everything down perfectly aligned. The tool drops between the rails (several different gauges are available) and holds the ends in place while you pin everything down. Curved Tracksettas are available for laying track on set radius curves too.

CROSSING BASEBOARD JOINTS

WHERE CAN I BUY COPPER-CLAD SLEEPERS?
Both Marcway and Eileen's Emporium can supply sleeper strip. It is usually sold in 12" lengths which you trim to length with your track cutter.

Cutting the track like this isn't essential if you don't plan on moving the layout. There's nothing wrong with track running straight over baseboard joints. This work is a precaution as the layout will be moved around and handled quite a bit in the future.

Plastic-based track is wonderful stuff but if the layout is to be taken apart to go to exhibitions or just for moving, it's possible to damage it at the ends of the board. Just catching a rail end will pull it out of the chairs, probably breaking them. Fixing this may well require the replacement of that section of track.

10 To avoid this, we remove the end sleeper either side of the baseboard joint and replace it with a copper-clad version soldered to the rails. Once fitted, the metal on the top surface of the sleeper has to be cut to stop a short circuit.

11 Next, the rails are cut on the joint with a slitting disk in a mini-drill. This is a very handy tool but you should wear eye protection while using it. The disk can disintegrate with bits flying off in all directions.

TOP TIP

Six Foot Way
To stop trains on adjacent tracks hitting each other as they pass, in the UK we traditionally separate them by six feet - a gap often called the 'six foot way'. On a model you need to ensure the same separation. You can do this with a ruler or a simple gauge like this one from Peco.

On curves, the distance between the tracks must be wider to allow for the swing of bogie vehicles like coaches. This problem becomes worse the tighter the curve.

TESTING, TESTING

Don't Hope The Problem Will Go Away - It Won't.
By the end of the job, you should find the stock can be given a shove at one end of the layout and still be running when it falls off the baseboard at the other end. Well, if you aren't quick enough to catch it anyway!

As you lay your track, it must be tested. You'll need a coach and wagon for the job; don't use your best stock, something secondhand or cheap is a better idea in case of derailments.

Push the vehicles around all the trackwork. If they jump or derail, investigate and rectify until everything flows smoothly. The chances are, at this stage, it's something quite simple. Is the track pinned down too hard? Has one side lifted? Has something become stuck under the sleepers? Are the curves too tight or do the rails line up badly at a joint?

THE BRM GUIDE TO BUILDING YOUR FIRST MODEL RAILWAY

HOW TO... WIRE THE LAYOUT

Adding electricity to power locomotives and accessories isn't as complicated as it may appear. Here we guide you through wiring a simple layout.

TRACK POWER

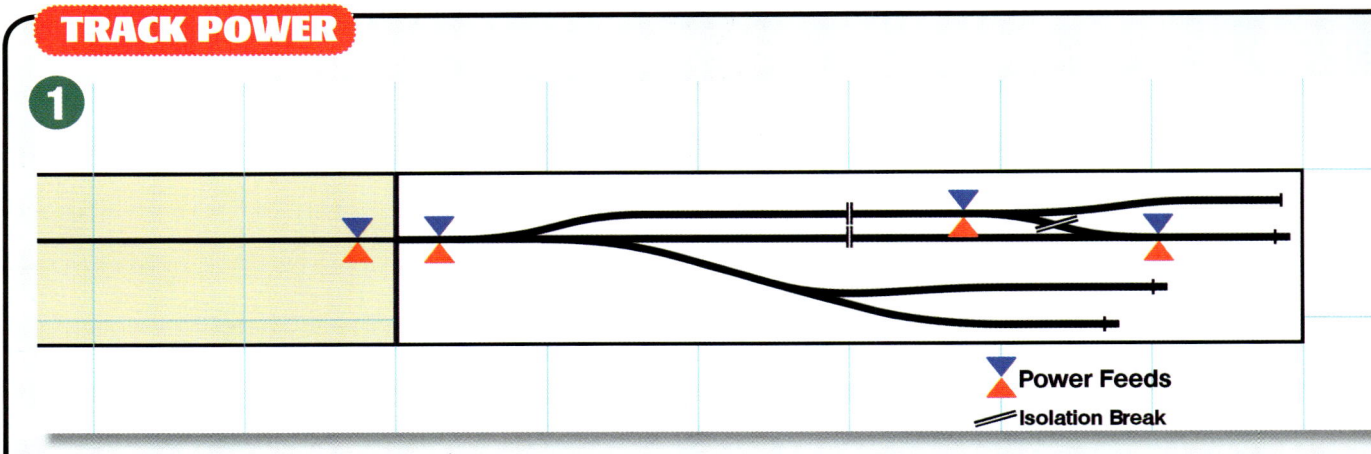

▼▲ Power Feeds
∥ Isolation Break

TOOLS FOR THE JOB
- Soldering Iron (20w or greater)
- Cored solder
- Wire strippers
- Small pliers
- Screwdriver

To keep things simple, 'Edgeworth' is wired for conventional 12V DC control. With a layout this simple, DCC isn't essential although it would be easy to make the change, just swap the DC controller for the DCC control unit if that's what you prefer.

Points operate using Peco solenoid motors which are switched using buttons on a control panel that plugs into the back of the layout. It's all simple technology put together by a simple person.

1 The wiring diagram shows the three track feeds needed to power the model. Each is at the toe end of a point and looks after a section of the layout. In addition to feeding power in, we need to stop it getting everywhere to avoid short circuits.

2 Take a look at this drawing of a crossover. If there are no isolating gaps between the running rails of the two points, in the centre the different polarities will meet causing a 'short circuit'. The overload light will appear on the controller and everything will stop. The solution to this is to insulate one side of the junction from the other using insulating fishplates.

3 The same thing can occur in the middle of the loops so we insulate one end from the other. We could use insulated fishplates here as well but as the baseboard joints are there, we'll allow those to do the job for us.

4 Feeding power into the rails is easily accomplished by soldering wires to the sides. If you tin both the wire and rail sides, soldering the two together is a matter of a couple of seconds with a hot soldering iron. Practice on scrap track first if you aren't confident. You can use power clips or even Peco pre-wired fishplates if soldering really does worry you but this is quite a good first soldering job for the beginner.

5 We'll be using a Gaugemaster 'Combi' Controller. This has it's own power supply that plugs into a wall socket. Screw terminals on the unit allow the 12V supply to be wired to the track. A 16V AC supply is available for powering point motors too.

The constant refrain in magazine layout articles is; 'I don't understand electricity so I did the wiring the simplest way I could'. Apparently it's all very complicated, far too challenging for the average person to understand.

This is odd considering many of us started with a train set that included a controller and power clip that plugged the wires into the rails. That all worked so why does everything become more complicated when we build a 'proper' layout? The truth is, it doesn't.

Two wires, one for each polarity, connect *via* the track and wheels to either side of the motor in the locomotive. Add electricity and the motor will turn.

If you look under any model railway, the chances are you'll see a lot of scary wires. My layouts do tend to look like someone has set a paint bomb off in a spaghetti factory. All you are seeing though, is lots of repetitions of the same simple circuit. It might look complicated but by taking one step at a time, it really isn't.

> It might look complicated but by taking one step at a time, it really isn't

TOP TIP

Tinning a wire

Tinning is the process of covering a bit of metal with solder. We do this to make soldering two things together simpler.

If your aim is to attach a wire to a rail, you need to bring these two together along with a hot iron and some solder, all at the same time. Assuming the rail is fixed to a board, you still need three hands to manipulate everything.

The trick is to melt some solder on the wire, then some on the rail. Let them both cool and then hold the wire on the rail, heat the joint to melt the solder that is now on both. That's a two handed job and a lot easier.

2 Because of the different polarity of the track feeds in the rails, a short circuit will occur at crossovers unless insulating fishplates are fitted, even if the points are set straight ahead.

3 Fitting insulating fishplates will isolate each rail and prevent short circuits happening.

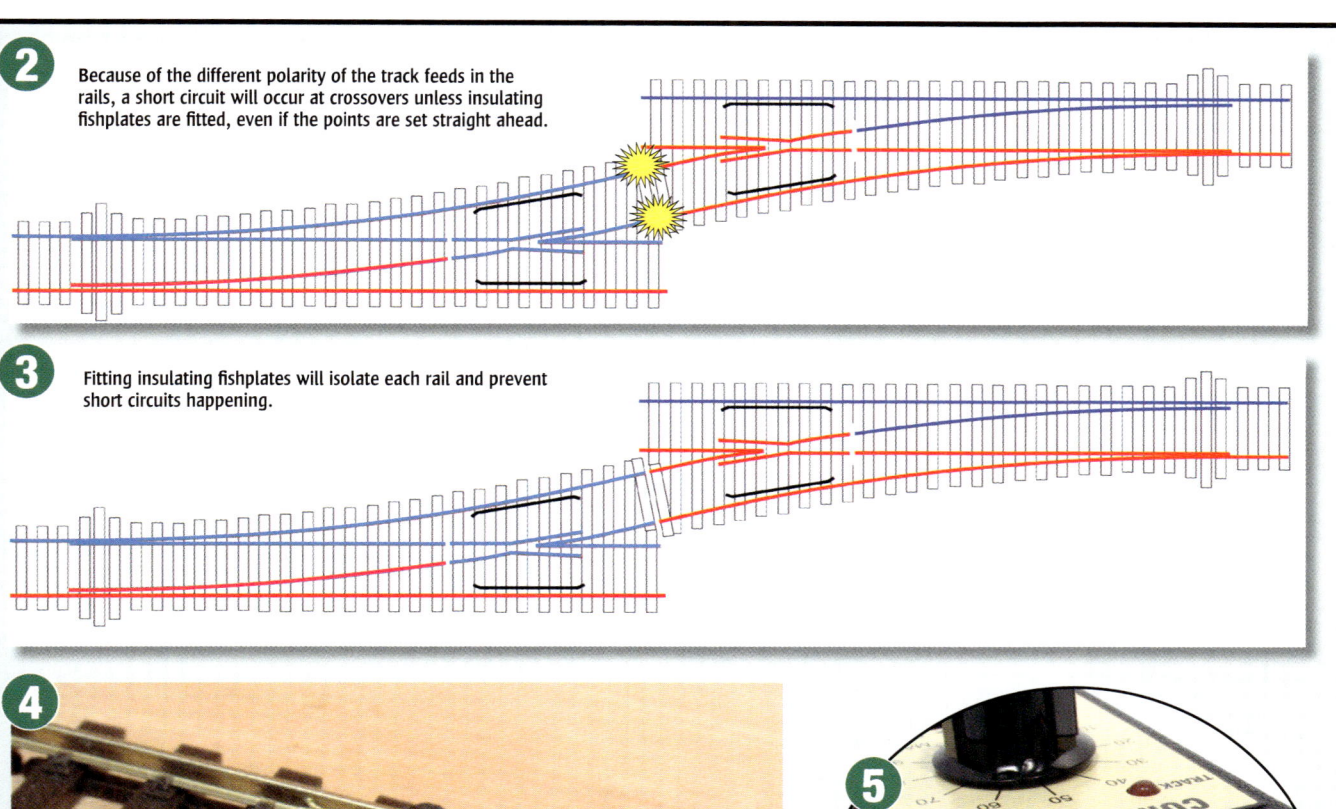

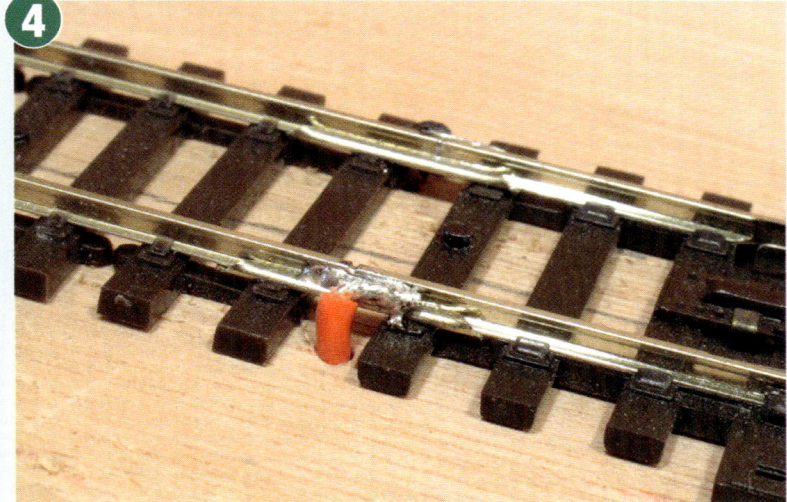

THE BRM GUIDE TO BUILDING YOUR FIRST MODEL RAILWAY

TOP TIP

TURNING THE SCREWS

Putting screws in under the board can be fiddly, but here's a handy hint: fill the slot in the head with Blu-tack and poke the screwdriver in to this. It ought to hold the screw in place long enough to get it started.

SWITCHING POINTS

6 While there's nothing wrong with flicking points by hand, most layouts opt for powered operation. We're going to use Peco point motors mounted under the baseboard. In my experience, these are easy to fit and reliable. Being screwed to the bottom of the board, if anything does go wrong, removal and replacement isn't a big deal.

Buying motors is a little fiddly as there are several variants. For under-baseboard use, you need the PL-10E and PL-12X adaptor base.

Instructions are included with each to show how to put them together to make up the units shown in the photograph. Three brass screws are also in the packet so fitting the motor is simply a case of inserting the pin in the tiebar, waggling it back and forth to make sure the point throws properly and screwing it down. Don't do the screws up too tightly as you can bend the plastic base and affect the switching. As long as the point changes when you push the pin from side to side, you're fine.

WIRING UP

We're going to build a control panel and operate the points using the cheap push buttons found on any model railway electronics stand.

Peco motors are solenoid units. There are two coils and when one of them is electrified, it pulls a steel rod running through the centre towards it. This rod holds the operating pin and so changes the point. All we need to do is give the appropriate coil a burst of power and it will work.

Each motor has four connections. On one side these are joined together and connected to one side of the Capacitor Discharge Unit (CDU, see right). On the other, they connect via push buttons. Press the button and you complete the circuit and energise one coil.

It's important that the coil only receives a burst of power, hence the push buttons. If you prefer a lever, both Peco and Hornby will sell you a passing contact switch lever. Do not use a toggle switch, you'll burn the coil out.

7 To connect the motor, Peco sells a wiring harness that plugs in to the sides. The wires aren't very long so it's a good idea to run them into some electrical 'chocolate block' connectors so longer wires can be connected to reach the panel.

8 Alternatively, solder wires to the tags on the side of the motor. Holes are provided in these so you can poke the wire through and it will hold in place while you apply heat and solder.

9 Either way, this is the basic circuit. Each motor has to be wired up and that accounts for an awful lot of the 'spaghetti' you see under a model railway (below).

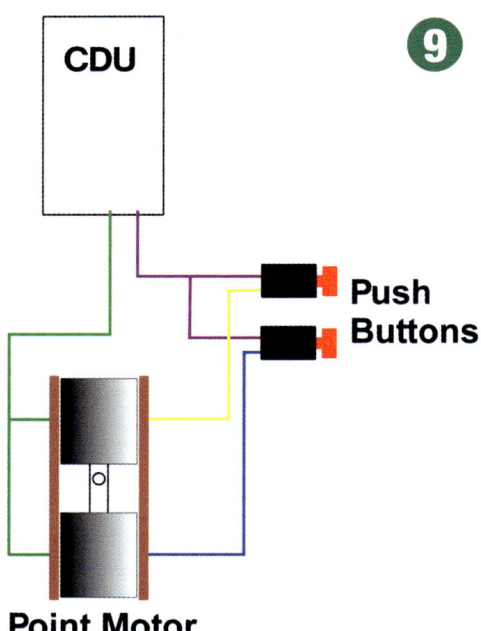

THE CONTROL PANEL

Control panels are very personal things. Some people like enough switches to rival a Space Shuttle. Others prefer a tiny box with buttons on it.

10 My preference is for a nice, clear mimic diagram and enough space for a mug of tea. Ours needs to be removable for transport, so multi-pin plugs and sockets will connect it to the layout.

If you aren't moving the layout, you can wire the panel straight to the board.

11 Construction is simple. Take a couple of rectangles of 3mm thick plywood and pin some two inch deep softwood around the edge of one to form a tray. The other piece of ply will be the top and needs a track diagram drawn on it which is fitted with switches.

You could paint the wood but I acquired some white-faced hardboard the same size as the ply. On this I made a diagram using 'Go Faster Strip' from a car accessory shop. Black looks nice but you can have neon pink if you prefer.

The stuff stays in place on a high-speed Vauxhall Corsa so it is more than good enough for our purposes. I laid out the horizontal lines, then added the junctions, finally cutting the lines back to give a diagram. Gaps were then cut where the switch holes which were drilled out to accept the push buttons.

12 Inside, one terminal on each button is joined up. The other needs a wire long enough to run to the connector fitting in the corner of the box. It all looks like a tangle of wires initially.

These need to be connected one at a time to the sockets and then on to the layout. This is a job made much easier if you support the layout on its front so the entire path of the wire can be traced. Follow each connection on each motor all the way back to the button.

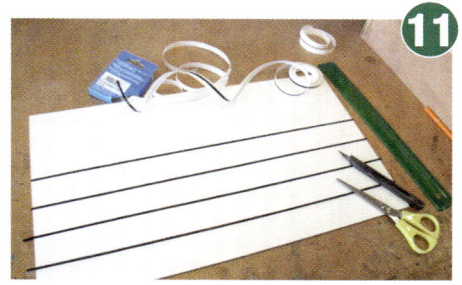

WHAT IS A CDU?

A Capacitor Discharge Unit is an electronic device that stores up a charge until it's required. Then it releases the stored electricity in one quick burst. This will be enough to switch several points at the same time, something that just connecting them to the output of a controller won't always achieve. The extra power also helps with sticky points and makes a layout more reliable.

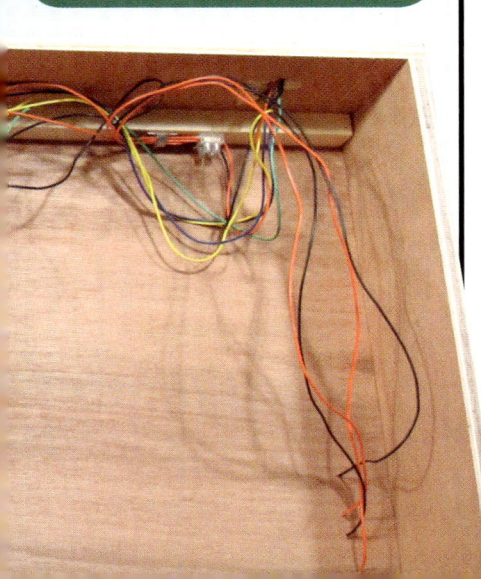

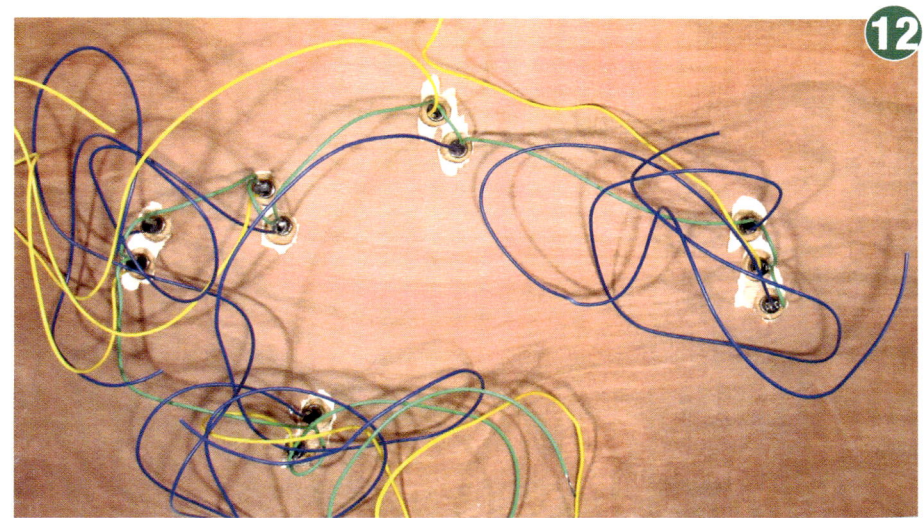

TIDYING UP

Once everything is working, fix the wires to the baseboard. While neat wiring is nice, don't lose sleep over it. The most important thing is that the wires stay put.

Self-adhesive cable clips are very quick and easy to use - stick in place and bend the metal legs over the wires. Over time though, they can lose their grip, so many people prefer nailing the clips in place. This can disturb the track, so a simple modification is to replace the nail with a small brass screw – far less vibration when fitting and easily removed if required.

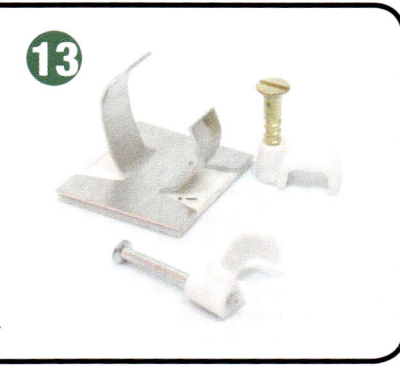

www.model-railways-live.co.uk

GAUGEMASTER.com
The Online Home of The Engine Shed

DCC CONTROL

DIGITAL CONTROL SYSTEMS

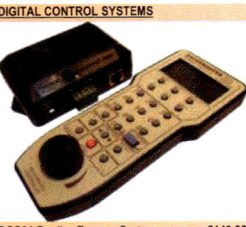

Code	Description	Price
DCC01	Prodigy Express System	£149.95
DCC02	Prodigy Advance2 System	£279.95
DCC03	Prodigy Advance2 Wireless Systm	£479.95

DECODERS

Code	Description	Price
DCC22	CLASSIC 2 Function Micro	£24.95
DCC23	CLASSIC 6 Pin Plug-in Decoder	£24.95
DCC27	OMNI 21 & 8 Pin Decoder	£18.95
DCC28	OMNI 6 Pin Decoder with Harness	£20.95
DCC29	OMNI Direct Plug Decoder	£19.95
BPDCC27	OMNI 21 & 8 Pin Decoder	£89.95
BPDCC28	OMNI 6 Pin with Harness (5)	£99.95
BPDCC29	OMNI Direct Plug Decoder (5)	£96.95
DCC30	Accessory Decoder 4 Accessories	£59.95
DCC31	Accessory Decoder Kato UniTrack	£15.95

DCC ACCESSORIES

Code	Description	Price
DCC11	Prodigy Extension Plate	£37.95
DCC13	Prdigy Adv2 Wireless Walkaround	£179.95
DCC14	Prodigy Adv2 Backlit Walkaround	£129.95
DCC15	"Decoder Doctor" Decoder Tester	£79.95
DCC40	Auto Reverse Module	£39.95
DCC49	Prodigy DCC Booster Unit 8 Amp	£179.95
DCC51	Prodigy Wireless Conversion Set	£259.95
DCC55	Prodigy Wired Computer Interface	£54.95
DCC60	Spare plug for Prodigy	£3.25
DCC61	Medium NEM 652 Socket (5)	£7.95
DCC62	Prodigy Universal Lead (2m)	£19.95
DCC63	Prodigy Adv Power Supply Unit	£24.95
DCC64	Prodigy Power Pack Lead	£6.95
DCC65	Prodigy Express Power Supply Unit	£25.95
DCC71	Prodigy Decoder Tester	£9.95
DCC72	8 to 21 Pin Adaptor	£4.50
DCC77	Prodigy Walkaround Adapter	£9.95

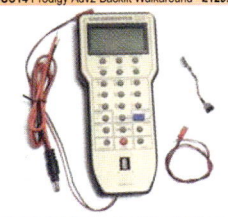

ANALOGUE CONTROL

MAINS POWERED CONTROLLERS

Code	Description	Price
GMC-COMBI	Single Track Controller	£39.95
GMC-100M	Single Track	£84.95
GMC-100MO	Single Track O Scale	£84.95
GMC-10LGB	Single Track G Scale	£99.95
GMC-10LGB5F	Single Track G Scale Fan	£169.95
GMC-P	Single Track Simulation	£99.95
GMC-PO	Single Track Simulation O Scale	£99.95
GMC-D	Twin Track	£94.95
GMC-DO	Twin Track O Scale	£164.95
GMC-DF	Twin Track Feedback	£99.95
GMC-DS	Twin Track Simulation	£164.95
GMC-TS	Three Track Simulation	£174.95
GMC-Q	Four Track	£169.95

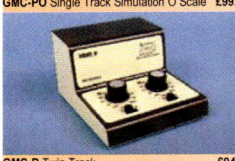

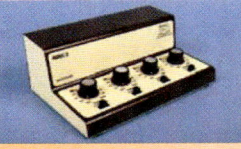

PANEL MOUNT CONTROLLERS

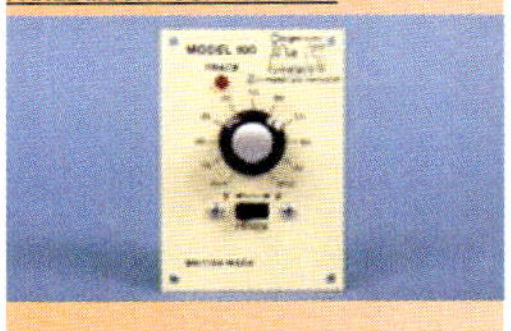

Code	Description	Price
GMC-100	Single Track	£34.95
GMC-100.O	Single Track O Scale	£44.95
GMC-100LGB	Single Track G Scale	£54.95
GMC-U	Single Track Simulation	£44.95
GMC-UF	Single Track Feedback	£39.95
GMC-UO	Single Track Simulation O Scale	£59.95
GMC-UD	Twin Track	£59.95
GMC-UDF	Twin Track Feedback	£59.95
GMC-UDS	Twin Track Simulation	£69.95
GMC-UTS	Three Track Controller Sim.	£79.95
GMC-UQ	Four Track	£84.95

HANDHELD CONTROLLERS

Code	Description	Price
GMC-W	Single Track	£39.95
GMC-WH	Single Track Feedback	£39.95
GMC-WS	Single Track Simulation	£59.95

MAINS POWERED TRANSFORMERS

Code	Description	Price
GMC-M1	Output 2 x 16v AC	£49.95
GMC-M1DC	Output 2 x 12v DC	£54.95
GMC-M2	Output 1 x 18v AC (2.5a)	£54.95
GMC-M3	Output 1 x 24v AC (1.25a)	£54.95
GMC-M4	Output 2 x 12v AC (1.25a)	£54.95

WALL MOUNTED TRANSFORMERS

Code	Description	Price
GMC-WM1	Output 1 x 16V AC or 12v DC	£19.95
GMC-WM2	Output 1 x 9v DC (0.6a)	£14.95

OPEN TRANSFORMERS

Code	Description	Price
GMC-T1	Output 2 x 16V AC (1a)	£24.95
GMC-T2	Output 1 x 18v AC (2.5a)	£24.95
GMC-T3	Output 1 x 24v AC (1.25a)	£24.95
GMC-T4	Output 2 x 12v AC (1a)	£24.95

MODULES

Code	Description	Price
GMC-SS1	Super Shuttle Unit	£34.95
GMC-SS1LGB	Super Shuttle Unit G Scale	£44.95

SEEP POINT CONTROL

POINT CONTROL STARTER SET

Code	Description	Price
GMC-PCSET	Point Control Starter Set	£49.95

Contains Mains Powered CDU, 3 x Point Motors, 3 x Reels of 10m Wire & 3 x Toggle Switches. Ideal for the beginner.

MAINS POWERED POINT CONTROL SYSTEM

Code	Description	Price
GMC-PCU1	Point Control Unit	£114.95
GMC-PCU2	Slave Unit for PCU1	£52.95

CAPACITOR DISCHARGE UNITS

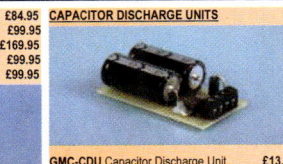

Code	Description	Price
GMC-CDU	Capacitor Discharge Unit	£13.95
GMC-MCDU	Mains Powered CDU	£24.95

POINT MOTORS

Code	Description	Price
GMC-PM1	Motor with Built-In Switch	£5.35
GMC-PM2	Motor No Switch	£4.95
GMC-PM4	Motor Latching Mechanism	£6.25

UNCOUPLERS

Code	Description	Price
GMC-EM1	N Electro Magnetic Uncoupler	£8.95
GMC-EM2	Coupling Adaptor Fret (20)	£4.95
GMC-TLU	OO Tension Lock Uncoupler	£10.95

TRACK

ELECTRONIC HIGH FREQUENCY TRACK CLEANERS FOR DC (ANALOGUE) USE ONLY

Code	Description	Price
GMC-HF1	Single Track Unit	£39.95
GMC-HF2	Double Track Unit	£49.95

AXLE-HUNG TRACK CLEANING PADS

Code	Description	Price
GM37	OO/HO Track Cleaning Pads (3)	£5.50
GM39	N Track Cleaning Pads (3)	£5.50

TRACK TESTER

Code	Description	Price
GM52	Multi Scale Track Tester	£4.95

OO SCALE FLEXIBLE TRACK

Code	Description	Price
GM90	900mm N/Silver Flexible Track (100)	£295
GM93	900mm N/Silver Blk Flexi Track (24)	£79.95
GM94	900mm N/Silver Brn Flexi Track (24)	£79.95
GM97	900mm N/Silver Brn Flexi Track (100)	£295
GM19	Code 100 (OO) Rail Joiners (24)	£2.45

OO SCALE TRACK ACCESSORIES

Code	Description	Price
GM45	OO/HO Re-Railer	£5.35
GM54	OO Buffer Stop	£1.85
BPGM54	OO Buffer Stop (5 Pack)	£8.35

Code	Description	Price
GM13	Pair of Leads (Joiners/Bare Wire)	£4.95
GM66	Hornby Type Track Pins 10mm	£2.60
GM67	Extra Long Track Pins 15mm	£2.60

N SCALE FLEXIBLE TRACK

Code	Description	Price
GM18	Code 80 (N) Rail Joiners (24)	£2.35

N SCALE TRACK ACCESSORIES

Code	Description	Price
GM46	N Re-Railer	£2.95
GM53	N Scale Buffer Stop	£4.50
BPGM53	N Scale Buffer Stop (Pack of 5)	£19.95

Code	Description	Price
GM57	N Lit Buffer Stop on Track	£9.25
GM58	N Buffer Stop Lights (Pack of 2)	£9.95
GM17	Pair of Leads (N Joiner/Bare Wire)	£4.95

OO GREY BALLASTED UNDERLAY SYSTEM

Code	Description	Price
GM114	OO/HO Granite Ballast (500g)	£3.55
GM117	OO/HO Granite Ballast (200g)	£2.35

Code	Description	Price
GM200	Flexible Ballasted Underlay (5m)	£22.95
GM204	Point & Crossing Ballasting Kit	£7.95

OO BROWN BALLASTED UNDERLAY SYSTEM

Code	Description	Price
GM111	OO/HO Brown Ballast (500g)	£3.55
GM210	Flexible Ballasted Underlay (5m)	£22.95
GM214	Point & Crossing Ballasting Kit	£7.95

N GREY BALLASTED UNDERLAY SYSTEM

Code	Description	Price
GM115	N Granite Ballast (500g)	£3.55
GM118	N Granite Ballast (200g)	£2.35
GM201	N Flexible Ballasted Underlay (5m)	£22.95
GM205	N Point & Crossing Ballasting Kit	£7.95

N BROWN BALLASTED UNDERLAY SYSTEM

Code	Description	Price
GM113	N Brown Ballast (500g)	£3.55
GM211	N Flexible Ballasted Underlay (5m)	£22.95
GM215	N Point & Crossing Ballasting Kit	£7.95

OO SCALE CORK TRACKBED SYSTEM

Code	Description	Price
GM251	3mm Cork Trackbed 4.5 x 50cm (6)	£8.95
GM252	3mm Cork Plates 15 x 50cm (2)	£4.50
GM240	For RH Sectional Points (2)	£3.95
GM241	For LH Sectional Points (2)	£3.95
GM244	For RH Sectional Curved Points (2)	£3.95
GM245	For LH Sectional Curved Points (2)	£3.95
GM247	For Y Sectional Points (2)	£3.95

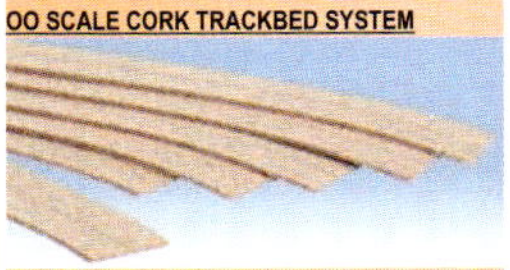

N SCALE CORK TRACKBED SYSTEM

Code	Description	Price
GM231	2mm Cork Trackbed 2.8 x 50cm (6)	£8.95
GM232	3mm Cork Plates 15 x 50cm (2)	£4.50
GM225	For RH Sectional Points (2)	£3.95
GM226	For LH Sectional Points (2)	£3.95

SCENICS

STARTER PACK

Code	Description	Price
GM194	Scenic Starter Pack	£24.95

GENERAL SCENIC MODELLING PRODUCTS

Code	Description	Price
GM100	Mod Roc (2.75m)	£4.50
GM119	Fine Plaster of Paris (1kg)	£3.95
GM130	1/16 Cork Sheet 3' x 2' (60 x 60cm)	£6.50
GM131	1/8 Cork Sheet 3' x 2' (60 x 90cm)	£10.50
GM167	Balsa Bundle 50 x 76 x 229mm	£1.95
GM168	Balsa Bundle 75 x 150 x 450mm	£9.95
GM55	OO Lit Buffer Stop	£6.95
GM66	OO Buffer Stop Lights (Pack of 2)	£9.95

GRASS & GRAVEL MATS

Code	Description	Price
GM20	Spring Grass Mat 100cm x 75cm	£7.95
GM21	Summer Grass Mat 100cm x 75cm	£7.95
GM22	Autumn Grass Mat 100cm x 75cm	£7.95
GM23	Gravel Mat 100cm x 75cm	£5.95
GM38	Spring Grass Mat 240cm x 120cm	£29.95

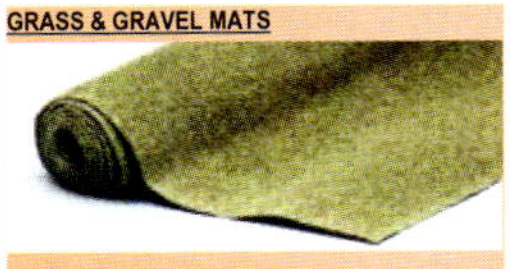

MEADOW MATS

Code	Description	Price
GM140	Meadow Mat - Spring 6mm Grass	£8.95
GM141	Meadow Mat - Meadow 6mm Grass	£8.95
GM142	Meadow Mat - Spring 12mm Grass	£11.95
GM143	Meadow Mat-Meadow 12mm Grass	£11.95
GM147	Meadow Mat - Beige 6mm Grass	£8.95
GM148	Meadow Mat - Beige 12mm Grass	£11.95

STATIC GRASS SYSTEM

Code	Description	Price
GM196	Static Grass Starter Set	£9.95
GM193	Puffer Bottle	£4.75
GM169	Static Grass Glue (250ml)	£6.95
GM170	Spring Grass Flock (30g)	£3.15
GM171	Summer Grass Flock (30g)	£3.15
GM172	Moorland Grass Flock (30g)	£3.15
GM173	Meadow Grass Flock (30g)	£3.15
GM174	Woodland Floor Grass Flock (30g)	£3.25

BUDGET SCATTERS

Code	Description	Price
GM101	Meadow Scatter (50g)	£1.85
GM102	Mid Green Scatter (50g)	£1.85
GM103	Dark Green Scatter (50g)	£1.85
GM105	Spring Green Scatter (50g)	£1.85
GM108	Earth Brown Scatter (50g)	£1.85
GM109	Black Scatter (50g)	£1.85
GM110	Red/Brown Scatter (50g)	£1.85
GM112	Imitation Coal (50g)	£2.35
GM116	Grey Tarmac Scatter (50g)	£1.85

LICHENS & HEDGES

Code	Description	Price
GM160	Light Green Hedgerow (1m)	£6.95
GM161	Dark Green Hedgerow (1m)	£6.95
GM164	Light Green Lichen (80g)	£4.75
GM165	Dark Green Lichen (80g)	£4.75
GM166	Assorted Lichen (80g)	£4.75

FOLIAGE

Code	Description	Price
GM150	Fine Light Green Foliage (30g)	£3.15
GM151	Fine Dark Green Foliage (30g)	£3.15
GM152	Fine Mid Green Foliage (30g)	£3.15
GM153	Fine Light Brown Foliage (30g)	£3.15
GM154	Fine Brown Foliage (30g)	£3.15

STANDARD TREES

Code	Description	Price
GM180	Plum Trees (3)	£6.95
GM181	Plum Trees in Blossom (3)	£6.95
GM182	Fruit Trees (3)	£6.95
GM183	Apple Trees (3)	£6.95
GM184	Birch Trees (3)	£6.95
GM185	Weeping Willow Trees (3)	£6.95
GM186	Poplar Trees (3)	£6.95
GM187	Pine Trees (3)	£8.50
GM188	Beech Trees (2)	£7.50

VALUE TREE ASSORTMENTS

Code	Description	Price
GM127	N Scale Tree Assortment (10)	TBA

BULK TREES

Code	Description	Price
GM128	OO Scale Spring Trees (10)	£10.95
GM129	OO Scale Summer Trees (10)	£10.95
GM120	Deciduous Trees (25)	£19.95
GM121	Mixed Trees (25)	£19.95
GM122	Fir Trees (25)	£19.95
GM123	Small Fir Trees (50)	
GM124	Deciduous Trees (25)	
GM125	Spruce Trees (25)	

MAKE YOUR OWN TREES

Code	Description	Price
GM195	Seafoam for Tree Making	
GM156	Light Green Scenic Leaves (50g)	£7.95
GM157	Mid Green Scenic Leaves (50g)	£7.95
GM158	Dark Green Scenic Leaves (50g)	£7.95

FLOWERS

Code	Description	Price
GM139	Flowerbeds	

Code	Description	Price
GM175	OO/HO Garden Flowers	
GM176	OO/HO Water Plants	
GM177	OO/HO Garden Plants	
GM178	OO/HO Wild Flowers	

GRASS TUFTS

Code	Description	Price
GM136	Spring Grass Tufts	
GM137	Summer Grass Tufts	
GM138	Flowering Grass Tufts	

BRICKWORK

Code	Description	Price
GM30	Plain Stone Wall Grey	
GM31	Grey Stone Wall & Buttresses	
GM32	Grey Stone Wall & Arches	
GM197	Stone Tunnel Wall	
GM198	Single Tunnel Mouth & Walls	
GM199	Double Tunnel Mouth & Walls	

BACKSCENES

Code	Description	Price
GM701	Large Valley Backscene	
GM702	Large Countryside Backscene	
GM703	Large Open Field Backscene	
GM704	Large Village Backscene	
GM705	Large Cloudy Sky Backscene	
GM706	Large Industrial Backscene	
GM707	Large Housebanks Backscene	
GM708	Large Pretty UK Town Backscene	
GM751	Small Valley Backscene	
GM752	Small Countryside Backscene	
GM753	Small Open Field Backscene	
GM754	Small Village Backscene	
GM755	Small Cloudy Sky Backscene	
GM756	Small Industrial Backscene	
GM757	Small Housebanks Backscene	
GM758	Small Pretty UK Town Backscene	

HIGHWAY / OO SCALE WIDE ROAD SYSTEM

Code	Description	Price
GM370	80mm Wide Tarmac Road (1m)	
GM371	80mm Wide Universal Curves (2)	

OO SCALE NARROW ROAD SYSTEM

Code	Description	Price
GM375	68mm Wide Tarmac Road (1m)	
GM376	68mm Wide Universal Curves (2)	

OO/HO SCALE VEHICLE LIGHTING KITS

Code	Description	Price
GM385	Standard Vehicle Kit	
GM386	Emergency Vehicles Kit (Blues)	
GM387	Service Vehicles Kit (Orange)	

N SCALE ROAD SYSTEM

Code	Description	Price
GM390	40mm Wide Tarmac Road (1m)	
GM391	40mm Wide Universal Curves (2)	

STRUCTURES

OO SCALE FENCING

Code	Description	Price
GM145	Country Fencing 290mm Length	
GM371	Garden Fencing 290mm Length	

OO SCALE LASER CUT KITS

Code	Description	Price
GM451	Wooden Fencing 300mm Length	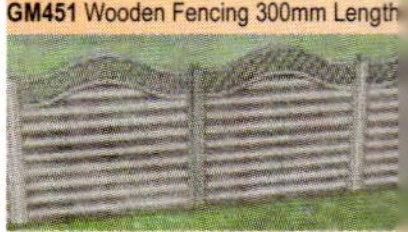
GM452	Lattice Fencing 300mm Length	

TENS OF THOUSANDS OF ITEMS ARE IN STOCK NOW. E & OE.
WE CAN DELIVER POST FREE TO MOST UK ADDRESSES

Gaugemaster Controls Ltd, Gaugemaster House, Ford Road
Arundel, West Sussex, BN18 0BN, United Kingdom

Tel - 01903 884488

Fax - 01903 884377 **E Mail** - engineshed@gaugemaster.co.uk

GAUGEMASTER

STRUCTURES

SCALE LASER CUT KITS (Ctd.)

453	Garden Shed Kit	£6.00

SCALE "FORDHAMPTON" PLASTIC KITS

rdhampton is a bustling market town on a busy inline running through the rolling South Downs. h both local and express services steaming ough, Fordhampton Station serves all kinds of ns from commuters travelling to and from ndon as well as excursions to the seaside at ghton! Wherever you are going the station ster will be happy to help you get to your stination.

401 Fordhampton Station £25.50

402 Fordhampton Signal Box £10.50

403 Fordhampton Footbridge £17.50

404 Fordhampton Level Crossing £11.50

405 Fordhampton 60s Estate House £15.95

406 Fordhampton Locomotive Shed £19.95
407 Fordhampton Carriage Platforms £9.95

408 Fordhampton Village Store or Pub £17.95

ok out for more additions to Fordhampton as and en planning permission is granted!

KESTREL DESIGNS

N GAUGE PLASTIC KITS

GMKD01	House	£4.25
GMKD02	Shop	£4.25
GMKD03	Bungalow	£3.50
GMKD04	Church with Porch	£5.75
GMKD05	House/Shop Unit with Glazing	£6.50
GMKD06	Two Shop Unit with Glazing	£6.50
GMKD07	Four House Unit	£6.50
GMKD08	Country Station	£8.50
GMKD09	Station Buildings	£5.25
GMKD10	Island Platform with Flat Canopy	£8.00
GMKD11	Flat Canopy	£5.75
GMKD12	Small Signal Box	£6.25
GMKD13B	Farm Rail Fencing Brown	£3.00
GMKD13W	Farm Rail Fencing White	£3.00
GMKD14	Telegraph Poles	£3.00
GMKD15	Windows Doors & Guttering	£4.25
GMKD16	Platforms (2)	£2.75
GMKD17	Platform Ramps (2)	£2.25
GMKD18	Station Yard Huts	£3.25
GMKD19	Weighbridge & Office	£4.25
GMKD20	Coal Office	£3.25
GMKD21	Level Crossing/Keepers Cottage	£5.75
GMKD22	Four Greenhouses	£3.00
GMKD23	Two Domestic Garages	£3.00
GMKD24	Water Tower	£3.75
GMKD25	Corner Shop	£4.50
GMKD26	Corner Pub	£4.50
GMKD27	Three Storey Townhouse	£5.75
GMKD28	Three Storey Town Shop	£5.75
GMKD29	Modern Station	£7.75
GMKD30	Modern Station Waiting Room	£5.50
GMKD31	Station Masters House	£6.25
GMKD32	Pair Pre War Semi Det. Houses	£7.00
GMKD33	Boilerhouse & Chimney	£6.25
GMKD34	Stable Block	£3.75
GMKD35	Cow Shed	£3.50
GMKD36	Barn	£5.75
GMKD37	Farm House	£7.25

GMKD38	Steel Footbridge	£7.25
GMKD39	Modern Industrial Unit	£5.75
GMKD40	Modern Fire Station	£7.00
GMKD41	Platforms Wide (2)	£3.25
GMKD42	Platform Ramps Wide (2)	£2.75
GMKD43	Goods Shed	£7.50
GMKD1000	Town Station	£16.95
GMKD1001	Old Factory with Chimney	£19.95

N GAUGE LASER CUT KITS

The same as the ultra detailed OO equivalents (GM451/GM452/GM453) - pack sizes vary from the 4mm versions though

GMKD51	Wooden Fencing	£5.00
GMKD52	Lattice Fencing	£5.00
GMKD53	Garden Sheds (2)	£5.00

N GAUGE VALUE KIT SETS

GMKD2000	Station Set	£14.95
GMKD2001	Town Set	£12.95
GMKD2002	Suburban Set	£14.95
GMKD2003	Farm Set	£16.95

TOOLS

MODEL RAILWAY MAINTENANCE

GM50	OO/HO Locomotive Wheel Cleaner	£39.95
GM47	N Gauge Wheel Cleaner	£34.95
GM51	Spare Pads for GM50	£17.95
GM49	Spare Pads for GM47	£17.95
GM59	N Scale Wheel Cleaner	£15.95

GM60	OO Scale Wheel Cleaner	£19.95
GM619	Precision Lubricator	£4.75
GM667	Superfine Oil Pen w/Teflon Particles	£5.75
GM668	Electrical Contact Oil Pen	£9.75

GENERAL MODELLING TOOLS

GM08	Modelstrip (115ml)	£6.95
GM26	Track Rubber	£3.15
GM27	Jumbo Track Rubber	£5.75
GM600	A2 Cutting Mat	£14.95
GM601	A3 Cutting Mat	£9.95
GM602	A4 Cutting Mat	£4.95
GM603	A5 Cutting Mat	£2.95
GM604	Round Nose Pliers	£6.75
GM605	Flat Nose Pliers	£6.75
GM606	Side Cutters	£6.75
GM607	Half Round Pliers	£6.75
GM608	Bent Nose Pliers	£6.75
GM609	S/Steel Tweezers (4)	£7.95
GM610	Double Ended Pin Vice	£5.75
GM611	Sawset 1 w/ Scalpel Handle	£9.75
GM613	Trim-away Knife	£3.50
GM614	S/S Scalpel & Blades	£4.95
GM615	Plastic Scalpel & Blades	£5.50
GM616	Cutting Knife & 5 Blades	£5.95
GM617	Pick-Up Tool	£5.95
GM618	Magnifier Tweezers	£3.95
GM621	Locking forceps Curved	£6.75
GM624	Swivel Top Pin Vice	£6.50
GM625	Curved Tweezer R/Action	£3.95
GM626	Straight Tweezer R/Action	£3.95
GM627	Blunt End Tweezer R/Action	£3.95
GM629	Cutting Discs (10)	£4.75
GM630	Screw Top Mandrels (3)	£4.25
GM631	Slitting Discs (10) & Mandrel	£6.75
GM632	Budget Needle File Set	£4.75
GM633	Glass Fibre Pencil 4mm	£4.75
GM634	4mm G/Fibre Refills (10)	£7.50
GM635	2mm Glass Fibre Pencil	£9.50
GM636	2mm G/Fibre Refills (5)	£6.50
GM638	Cutting Broaches 0.6-2.0	£15.50
GM640	Archimedian Drill Stock	£5.95
GM641	HSS Jbbrs Drills 0.5 (5)	£3.95
GM642	HSS Jbbrs Drills 0.8 (5)	£3.95
GM643	HSS Jbbrs Drills 1.0 (5)	£3.95
GM644	HSS Jbbrs Drills 1.2 (5)	£3.95
GM645	HSS Jbbrs Drills 1.5 (5)	£3.95
GM646	HSS Jbbrs Drills 1.8 (5)	£3.95
GM647	HSS Jbbrs Drills 2.0 (5)	£3.95
GM648	Microbox Drills 0.3-1.6	£10.95
GM649	Microbox HSS Twist Drill Bits 61-80	£10.95
GM650	HSS Jbbrs Drills 0.3 (5)	£3.95
GM651	HSS Jbbrs Drills 0.4 (5)	£3.95
GM652	HSS Jbbrs Drills 0.6 (5)	£3.95
GM653	HSS Jbbrs Drills 0.7 (5)	£3.95
GM654	HSS Jbbers Drills 0.9 (5)	£3.95
GM655	Spare Blades for GM614	£2.50
GM656	Spare Blades for GM616	£2.50
GM660	Pick n Place Twin Pack	£7.75
GM664	Economy Sprue/Plastic Cutter	£4.50
GM666	Clip On Magnifying Eye Glass	£6.50
GM669	Pin Pusher with Depth Stop	£9.95
GM670	Deluxe Paintbrush Set	£9.95

GM683	Soft Grip Knife Set with Blades	£6.95
GM684	Spare Blades for GM683	£1.50
GM693	Value Model Railway Drill	£9.95
GM694	Mains Powered Value Drill	£16.95
GM695	Model Railway Screwdriver Set	£4.95
GM696	Masking Tape 6mm x 18m (2)	£2.25
GM697	Masking Tape 10mm x 18m (2)	£2.95
GM698	Masking Tape 18mm x 18m (1)	£2.75

RAZOR SAWS

GM672	Razor Saw Superfine	£10.95
GM673	3 in 1 Saw Set	£13.95
GM674	Razor Saw Fine	£10.95
GM675	Razor Saw Medium	£10.95
GM676	Aluminum Mitre Box	£14.95
GM677	Fine Woodcraft Saw	£10.95
GM678	Flush Cutting Saw	£14.95
GM679	Universal Razor Saw	£11.95

SOLDERING IRONS & BITS

GM680	15W 230V Soldering Iron	£14.95
GM681	25W 230v Soldering Iron	£16.95
GM682	40W 230v Soldering Iron	£18.95
GM685	15W No.6 Tip	£3.50
GM686	15W No.8 Tip	£3.50
GM687	25W No.6 Tip	£3.75
GM688	25W No.7 Tip	£3.75
GM689	25W No.8 Tip	£3.75
GM690	40W No.6 Tip	£3.75
GM691	40W No.7 Tip	£3.75
GM692	40W No.8 Tip	

SOLDERING ACCESSORIES

GM01	Low Melt Solder 70 degrees (20g)	£4.25
GM02	Solder 180 degrees (20g)	£3.95
GM03	White Metal Flux	£5.95
GM04	Brass Flux	£5.95
GM05	Non Acid Safety Flux	£6.25
GM06	Solder Wire 145 Degrees	£4.85

ELECTRICS

SWITCHES

GM501	Slide Switch DPDT	£1.65
GM502	Slide Switch DPDT (C/off)	£1.65
GM503	Toggle Switch SPST	£2.30
GM504	Toggle Switch DPDT	£2.60
GM505	Mini-Toggle DPDT (C/off)	£3.10
GM506	Mini-Toggle DPDT	£2.70
GM507	Mini-Toggle SPST	£2.40
GM508	Mini-Toggle SPDT	£2.40
GM509	Mini-Toggle SPDT (C/off)	£2.40
GM510	Mini-Toggle for Point Motors	£2.65
GM511	Mini-Toggle for G Point Motors	£3.60
GM512	Push to Break Black (5)	£5.95
GM513	Push to Make Black (5)	£2.75
GM514	Push to Make Blue (5)	£2.75
GM515	Push to Make Green (5)	£2.75
GM516	Push to Make Red (5)	£2.75
GM517	Push to Make White (5)	£2.75
GM518	Push to Make Yellow (5)	£2.75
GM519	Rotary Switch 1 Pole 12 Way	£2.75
GM520	Rotary Switch 2 Pole 6 Way	£3.70
GM521	Rotary Switch 3 Pole 4 Way	£3.70
GM522	Rotary Switch 4 Pole 3 Way	£3.70
BPGM501	Slide Switch DPDT (25)	£12.95
BPGM502	Slide Switch DPDT (C/off) (25)	£12.95
BPGM503	Toggle Switch SPST (25)	£34.95
BPGM504	Toggle Switch DPDT (25)	£42.95
BPGM505	Mini-Toggle DPDT (C/off) (25)	£44.95
BPGM506	Mini-Toggle DPDT (25)	£42.95
BPGM507	Mini-Toggle SPST (25)	£34.95
BPGM508	Mini-Toggle SPDT (25)	£34.95
BPGM509	Mini-Toggle SPDT (C/off) (25)	£39.95
BPGM510	Mini-Toggle for Point Motors (25)	£44.95
BPGM513	Push to Make Black (25)	£9.95
BPGM514	Push to Make Blue (25)	£9.95
BPGM515	Push to Make Green (25)	£9.95
BPGM516	Push to Make Red (25)	£9.95
BPGM517	Push to Make White (25)	£9.95
BPGM518	Push to Make Yellow (25)	£9.95

WIRE

GM10	Wire Red/Black/Green (10m of each)	£5.95
GM11BK	Wire Black 7 x 0.2mm (10m)	£2.15
GM11BL	Wire Blue 7 x 0.2mm (10m)	£2.15
GM11BN	Wire Brown 7 x 0.2mm (10m)	£2.15
GM11GN	Wire Green 7 x 0.2mm (10m)	£2.15
GM11GR	Wire Grey 7 x 0.2mm (10m)	£2.15
GM11O	Wire Orange 7 x 0.2mm (10m)	£2.15
GM11P	Wire Pink 7 x 0.2mm (10m)	£2.15
GM11P	Wire Purple 7 x 0.2mm (10m)	£2.15
GM11R	Wire Red 7 x 0.2mm (10m)	£2.15
GM11W	Wire White 7 x 0.2mm (10m)	£2.15
GM11Y	Wire Yellow 7 x 0.2mm (10m)	£2.15
BPGM11BK	Black Wire 7 x 0.2mm (100m)	£7.95
BPGM11BL	Blue Wire 7 x 0.2mm (100m)	£7.95
BPGM11BN	Brown Wire 7 x 0.2mm (100m)	£7.95
BPGM11GN	Green Wire 7 x 0.2mm (100m)	£7.95
BPGM11GR	Grey Wire 7 x 0.2mm (100m)	£7.95
BPGM11O	Orange Wire 7 x 0.2mm (100m)	£7.95
BPGM11P	Pink Wire 7 x 0.2mm (100m)	£7.95
BPGM11R	Red Wire 7 x 0.2mm (100m)	£7.95
BPGM11W	White Wire 7 x 0.2mm (100m)	£7.95
BPGM11Y	Yellow Wire 7 x 0.2mm (100m)	£7.95

GENERAL ELECTRICAL ACCESSORIES

GM12	Pair Connecting Leads (Pin/Bare Wire)	£4.55
GM14	Crimped Pin Terminals (6)	£2.95
GM15	Ring Terminals (6)	£1.95
GM16	Pair Connecting Leads (Pin/Pin)	£4.95
GM28	Crocodile Clips Red/Black Pair	£1.65
GM29	Knob for Rotary Switches & Pots	£2.75
GM40	1.5a Rectifier	£4.95
GM41	Thermal Cut-Out 1 Amp	£3.95
GM42	Thermal Cut-Out 2.5 Amp	£3.95
GM75	PS6 6-Way Din Plug/Socket	£2.95
GM77	12-Way Poly Terminal Block	£1.95
GM89	Pack of 5 Amp Fuses (5)	£2.65

LIGHTING

GM61	Micro LED White (4)	£7.95
GM62	Micro LED Red (4)	£7.95
GM63	Micro LED Blue (4)	£7.95
GM64	Micro LED Orange (4)	£7.95
GM69	Grain of Wheat Bulb 12v Yellow (5)	£3.95
GM70	Grain of Wheat Bulb 12v Red (5)	£3.95
GM71	Grain of Wheat Bulb 12v Clear (5)	£3.95
GM72	Grain of Wheat Bulb 12v Green (5)	£3.95
GM73	Grain of Wheat Bulb 12v Orange (5)	£3.95
BPGM69	GOW 12v Yellow (100)	£49.95
BPGM70	GOW Bulb 12v Red (100)	£49.95
BPGM71	GOW Bulb 12v Clear (100)	£39.95
BPGM72	GOW Bulb 12v Green (100)	£49.95
BPGM73	GOW Bulb 12v Orange (100)	£49.95
GM80	LED Green 3mm 12v (5)	£2.25
GM81	LED Red 3mm 12v (5)	£2.25
GM82	LED Yellow 3mm 12v (5)	£2.25
GM83	LED Green 5mm 12v (5)	£1.95
GM84	LED Red 5mm 12v (5)	£1.95
GM85	LED Yellow 5mm 12v (5)	£1.95
GM76	Resistor 1K Ohm for LEDs (10)	£1.60

MAGNETS

GM86	Small Magnets (10)	£5.50
GM87	Medium Magnets (10)	£5.75
GM88	Large Magnets (10)	£6.00
GM98	3v Bulbs (10) & Capacitors (5)	£5.95
GM99	Pack of Reeds & 5 Magnets	£13.95

UNIVERSAL RELAY SWITCH

GM500	Universal Relay Switch (Single)	£5.25
BPGM500	Universal Relay Switch (3)	£13.95

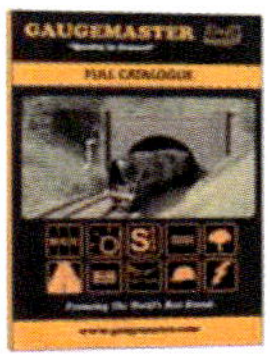

GM353 CATALOGUE
128 Page Full Colour Catalogue
£3.95

GAUGEMASTER Limited Edition News

dapol **N SCALE**

DAGM220 Cl66 DB Schenker - £89.95
66 001 **IN STOCK NOW**

DAGM231 IC Executive Pristine £69.95
73 142 Broadlands

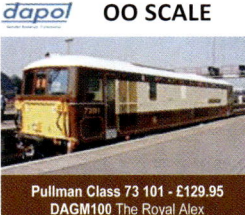

DAGM232 First GBRf - £69.95
73 141 Charlotte

DAGM233 South West Trains - £69.95
73 235

DAGM234 Southern Livery - £69.95
73 202

DAGM235 Pullman - £69.95
73 101 The Royal Alex
(DAGM230 is already sold out)

dapol **OO SCALE**

Pullman Class 73 101 - £129.95
DAGM100 The Royal Alex
DAGM101 Brighton Evening Argus
300pcs of each only

GM354 2015 NEW ITEMS BROCHURE
28 Pages. Free from your local dealer or direct from us.

RANGES STOCKED

Airfix
Antex
Atlas
Bachmann
Berko
Busch
Capital Transport
Carrera
Cartrix
Classix
Dapol
DCCconcepts
Deluxe Materials
DM Toys
Dornaplas
EFE
Faller
Fleischmann
FlySlot
Gaugemaster
Graham Farish
Harburn Hamlet
Heljan
HMRS Transfers
Hobbytrain
Hornby
Humbrol
Ian Allen
Jagerndorfer
Kadee
Kato
Kestrel Designs
Kibri
Knightwing
LGB
Lifelike
Lightcraft
Marklin
Mehano
Metcalfe
Middleton Press
MiNis
Minitrains
Modelcraft
Model Scene
MRC
Ninco
Noch
NSR
Oxford Diecast
Oxford Rail
Parkside Dundas
Peco
Piko
Plastruct
Pola
Preiser
Racer
Railmatch
Ratio
Revell
Roco
Rokuhan
Rotacraft
Scalextric
Scenix
Seep
Seuthe
Sideways
Slaters
Slot It
Slotwings
Spraycraft
Springside
SRC
Superquick
Tiny Signs
Tracksetta
Train Tech
TrainSave
Trumpeter
Trix
Viessmann
Vollmer
Vulcan Slot
W & T
Walthers
Wiking
Wills
Xuron

CONTACT US FOR A FREE PRICE LIST
HUGE BREADTH OF STOCK, VISIT OUR WEBSITE FOR LIVE STOCK INFORMATION

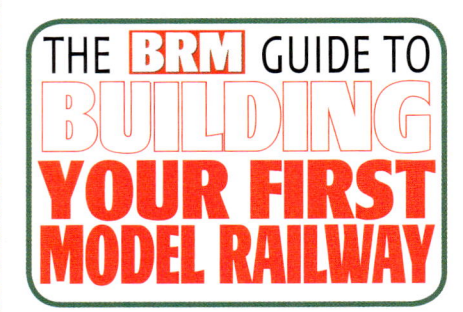

THE BRM GUIDE TO BUILDING YOUR FIRST MODEL RAILWAY

HOW TO... BALLAST TRACK

With the track laid, the job moves to ballasting. Here's our simple guide to giving your track a more realistic look.

Real railways don't use massive pins to hold the track in place. Instead, it sits on a bed of ballast allowing water to drain away as well as absorbing energy. Although railways in the UK predominantly use granite ballast, limestone was once popular in areas where it was available locally.

The quality of ballast varies depending on the type of track too. Running lines get the best and in the past would be maintained by track gangs being re-packed and cleaned as necessary. In steam days, linesmen would be responsible for minor maintenance on sections of track - awards were given to those who kept the tidiest 'length'.

Sidings received secondhand ballast, poor quality material, even ash or clinker - something steam railways had in enormous quantities. If you look at old photographs, the difference between this and the main lines is obvious. On a small scale model, ballast is purely decorative, but without it the track doesn't look right. Because of this we work in the opposite way to the prototype - track is laid and tested then the ballast is added.

The actual work is time-consuming but not difficult. Simply pour ballast on the track, tidy it up and then glue it into place. As this is a first layout, we've kept things simple with a single grade of ballast. If you want to become an expert in the subject, I recommend the 2mm Scale Society's book *Track: How It Works and How To Model It*. Even for modellers working in larger scales, the information on what can be a complex subject is very useful.

One problem with model ballast is that it's heavy. A quick survey of local model shops showed me that the one brand they all carried was Javis, so we've used its fine granite chips on 'Edgeworth'.

Obviously, there are many other options but I'd recommend picking them up at an exhibition at

CAN I REMOVE OLD BALLAST FROM TRACKWORK?

It all depends on how the ballast was glued down in the first place. Assuming PVA was used then a damp (not dripping wet) pad of kitchen towel placed on the track and left for a while can soften the glue enough to make it possible to lift the track and leave the stones.

STEP-BY-STEP GUIDE

1 Before starting work, the copper-clad sleepers at the baseboard ends were painted with Phoenix Precision track colour. You could paint all the track at this stage, especially if you plan to spray it.

2 Use leftover sleepers to fill any gaps. Cut away the rail chairs and they should slide in. As you can see, I nearly forgot this step - it needs to be carried out before the stones are poured.

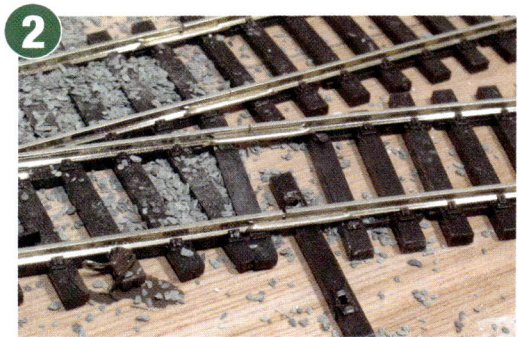

3 Sprinkle small amounts of ballast over the track, working on small sections at a time.

TOP TIP
Before dripping glue all over the layout, pull the baseboards apart slightly. That way the glue won't get between them and stick them together!

IS THERE AN EASIER WAY TO DO THIS?

Certain brands such as Kato, Fleischmann, Roco and Atlas offer track with plastic 'ballast' moulded as part of the trackbed. Aesthetically, it's not as pleasing as properly ballasted track, but it would be worth considering if you want to speed things up or need to take up your track regularly.

Another popular option is Gaugemaster's ready-ballasted foam underlay, which combines the sound-deadening properties of foam with a realistic ballasted appearance. See www.gaugemaster.com

Greenscene, Poppy's Woodtech and Proses, amongst others, sell ballasting tools too. These are hoppers that you place over the track, fill with stone and then slide along the rails. They deposit the ballast neatly along plain track. You'll still need to do the points by hand, but if you've a lot of running line, the tools are worth buying.

To the right you can see what we are aiming for. Nice neat ballast with nothing on the sleeper tops. On the left, the track gang must have been interrupted or perhaps they were in a hurry. The different sizes of stone used on the prototype show up here too, on the far left the sidings are ballasted in very fine grit or even ash whereas the running line makes use of granite.

the end of the day as carrying a pound or two of stone around can be wearing. Worse, postage can be expensive if you use mail order.

Granite might be the 'correct' material but it reacts poorly with PVA glue and changes colour slightly to a greenish hue. We'll tackle this with some weathering later. In the meantime, next time you take a trip on the train, have a good look at the track. There's a lot more to it than you might think. **BRM**

TOOLS FOR THE JOB
- Pipette
- Soft ½" paintbrush

WHAT WE USED
1.5lb Javis fine ballast - £3.35

The first question to ask is: "What sort of stone was the line I am modelling ballasted with?" On the left, Javis granite ballast, on the right, Hornby SkaleScenes fine gravel to represent limestone ballast.

How fine should ballast be? Both these are Limestone ballast from Geoscenics, on the left 7mm scale/O gauge, on the right OO gauge/4mm scale. Some people would look for N gauge ballast even in OO as they prefer even smaller sized stones.

4

Above Use a half-inch wide paintbrush at a shallow angle to brush the stone along the track. Try to keep the sleeper tops clear as it all looks a lot neater. Try to keep the edge of the stones reasonably straight and a few millimetres from the end of the sleepers.

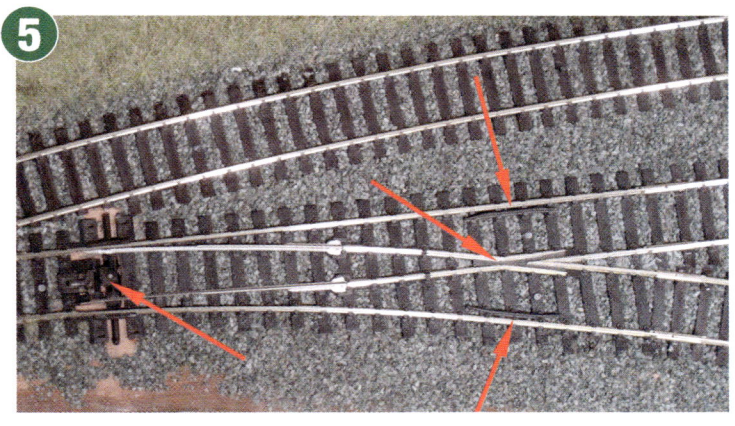

5

Around the points you need to be especially careful. Try to keep stone out of the crossing and behind the checkrails. I keep the tiebar clear too, painting and weathering the baseboard here will make the lack of ballast less obvious, it's more important to keep things working.

6

Right Fix the stone in place with a 50/50 mix of PVA glue and water. Add a drop of washing-up liquid to this as it will reduce surface tension. Let the mix stand for an hour before applying it to the track with a pipette. Work along the outside of the rail – the glue will soak through to the centre and use the minimum around pointwork. You can always add more if required.

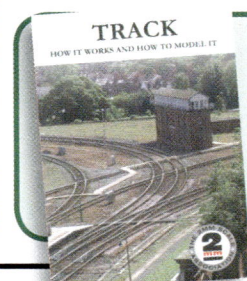

USEFUL READING
If you really want to know how to model great looking track, the 2mm Scale Society's book *Track: How it Works and How To Model It* provides a wealth of information. Price £15.00
W: www.2mm.org.uk/products/trackbook

THE BRM GUIDE TO BUILDING YOUR FIRST MODEL RAILWAY

HOW TO MODEL...
A BAC

A good quality backscene will add a large degree of realism to your layout.

Why does a model railway need a backscene? I suppose you can argue that it doesn't really. Many people don't bother with one, preferring to get on with the 3-D modelling. Sometimes a tall background can get in the way of access to the model. This can be a problem if you are using three-link couplings or are just a bit on the short side and operate from behind the layout.

For most of us though, if the background to our model is some lovely floral wallpaper or the jumper-clad bellies of our operators, then something more realistic is essential.

If your backscene does its job then as well as covering up undesirable sights, it will make the model appear larger. The key to doing this is pale colours. If you look at a view in real life, as things get further away they are paler. The atmosphere adds a blue tinge to the colours too.

Technical details like this won't worry us when using commercial backscene sheets, but if you fancy yourself as a bit of an artist then sketching in some hills using watercolour or poster paints isn't too difficult. Practice on some paper before attacking the layout and you might be pleasantly surprised how effective your efforts are.

Painting hillsides has always defeated me so I prefer a commercial backscene. These can be a bit of a mixed bag. Some try to include too much detail or get all the perspective wrong, but there is plenty of choice, so spend some time taking your pick before sticking it to the backs of the layout. Once the scenery work starts, it's almost impossible to change your mind!

Talking of scenery, there is a need to disguise the transition from 3-D model to 2-D background. Having spent time on my backscene, I then normally end up trying to hide it from view as much as possible. We'll look at this in more detail later. **BRM**

> "If you don't want your operators' tatty jumpers as the background to your modelling, you'll need a backscene!"

TOOLS FOR THE JOB

- Household filler
- Sharp knife
- Masking tape
- Sky blue base colour
- Your chosen backscene
- Deluxe Materials View Glue

KSCENE

PECO BACKSCENES
We used two SK-12 (Country Landscape) and a single SK-16 (Town Provincial) large sheets plus the SK-14 (Conversion Landscape) for an added hill. All sheets are £1.35 each and available from all good model shops.

STEP-BY-STEP GUIDE ▶

1

'Edgeworth's' backscene is built into the baseboards using the same 9mm plywood as the rest of the layout. At 10" high, it adds strength to the boards, one of the benefits of including it in the initial construction.

2

Using some household filler, I've rounded the inside of the corner a little. A hard vertical line in the sky looks odd and so the greater the curve you can introduce here the better.

www.model-railways-live.co.uk 45

THE BRM GUIDE TO BUILDING YOUR FIRST MODEL RAILWAY

STEP-BY-STEP GUIDE ➡

3 Scenic work can be messy, so covering the track, especially the pointwork, with cheap masking tape is a good idea. A few minutes spent now can save you hours digging blobs of paint out from between sleepers.

4 It's not difficult to chose a suitable base colour. This matchpot is labelled 'Sky' and the contents are unsurprisingly, a pleasant sky blue colour. 'Edgeworth' used one-and-a-half pots of paint to provide three coats making the testers a very economical choice.

5 What sort of backscene to use? Peco's painted version or a Gaugemaster photographic type? I felt the later was too strongly coloured for a small layout, so plumped for the more traditional and cheaper option.

6 Peco backscenes are intended to match up when used end-to-end. While the scenery might, colours vary between batches, so you need to check them against each other in the shop. Here, we'll need a strategically placed tree to hide the join.

7 While the backscenes include sky, I cut this away with a sharp knife as the blue paint is easier to maintain on a model that will be subject to handling. Also, we can hide joins in hillsides, those in the sky are more obvious. If you decide to do this, take your time around details such as buildings and tree tops.

8 As well as full sheets, Peco sells extra sections to be cut out and overlaid to add variety to the scene. The colours appear stronger than the normal sheets which will make them appear closer to the viewer.

9 Taking layering to an extreme, on 'Melbridge Dock', I used a Peco scene as intended behind an overbridge, but to avoid seeing the same image again elsewhere, chopped out individual buildings and re-arranged them behind the gates in the centre of the model. As well as providing variety, this also gives the background a mild 3-D effect.

46 www.RMweb.co.uk

Deluxe Materials 'View Glue' is liberally applied to the back of the paper to fix it to the woodwork. Smooth out any bubbles and then leave to dry. Any slight wrinkles should pull out automatically as the glue sets. It's just like hanging wallpaper - the paste intended for this will work nearly as well if used sparingly so as not to soak the paper.

10

11

Just adding the backscene makes the model look larger and certainly brightens the boards up.

THE PERILS OF PRODUCING A PHOTOGRAPHIC BACKSCENE

Using a large photograph as a backscene can be incredibly effective as you can see here on 'Black Country Blues'. Here, the image has been made up by stitching lots of images together electronically and then taking the resulting file to a commercial printer to produce a long flexible sheet.

Crucially, the colours on the image are toned down and the whole thing lacks sharpness, all of which stops it dominating the scene. Producing a backscene this way isn't cheap - you can spend as much as buying a couple of large OO gauge locomotives doing it. You also need to work out how to hang the scene at the back of the layout. Most people keep it separate, supported on special uprights, but this is another job when setting up the layout that might need several pairs of hands.

How we made the 'BCB' backscene...
Find out how Andy York made the amazing backscene on 'Black Country Blues'. **Download the April 2013 issue of BRM from just £3.99.** For more information go to: **www.model-railways-live.co.uk/digital**

MY LAYOUT

▶ On my layout, 'Flockburgh', we used an early photograph background glued to the backscene boards. Sadly the colours were very strong so it didn't look right until the layout in front was brightly lit. Worse, the paper at the baseboard ends became battered as the layout was transported around the country. You can't repair this and replacement wasn't an option.

▶ Our solution was to add a tall chimney over the join. Held in place with Blu-Tak, it works well and the shadows cast aren't as obvious in real life. Fortunately there is only one join, or we'd need a lot of chimneys!

www.model-railways-live.co.uk 47

THE BRM GUIDE TO BUILDING YOUR FIRST MODEL RAILWAY

HOW TO MODEL...
HILLSIDES & RETAINING WALLS

It's time to start landscaping the layout. Follow this guide to make your lightweight hillsides with detailed retaining walls.

STEP-BY-STEP GUIDE

1 Bigger hills demand more effort. Above 'Edgeworth's' fiddleyard exit we're planning a road bridge, so the ground needs to be built up as high as the top of the trains. Polystyrene sheet is the easiest way to achieve this. Ceiling tiles are cut roughly to shape and then glued together with PVA.

2 *Above* The messy part - have a vacuum cleaner handy as you shape the hills with a surform tool normally used for wood. A rasp works as well and the job can be carried out with a knife if you don't have access to either.

Below A plaster skin over the hills makes them easier to work with. On its own the polystyrene can be attacked by some types of paint and this step will also remove any final steps in the hillsides. We've used Geoscenics plaster bandage, cut in to squares, dipped in water and then smoothed over the polystyrene. Two coats are a good idea, or a single one with a skim of wall filler - one layer feels a bit weak on its own.

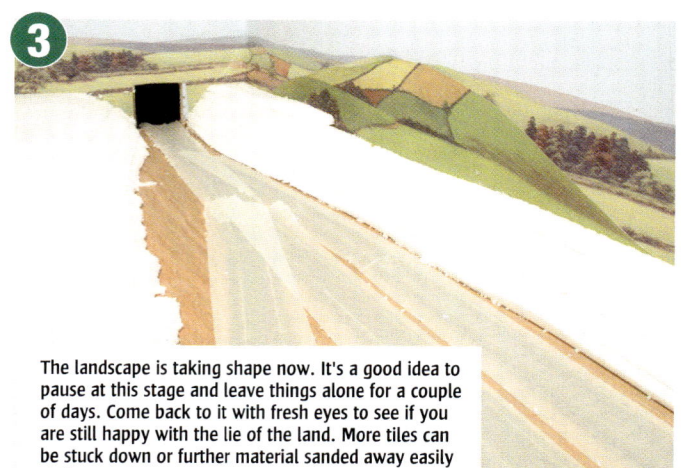

3 The landscape is taking shape now. It's a good idea to pause at this stage and leave things alone for a couple of days. Come back to it with fresh eyes to see if you are still happy with the lie of the land. More tiles can be stuck down or further material sanded away easily at the moment.

4

One of the aims for any modeller building a railway is to make it appear as those it has been set into the landscape rather than the hills springing up around the track. The real thing was cut through the countryside by sheer back-breaking effort of large groups of navvies rather than the other way around.

We don't have to work nearly as hard of course. For most of us, a few modest hills will suffice. You might even think that you'll be able to get away without any work, after all there are plenty of areas where the ground at first glance appears to be flat.

Don't be fooled though. I made this mistake with my first layout. Visiting the area, we didn't see any hills or valleys. Flock powder was stuck straight to the baseboard and sadly, it looked exactly like we had done this. A refurbishment incorporated some mild contours made from plaster and the layout looked a lot better for it.

'Edgeworth' isn't really big enough to allow for extensive earthworks but the model will gain a lot of visual interest if we bring trains in through a low cutting so I've build the ground levels up a bit around the track.

For this I'm using polystyrene sheets, bought as ceiling tiles as they were easily available and we didn't need much material. There are lots of other options though - most types of sheet building insulation are ideal, being light and easy to carve. A trip to a builders' merchants should furnish the modeller with enough to build a miniature mountain range.

The sharp eyed and stingy might prefer to keep an eye on local skips as off-cuts thrown out by builders will probably be large enough for our purposes. Obviously you need to ask before helping yourself but normally the owners are only too happy to have people taking the stuff away with them. **BRM**

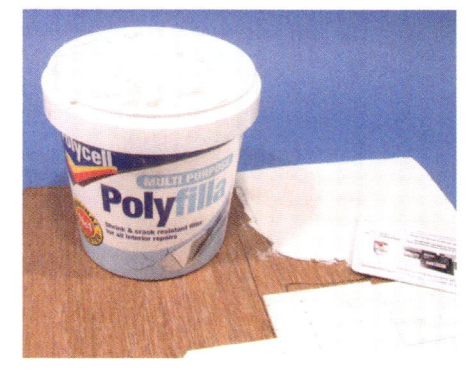

'Time for the messy bit – building scenery!'

For minor lumps and bumps in the scenery, there's nothing better than some household filler from a DIY store. This pub garden was featured in the June 2013 issue of **BRM**. A 2/3 millimetre high mound was needed.

SUPPLIER
Geoscenics Plaster bandage – 270cm x 15cm roll - £3.50
(We used 1 ½ rolls on the hills to provide 2 layers)
W www.geoscenics.co.uk

5 Paint the ground a nice earthy colour. Emulsion matchpots are ideal and cheap. I have a collection of mud tones that are mixed up to vary the shade or earth. Just slap it on with a 1" brush. There's no science to this bit.

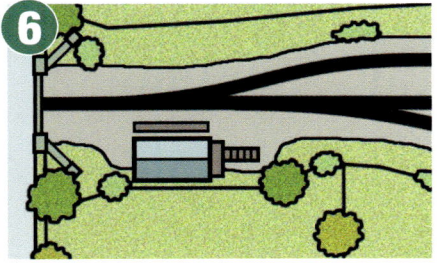

6 The plan calls for the signalbox to be set into the hillside. We could have built this into the hill during construction, but it seemed easier to do the job afterwards – just like the prototype.

7 **Above** Cut through the plaster skin with a craft knife. It should cut reasonably cleanly and lift away. The polystyrene can then be excavated from the hole.

Right I checked that the signalbox fitted and enlarged the hole as required. While the tape measure might suggest all is OK, there's nothing to beat putting the building in place to see if it looks right. There should be space for a man to walk around all sides of the building.

8

9 In real life there would be a retaining wall to stop the earth slipping into the hole. On the model this is made from cardboard cut to size then covered with Slater's Plastikard. Use PVA to fix the parts here - solvent based glues will eat the polystyrene.

10 With the 'box in place, the finished section of landscape looks great. The final 'bedding in' of the building will take place after the ground has been covered with greenery.

THE BRM GUIDE TO BUILDING YOUR FIRST MODEL RAILWAY

HOW TO MODEL...
GRASS AND FLOCK

Applying grass to layouts has been made easier. Here's a quick guide to electrostatic grass and applicators.

One area of our hobby that has improved in leaps and bounds in the last few years is the modelling of grass. Once, hillsides were simply painted green. If the modeller sprinkled a little sawdust in to the wet paint to provide some texture they were hailed as an expert.

Then along came flock powders; dyed sawdust or ground foam that you sprinkled over glue and available in a selection of textures and colours. While not perfect, the cheaper varieties faded to yellow as soon as they saw sunlight, we took to this material thanks to a combination of ease of use and respectable results.

The limitation of flock is that it isn't fibrous. Producing a neatly mowed lawn was easy, long grass, less so. Some experimented with medical lint, dyed, stuck in place and then peeled away from the scenery. The effect was good but it's quite hard work and colouring the material is messy. Planting individual tufts of grass might be possible in tiny areas, but you'd have to be pretty committed to cover a field this way.

More recently, electrostatic grass has become an indispensable part of the tool kit. Nylon fibres are given an electric charge either with a battery-powered tool or by puffing it out of a polythene bottle - this makes the 'grass' stand on end. The effect will be familiar to anyone whose childhood toys included an Action Man – his hair was applied using similar technology, but on an industrial scale. The effect is very impressive and with care, many different types of undergrowth can be produced.

The trick to getting the best from any scenic material is to select the best colours. Nature tends to produce yellow-greens, but manufacturers will happily sell packs of blue-greens or lurid neon greens. On 'Edgeworth' most of our grass is a 50/50 mix of beige and green to represent a summer scene where the dry weather is bleaching the colour.

Covering the hillsides with grass provides a massive visual change to any layout and it's one that doesn't take very long at all. All the work shown in the photographs took place in an hour. Maybe the initial results are a bit bland, but this is just a first coat to cover the plaster. On *page 90* we'll look at detailing the landscape with different colours and types of plants. **BRM**

Spend an hour covering the ground with grass and you'll be amazed just how much the model has changed.

Our hillsides covered with grass. At the moment the effect is good but a bit uniform. We'll look at bringing it alive later on. Another pass with the vacuum is required - those fibres get everywhere.

STEP-BY-STEP GUIDE

TOOLS FOR THE JOB
- Greenscene Flockit, £80.00
- W www.green-scene.co.uk
- Noch/Gaugemaster puffer bottle, £4.50
- W www.gaugemaster.com

Flock powder is made by dying foam rubber and then grinding it up. Both the colours here are Hornby products – on the left coarse turf R8881 Burnt Grass, on the right finely ground R8882 Moss green.

Static grass is made from fibres and can be bought in different lengths. These are from Woodland Scenics – Medium green (left) and Wild honey (right). Although they appear to have formed clumps, a shake will separate the fibres.

To get the best from static grass, you need a tool to give the fibres an electrical charge before they are sprinkled on the scenery. It can be as a simple as the Noch polythene puffer bottle or one of the many electrical devices such as the Greenscene Flockit.

The business ends of the tools. The fibres are blown or shaken through the holes or mesh onto the layout. This provides the static charge which makes them stand up.

1 Moving on to the model, stage one is to paint the scenery with PVA glue. Diluting the glue with a little water makes it easier to brush. Work on areas of about a square foot at a time, any more and the glue might form a skin before the fibres hit it.

2 Before using the applicator, the earth lead needs to be clipped to a pin stuck in the wet glue. The power is switched on and the device is shaken allowing the fibres to fall.

3 Be generous with the fibres and the excess can be vacuumed away, a step that ensures those left are stood like grass. Holding a handkerchief over the nozzle collects the fibres, which can be re-used and put back in the applicator tool.

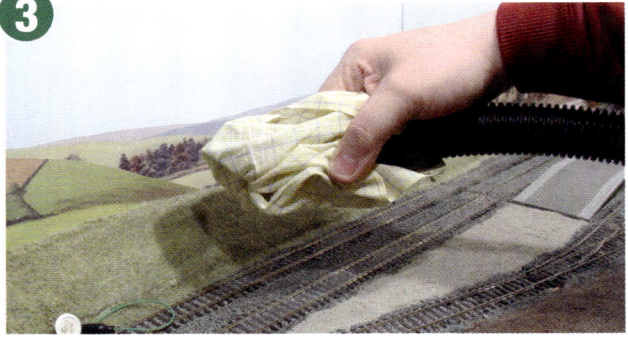

4 Puffer bottles are really great for blasting fibres under trees and into the corners around buildings. Just apply a small spots of PVA where you want greenery and puff the bottle containing the grass at them.

5 Flock powder simple needs to be sprinkled onto a glue base. Here we've built up layers of coarse flock to represent undergrowth and hide gaps under the fence!

THE BRM GUIDE TO BUILDING YOUR FIRST MODEL RAILWAY

HOW TO MODEL...
A STATION PLATFORM

In the UK and Ireland, we don't have to climb up the sides of coaches to board trains. 'Edgeworth' needs a platform.

I have a slight confession to make. In my modelling career, I've never actually built a kit for a station platform. To date, the platforms I have built - a grand total of two - were scratchbuilt.

This isn't because I'm clever, it's just that platforms are simple structures and it seemed quicker to make something from cardboard rather than try to force a kit to match the line of my station trackwork. If you can cut two sides and a top, you can build your own platform too. In fact, if you try the Peco kit version, that's pretty much how it works with pre-cut sides.

'Edgeworth' has nice straight track in the platform so it ought to be ideal for a kit-built solution. Looking around, it seemed sensible to stick with the Ratio range since the stone sides matched the other buildings and also the other options didn't appeal. Hornby produces some plastic platform sections that appear very modern, or solid resin ones that would have added quite a lot of weight to the layout. They featured brick sides anyway, so would have looked odd with all the stone buildings.

The Ratio kit is designed to be flexible. Modellers can change both the length and width of the finished product to suit their situation. Each kit links to the next so if you need a very long platform, just buy more kits.

One missing element to the range is a location for the station building to sit. This caused me a fair bit of head-scratching. If I've missed something obvious, I'm sure someone will tell me, but it appears that the building is supposed to float in mid-air, or at least you have to perform some major surgery on the platform kit to support it.

I chose to make a raised section using a leftover length of platform edge and some strips of 2mm thick plastic sheet. You could use the same technique to do the whole job without kits if you prefer.

Whatever you do, don't forget to test some rolling stock along all faces of the platform before you fix it in position. If possible, run a locomotive by it too. GWR steam locomotives are especially problematic because of the wide outside cylinders on some classes. **BRM**

Ratio kits each contain two identical mouldings. The idea is that they are flexible enough to make the platform to your requirements.

HOW WIDE IS A PLATFORM?

The simple answer is as wide as it needs to be. Some seaside stations had very wide platforms to accommodate the holiday crowds, others in cities had narrow platforms because the frequent train services meant that the numbers waiting didn't require as much space.

The basic rule is that there should be a minimum of 6' from the station building to the edge of the platform. In OO gauge, that's 24mm. This is a minimum though and normally there is much more space than this.

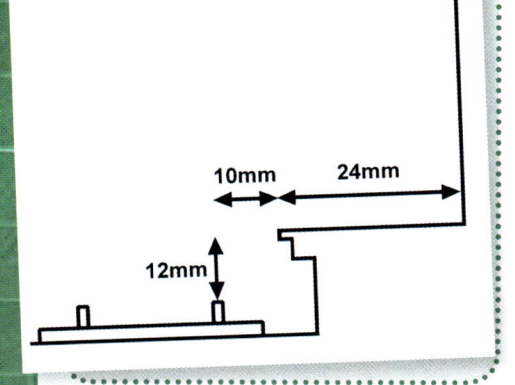

Assembly is simple enough. If you require edging stones on both sides of the top, stick these in place and then add the supporting walls. Connectors are included for joining sections together. At the sloping end, the top surface has to be cut and re-attached on the angled walls.

STEP-BY-STEP GUIDE

1

Before fixing the platform in place, make sure your rolling stock runs past it without clouting anything.

WHAT'S AN OLFA CUTTER?

The Olfa tool is designed to cut plastic card in a different way to a knife. Instead of the blade forcing its way in to the material, it removes a sliver of material. This allows the modeller to scribe panel lines or stones with single passes of the tool. More than this and you cut through the sheet, without distorting it like a knife.

As well as cutting plastic card, the tool will also score thin metal enough that it can be snapped along the line.

The cutting tool is available from many model railway traders for around £7.00. The version on the right has a retractable blade with a compartment to store spare blades. Mind you, I'm still on my first, even after ten years of use on plastic and metal so they're economical.

2

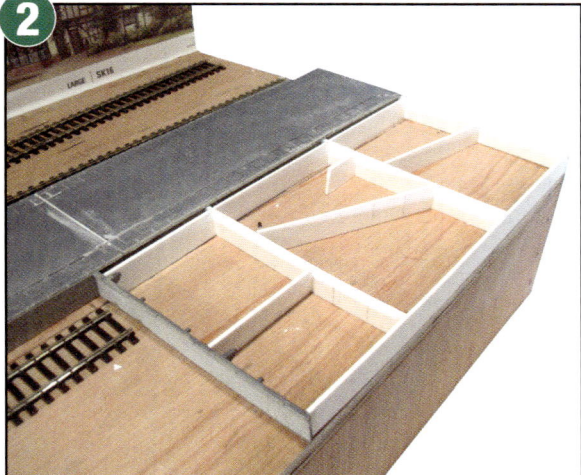

3

Left To provide somewhere for the station building to sit, I scratchbuilt some extra platforms. The first stage is to build a supporting structure using thick plastic card or cardboard.

Right This is topped with more plastic card. Along the edge some matching slabs were scribed using an Olfa cutter.

4

After filling the joints, the platform was painted, the sides to match other stonework on the layout and the top surface with Precision faded tarmac. A wash of dark grey highlighted the edging stones. Once dry, everything received a dusting with dark brown and grey weathering powders.

www.model-railways-live.co.uk 53

THE BRM GUIDE TO BUILDING YOUR FIRST MODEL RAILWAY

HOW TO MODEL...
ROADS AND PAVEMENTS

It's vital to match your roads and pavements to the period being modelled. Let's take a look at how this was achieved on some other layouts.

We all know what roads look like. Grey slabs of tarmac with potholes and drain covers that we bump over as we drive to work.

It wasn't always so. Tarmac as a road surface is a relatively new phenomenon. It wasn't until after the Second World War that many roads in the countryside were treated in this way. Photographs of Sussex in the early-1950s show road rollers laying the first solid surfaces.

Before this, country roads were often surfaced with crushed stone or gravel. 'Edgeworth' is set in the 1930s; it's by no means certain that our area of the country would have moved on from this. As it happens the only significant road surface on the model is the station forecourt. Because this area looks more in keeping with the pale stone buildings, we'll assume it hasn't been re-surfaced.

The other section on the plan is at the entrance to the model, but for space reasons it's little more than a few millimetres wide, so not much help. Instead of Edgeworth, we'll take the opportunity to look at other models and see how they produced roads in model form. **BRM**

POTHOLE ROAD KIT

Geoscenics Road Pothole kit is a grey powder that forms a surface as rough as you require. Other colours can be mixed in to give some variation in shades.

Paving slabs are best modelled by scribing either a cardboard (as shown here) or plastic card surface and then painting this with different shades of grey.

Our station forecourt is a sprinkle of fine chinchilla dust. Its colour is pretty good straight from the box, but once the building is bedded down we'll use some weak washes of poster paint to add variation.

The roads around Hellingly in Sussex didn't see tarmac until the 1950s so for my model of 'Hellingly Hospital' asylum, set in 1900, I used sawdust left over from sanding a floor. This was sieved to remove the bigger lumps and then stuck down with PVA glue. Washes of poster paint were enough to tint the edges and show where mud had gathered along the verge. ANDY YORK

Above Set in the 1920s, the roads around 'Pendon Parva' are made from crushed stone and chalk. Tarmac is a long way in the future. A smooth plaster surface suitably painted would represent this. ANDY YORK

Right The 'Black Country Blues' team used plaster or household filler to represent tarmac. Once dry and shaped to give the road a camber, the surface was painted with grey acrylics. ANDY YORK

Below To model repaired areas, the road was masked with tape and then the rest of the road airbrushed a slightly lighter colour. Note the manhole and drain covers, available as etched items. ANDY YORK

TOP TIP

White and yellow vinyl lines are available from model shops under the brand name 'Trimline'. Each pack contains 2.5 metres of lines in different widths. It's self-adhesive and flexible, so easy to lay around corners. It's shiny, so paint over it with matt varnish.

USEFUL EXTRAS

Etched manhole covers and drains area available from Langley Models.
W www.langley-models.co.uk

www.model-railways-live.co.uk 55

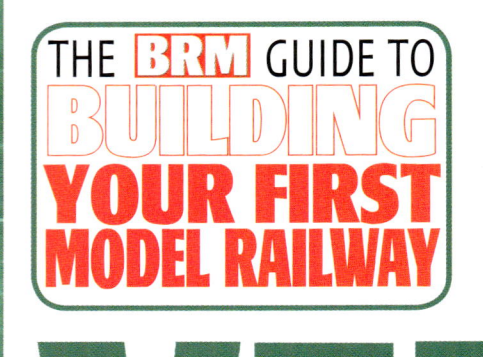

THE BRM GUIDE TO BUILDING YOUR FIRST MODEL RAILWAY
ROAD VEHICLES

Motor vehicles would have been fairly scarce in our rural 1930s scene, but they're essential for most layouts from the 1940s onwards.

A couple of AEC Monarch lorries built from Cooper Craft plastic kits and painted into a fictitious livery. Building a fleet like for a factory on your layout is a great way to give it a sense of place.

In recent years, assembling a suitable fleet of road vehicles for a model railway has become much easier than it used to be. Large numbers of accurate die-cast models are available in all the popular scales, often costing less than the equivalent kits and certainly being a lot easier to use.

All those pretty models can cause people to fill a layout with glossy and brightly-coloured cars with the result that every sleepy country lane looks like rush hour on the M25.

The problem is that we tend to forget just how recent mass car ownership is. Thinking back to the 1970s, the number of two-car families was minuscule and 15 years earlier, if there were ten cars in the street then you were in the wealthy part of town.

Between the wars, most people travelled by bicycle or perhaps motorcycle and sidecar. The doctor might have been mobile but very few others were that lucky. It's why everyone travelled by train or bus.

Talking of buses, these were far more numerous than they are now. If you want a model, don't forget that the correct company matters. With so many accurate liveries on sale, there's no excuse nowadays for London Transport Routemasters to appear outside the capital.

Spend few minutes studying photographs of the area you aim to portray in the era you are modelling it. Your model will look all the better for it. **BRM**

A whitemetal kit based traction engine on my 'Hellingly Hospital' layout. Steam-powered vehicles were a common sight into the 1950s and could still be found in use into the early-1960s.

At the end of the First World War, thousands of surplus lorries were repatriated and sold off by the army. Many ex-servicemen bought them to set up haulage businesses. This model is a resin kit from W^D models.

Any steam era town scene needs a Scammell mechanical horse. The older version (left) is a Langley whitemetal kit while it's more modern brother is from a Dapol plastic kit. These vehicles nipped around town performing local deliveries, hence the well-loaded trailers.

www.model-railways-live.co.uk

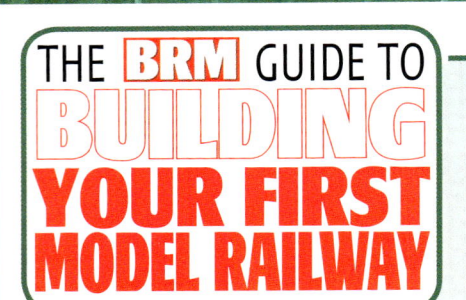

THE BRM GUIDE TO BUILDING YOUR FIRST MODEL RAILWAY

REPAINTING A ROAD VEHICLE

Modern die-cast road vehicles are great but sometimes even with the huge range available, what you want isn't easily available. Maybe you fancy creating miniature versions of cars you or your family once owned?

1 The first step is to take the model apart. Some cars have screws in the bottom that you can undo and then the model falls apart. Others are riveted. This needs to be drilled out gently with a large bit.

2 Most die-cast vehicles split down like this; body, chassis, glazing and interior.

3 Something you rarely see nowadays is a car with one wing replaced but not repainted. When blue diesels ruled the railways, it was a common sight and easy enough to model. Just mask off the panel to be repainted before giving the part a coat of red oxide colour.

4 The finished model has been matt varnished and weathered with powders. It won't be passing many more MOT tests!

Why not use die-cast models to re-create miniature versions of cars once owned by you or your family?

Above The post-war years saw a boom in private motoring represented by this combination of a Standard Vanguard and caravan. Both are die-cast models that have been matt varnished.

Left This 1963 Austin Paralanian Camper is an Oxford Diecast model that has been matt varnished and then dirtied by covering with weathering powders then wiping them off with a wet thumb.

GOLDEN VALLEY HOBBIES

www.goldenvalleyhobbies.com

OUR GUIDE TO CREATING REALISTIC ROADS

For many modellers the only option when it came to creating roads and pavements was to sprinkle a small width of 'Tarmac' coloured scatter across your model. Although quick and simple, it did not look too realistic, tended to fade over time and did not provide an option for adding road markings.

So take a look at this great product - Roadway on a roll! This is a special flexible, self-adhesive product – and not to be confused with spray painted masking tape!

BUS 6033 OO/HO Black Tarmac Roll 1m 80mm .. £5.00
BUS 7086 OO/HO Motorway Roll 2m 66mm... £7.80
BUS 7087 N Black Tarmac Roll 2m 40mm £5.30
BUS 7096 HO/OO Starter Pack £11.80
BUS 6039 OO/HO Grey Tarmac Roll 1M 80mm... £5.00
BUS 7097 N Roadway starter pack £9.30
BUS 6038 HO/OO Road and pavement 1m £6.90
BUS 8139 N Road and pavement 1m £3.50

Off the Beaten track...
Fancy adding a few Land Rovers and Tractors? Then the muddy lane is just ideal for the models.
Complete the lane with these flexible hedges and agricultural models.
BUS 7084 OO/HO Muddy Lane 1m 23mm £4.20
BUS 7155 OO/HO/N Premium Hedge 1m £3.50
BUS 7150 OO/HO/N Budget Hedge 1m £4.40
BUS 40169 HO Muddy Combine Harvester £30.80

New or faded tarmac?
Unless Tarmac is new or wet, when looked at you realise it is not Black. So, the basic range of roadways comes in both Black and Grey. Roads vary in width and so does this roadway. You can use several widths for each scale. There are also starter packs available which contain a length of roadway, a tarmac sheet (for market places and car parks), road signs, crash barriers and transfers to mark the road with. These are great value and contain everything required to get started.

For non motorised vehicles...
Also produced in the range are smaller strips of roadway, which allows you to add Cycle Tracks and Pavements. A pavement is typically: OO/HO = 25mm N = 12mm so you simply cut down the rolls to the required width. The cycle path contains 2 rolls - one red and one grey track.
BUS 7093 OO/HO/N Tarmac Pavement 2M x 55mm £5.10
BUS 6029 OO/HO Paving Slabs Assorted sheets £4.10
BUS 1018 OO/HO Crowd control barriers (20) £5.20
BUS 1005 OO/HO ESSO Small Petrol Station Kit £25.60
BUS 1057 OO/HO Basketball court and fence £15.20
BUS 7082 OO/HO Cycle Path 1m 14.5mm £4.80
BUS 6013 OO/HO Bikes and Scooters (8) £6.90

Something more traditional?
And it's not just Tarmac, there are also flexible roadways covered in cobbles. The cobbles rolls come in two widths: OO/HO = 80mm N = 40mm. The sheets are 560x330mm. Lastly why not add a flower stall and fruit and veg stall to complete your market scene?
BUS 6031 OO/HO Curved Cobbles 2m £8.40
BUS 7078 OO/HO Cobbled Street 1m £5.50
BUS 8131 N Curved Cobbles 2m £6.10
BUS 7079 N Cobbled Street 1m £3.90
BUS 7088 OO/HO Cobble Sheet £10.50
BUS 7089 N Cobble Sheet £10.50
BUS 1072 OO/HO Large Flower stall £14.80
BUS 1070 OO/HO Fruit and Veg stall £14.80

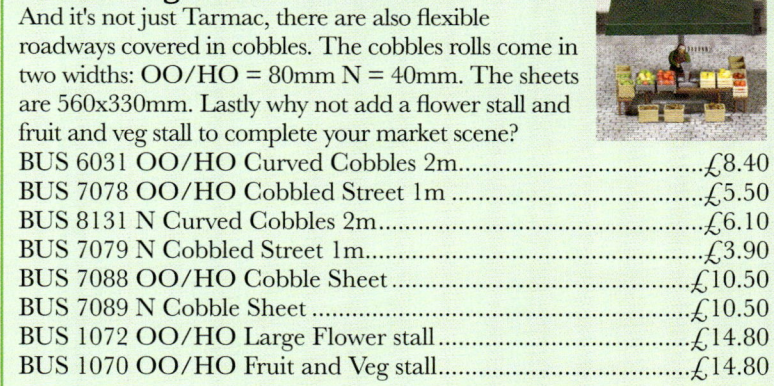

and Finally...
You can add your own touch to the roadway system with a range of extras. Roundabouts and crossings which match your roadway? Then there is a pack of road markings to compliment the flexible roadway sheet - ideal for junctions and gap filling. Finally, there are some road symbols and crash barrier packs.

BUS 1101 OO/HO Roundabout and grass centre............. £8.50
BUS 1102 N Roundabout with grass centre...................... £7.20
BUS 7074 OO/HO 4 way crossing...................................... £6.90
BUS 7075 N 4 way crossing... 6.10
BUS 1136 OO/HO Rubbish and Recycling Set................. 7.30
BUS 6027 OO/HO Modern Euro Road Signs 6.40
BUS 7076 OO/HO Car Park sheet 200x160 .... 4.30

BUS 7077 N Car Park Sheet 120x100............................. 3.40
BUS 6022 OO/HO Crash Barriers 90cm 4.30
BUS 8122 N Crash Barriers 90cm 4.30
BUS 7196 OO/HO Street Markings, 1 sheet 4.30
BUS 7197 N Street Markings 1 sheet 4.30
BUS 1105 OO/HO Potholed street 5.50

01981 241237
www.goldenvalleyhobbies.com | info@goldenvalleyhobbies.com

Expo Drills & Tools
www.expotools.com

6000+ quality products available for Model Railways!
This is just a small selection from the ranges we offer!
Please buy from your local stockist wherever possible. You can find them, and view all of our products at: www.expotools.com   TRADE ENQUIRIES WELCOMED.

Code	Price	Description
A74310	£2.95	5ml 6pc Syringe Set. Ideal for applying oils & adhesives accurately
A74311	£2.95	10ml 4pc Syringe Set. Ideal for applying PVA wood glue or oils and greases accurately
AB602	£109.95	Complete Airbrush and Compressor Deal
26211	£27.95	Expo Turntable Motorising Set
71250	£11.95	Rotating Self Healing Cutting Mat (300mm x 300mm)
75090	£8.95	Expo Modellers Hand Drill with 3 Jaw Chuck
AB500	£89.95	Expo Portable Spray Booth
75589	£26.95	Xuron Professional Photo-Etch Scissors
25182	£9.95	HO/OO Gauge Fibre Optic Scale Yard Lamp
25191	£9.95	O Gauge Fibre Optic Scale Gas Lamp
75570	£17.95	Xuron Track Cutter
44010	£2.75	Milliput Standard, Yellow-Grey
11508	£6.00	8pc HSS Drill Set (Sizes 0.5 - 2.00mm)
11516	£9.00	16pc HSS Twist Drill Set (Sizes 0.5 - 2mm)
71530	£4.95	Bending & Shaping Tool
44500	£4.95	Paint Remover. Safely removes most paints from most plastics!
73960	£59.95	Table Top Round Magnifying Lamp
79521	£25.95	Multi Position Vice with 3 inch Jaws
75040	£9.95	Professional Archimedes Drill Set
12820	£9.95	Professional Micro Chuck Set
75070	£9.95	Precision Pin Vice with 3 Jaw Chuck
26241	£5.95	Worm Gear and Pinion Puller
72506	£14.95	Miniature 10pc Diamond Needle File Set in wallet
72512	£7.95	5pc Diamond Needle File Set with soft grip handles
74360	£9.95	Hot Wire Polystyrene Cutter
73012	£5.00	Watchmakers Hammer
74325	£7.95	Professional Precision Oiler
74326	£5.95	Oil Bottle (15cc of oil) Perfect for 74325
PDX351 / PDX351D	£7.60 Each	N Gauge Ready Painted Model GWR Home Signal / GWR Distant Signal
PDZ19	£8.00	OO Gauge Painted Loco Crew (Ready Painted Model)
PDX76	£6.25	N Gauge 1950's Motorbike, Sidecar & Rider (New! Ready Painted Model)
PDZ40	£9.50	PD Marsh OO Gauge 1950/60 Fire Crew (New!)
PDZ41	£9.50	PD Marsh OO Gauge 1970/80 Fire Crew (New! Ready Painted Model)
PDZ37	£8.00	OO Gauge Belishas Bus Stop & Postbox (Ready Painted Model)
PDZ104	£11.95	OO Gauge 1950's AA Motorcycle Patrol (Ready Painted Model)
95865	£12.50	Ancorton OO Terraced Cottages (Half-Relief) OOTH4
95818	£10.00	Ancorton OO Gauge Water Tank Kit
95503	£5.50	Ancorton OO Gauge Camping Tents (3D Printed Model)
95426	£8.50	Ancorton N Gauge Platelayers Hut/Sleeper Built (RTP) (3D Printed Model)
95425	£7.50	Ancorton N Gauge Stone Built Lineside Building (3D Printed Model)
95432	£19.99	Ancorton Ready Made N Gauge 3D Printed Leisure Narrow Boat (RTP)
95832	£15.00	Ancorton OO Gauge Railway Bridge Kit Kit

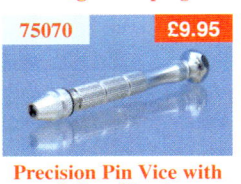

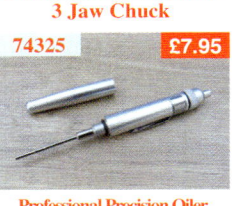

New Landscape Scenics Items Now Available!!!

Code	Price	Description
LS94294	£13.95	Professional 4 Inch Pine Tree Pack. Pack of 2. HO Gauge.
LS95553	£9.50	Corn Stalks (pack of 28) O Gauge Very Accurately Detailed Flowers
LS95582	£7.95	Hay Bales Assorted (HO/OO Gauge) 35 Pieces (15 Round/20 Rectangular)
LS95583	£9.95	Hay Bales Assorted (O Gauge) 35 Pieces (5 Round/16 Rectangular)
LS95584	£7.95	Boxwood Plants & Hedging (HO/OO Gauge) 20 Pieces
LS95585	£9.95	Large Boxwood Plants & Hedging (HO/OO Gauge) 15 Pieces
LS95594	£7.95	Primula Flowers (HO/OO Gauge) 32 Pieces
LS95596	£7.95	Allium Giganteum Flowers (HO/OO Gauge) 30 Pieces
LS95607	£7.95	Hibiscus Flowers (HO/OO Gauge) 18 Pieces
LS95608	£9.95	Large Hibiscus Flowers (HO/OO Gauge) 8 Pieces
LS95609	£7.95	Assorted Hydrangeas (HO/OO Gauge)

Code	Price	Description
72504	£16.95	Expo 6pc Superior Steel Needle File Set with Handle and Wallet (New!)
78130	£18.95	Expo Professional Ratchet Socket and Hex Key Set (New!)
78090	£14.95	Expo Professional 8pc Super Thin Combination Spanner Set (New!)
74365	£9.95	Expo Hand Held Guillotine (cuts up to 12mm thickness!) (New!)
79920	£14.95	Expo Professional Rapid Cable Stripper (New!)
77550	£34.95	5 in 1 Butane Gas Torch Set (New!)
78215	£5.95	2 Inch Stainless Steel Square
75110	£7.95	EXPO High Quality Pin Pusher 2mm
75120	£7.95	EXPO High Quality Pin Pusher 3mm
70515	£7.95	3pc Set of 4mm Scratch Brushes
79031	£9.95	Expo 8pc High Quality Tweezer Set in Wallet
71203	£10.00	Cutting Mat A3 Size (450 x 300mm)
74300	£5.00	Precision Oiler
70372	£15.00	6pc Cutting Broach set in wallet Covers sizes: 1.2 - 3.2mm
A23040	£7.95	Plug Together 12 Way Connector Block Set
A28015	£7.95	Pack of 5 SPDT Miniature Biased Switches
A23000	£4.50	Pack of 10 Micro Spade Connectors with Heat Shrink
46060	£5.75	Deluxe Materials Roket Card Glue (50ml)
74104	£4.95	OO Gauge Scale Rule 4mm = 1 foot (N/HO & O Gauge also available)
73520	£9.95	4pc Modelmakers Tool Kit in Wallet
59504	£6.50	2 Sheets of Tree Foliage

Code: 77510 3 in 1 Low Temperature Soldering Station

New!

A fantastic 3 in 1 soldering station - suitable for Modelling, Soldering and Pyrography.
· For mains operation - fitted with a British plug
· Soldering Iron 24V/30W
· Soldering Iron Stand
· Complete with 6 Tips
· Full instruction manual included

STAR TEC

Manufactured in Germany

(High power version also available - code 77520)

£69.95

Code: AB605 EXPO Super Detail Airbrush Set

Look whats included:
✓ Gravity Feed Airbrush
✓ Compressor
✓ Braided Air Hose
✓ Metal Storage Case
✓ Pipette
✓ Instructions

New!

Labelled: Metal Case, Airbrush, Pipette, Mains Power Cable, Braided Air Hose, Compressor

Fantastic New Airbrush Set Complete Set Only: £69.95

Expo EZE-Wire

The simple way to wire point motor's! All you need is the appropriate EZE-Wire switch harness to go with your point motor, nothing else to buy! No soldering or crimping is required!

No Soldering Required - connections are as simple as 1,2,3!

1. Slide the heat shrink tube provided over one of the wires to be connected
2. Push the micro connectors together
3. Slide the heat shrink over the joint and heat with a hair dryer or gas torch

28070 EZE-Wire Point Motor Harness for Peco Point Motors £6.95

28071 EZE-Wire Point Motor Harness for Hornby Point Motors £6.95

28069 EZE-Wire Point Motor Switch Box £17.95

For simple wiring & operation of 1 to 5 Model Railway point motors. For use with a suitable power source of 12-24volts.

Albion Alloys -
Precision Metals for the Creative Model Maker

A vast range of Albion Alloys products available through Expo Tools. To view the full range and find your local stockist please visit:

www.expotools.com

We ask that you support your local model shop by buying from them. You can see a list of our principal stockists on our website. In case of difficulty obtaining items you can order direct on our website.
www.expotools.com   TRADE ENQUIRIES WELCOMED.

Expo Drills & Tools, Unit 6, The Salterns, TENBY SA70 7NJ. Tel: 01834 845150 (Mon to Fri 9am-5pm)

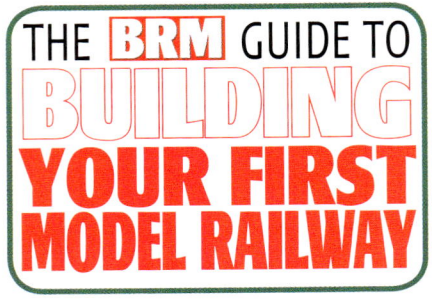

THE BRM GUIDE TO BUILDING YOUR FIRST MODEL RAILWAY

HOW... BUILDINGS MAKE A LAYOUT

Phil Parker shows how choosing the right type of buildings can help to define the character, period and function of your layout.

A wise man once said that you shouldn't need to see any trains on a model railway to be able to work out where it is set and which period is being modelled. A big part of being able to do this will involve the buildings you chose.

Look around you and there are plenty of wonderful prototypes that just cry out to be modelled. If your mobile phone has a camera then you have the ideal tool for 'collecting' them as you walk around. Over the years, I've photographed many interesting buildings, here is just a small collection. **BRM**

Above If you need a bit of colour and are modelling a seaside line, then how about some beach huts? These are from Paignton and could be easily converted from garden sheds, as we showed in the July 2013 issue of **BRM**.

Above Some buildings just ooze character. This tiny boat repair shop comes from the Isle of Man. A model could be just the thing to fill and odd corner.

Right In the centre of Birmingham, visible from the trains into Moor Street station, is this old building supplies warehouse. Now converted and brightened up, it still retains a certain 'Bates Motel' feel.

Above Not an impressive building, it's the sort of thing you see often and ignore, but it has character and could be fitted in on most layouts. The palm tree belies the Scottish location.

Above Every country station needs a goods shed. Fortunately, many survive including this example on the Severn Valley Railway.

Left Even without the name you can tell this is a Far North of Scotland station. Many lines had very distinctive architecture and this needs to be represented on a model if it's to look right.

Above Post-war architecture involved an awful lot of prefabrication such as the Welshpool Post Office. This sort of thing is quite a rare sight on model railways but common enough in real life.

Left Weymouth Harbourmaster's office on my layout 'Melbridge Dock'. Scratchbuilt from cardboard and plastic sheet, it's based on a plan in an old model railway magazine. Despite this being published over 40 years ago, plenty of visitors to exhibitions still recognise it.

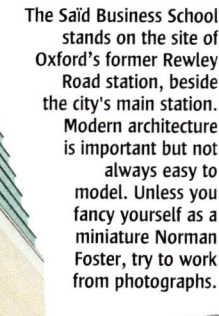

The Saïd Business School stands on the site of Oxford's former Rewley Road station, beside the city's main station. Modern architecture is important but not always easy to model. Unless you fancy yourself as a miniature Norman Foster, try to work from photographs.

Above Left A 'Tin Tabernacle' that became a village hall and now awaits demolition. The corrugated iron building has been extended with brick toilets but doesn't look as though it's seen a coat of paint in years.

Above Don't forget the little buildings! This wooden hut tucked alongside the locomotive shed on my model of the Hellingly Hospital Railway is based on a design used by contractors building the Great Central Railway in the 19th century. It's an old-fashioned portable building for the workers.

Above Warehouses are huge but often made up of repeated designs. This example from Gloucester would make an excellent backdrop for an industrial layout and could easily be made taller or shorter.

www.model-railways-live.co.uk 63

THE BRM GUIDE TO BUILDING YOUR FIRST MODEL RAILWAY

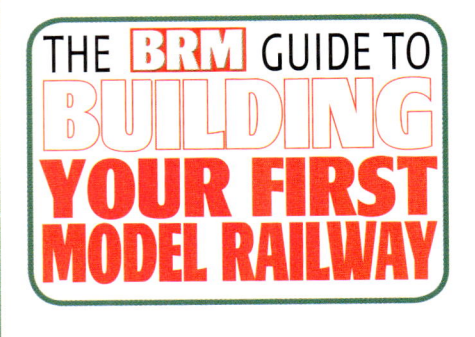

WHAT SHOULD I BUILD?

CARD KITS

For
- Normally easy to build
- A great introduction to making buildings
- Some kits are downloaded from the web at any time of day
- Reprint as often as you need
- Usually cheap
- Can assemble with non-smelly glues like PVA

Against
- Often very flat looking
- Limited detail
- Not a huge selection
- Colours can fade in sunlight

Card kits come in a bewildering variety of styles. At their most basic you find simple and slightly cartoony buildings printed on thin card in a limited number of colours. These might fill a gap on the layout but you'll probably want to replace them with something better eventually. Most kits are manufactured on thick cardboard and are pre-cut for ease of assembly. The model you produce will look good and be sturdy enough to withstand you moving it around if you aren't sure where it will end up being positioned. Some of these kits now come with laser-cut wood details and can be made up into very attractive models.

Above all, a good card kit is fun to assemble. The biggest problem is that you might enjoy building them so much that you end up with more buildings than you have space for.

The most sophisticated kits will produce a photo-realistic model that will stand scrutiny with the best of them. These take patience and often a bit of practice to construct but will reward the modeller with a superb building that can be assembled in very little time.

SCRATCHBUILDING
For
- The ultimate in flexibility
- You can have anything you want
- Very satisfying
- Cheap

Against
- Time consuming
- Helpful to have a stock of materials
- It can be difficult to find suitable plans

If you really must have that building, if no other will do, then the chances are you'll have to scratchbuild.

People have produced model buildings this way since our hobby was first invented and they'll carry on forever. Many really enjoy the process, some don't bother with the rest of the model and just concentrate on the buildings. They are certainly popular at the model railway club when volunteering to take on some of the more complex structures.

PLASTIC KITS
For
- Lots of surface detail
- Easy to assemble

Against
- Very limited selection
- Often non-British designs
- Might be an odd scale

TOP TIP
Some kits are printed with water-soluble inks. If this is the case don't use PVA, go for a solvent based glue such as UHU instead. To make sure, trying rubbing some glue on a bit of printing you won't see later.

Model buildings is an area where plastic kits have never made much of an impact. We all know the Airfix range dating back to the 1960s, now available from Dapol, but they are certainly showing their age. Having said that, plastic is a very forgiving medium in which to work and you can chop and hack the model around to improve it. Old magazines and the Internet are both great resources for instructions on doing this - see the July 2015 issue of **BRM**.

Beyond this, care is needed to make sure your building is a British prototype or at least looks like one. Check the scale too, European and American models will be to 1:87 scale rather than 1:76 for OO. Wargaming kits are likely to be 1:72 scale. N gauge modellers face similar problems with British N being 1:148 scale, rather than the 1:160 used everywhere else in the world.

This might not matter of course, buildings come in different shapes and sizes and if the model looks right in it's setting, it is right. You can even consider using HO models on a OO layout, placing them at the back to force perspective and make the layout look deeper than it really is.

www.model-railways-live.co.uk **65**

RESIN MODELS

For
- Nothing easier, ready-to-plant
- Usually well detailed

Against
- Identical models on lots of layouts
- Large buildings are heavy and can be fragile
- Most are limited editions so you need to buy when you see
- Can be pricey
- Sometimes the model is compressed in scale to make it fit.

There's nothing easier to use than a resin 'ready-to-plonk' building. Take it out of the box, place it on the layout and you're done.

The trouble is, that building on your layout is the same as the one on your friend's layout. And the same as one on his friend's layout too. Maybe this isn't a problem, after all it's your layout so you get to do what you want, but if you fancy putting your model on show, do you really want the people hanging over the barrier spotting where you bought each structure?

On the other hand, there are many prototypes, such as carriage sheds and coaling towers, where the same design was used in many locations so this isn't unprototypical.

For many layouts, buildings play an essential role in setting a location or scene. The stone buildings seen here on Ron North's layout 'Halland' portray the feel of a rural station set in the borders. The idea was spurred by the acquisition of the resin station building. Note the other less permanent wooden structures dotted around the scene, many built from kits, others scratch-built.

AC Models

Tel: 02380 610100 www.acmodelseastleigh.co.uk

Your one stop shop for the model enthusiast, selling brand new and near-new model trains, slotcars, sets and diecast toys at very special prices direct from our website or our shop in Eastleigh. We stock Hornby, Bachmann, Airfix, Scalextric, Lilliput, Spectrum etc and much more.

Both shops are **closed on Wednesdays and Sundays**

Gift vouchers available

WE HAVE EXPANDED TO NO9 HIGH STREET
New Radio Control Department,
Spares Department and Games Workshop now at No.7
www.acmodelsspares.co.uk

7 High Street, Eastleigh, Hants, SO50 5LB
email: info@acmodelseastleigh.co.uk

---

bright ideas from TRAINTRONICS

Model Railway & Train Accessories

OO and N gauge Signals and Signal heads

DCC for your model Railway

Model Railway Sounds and More in store.

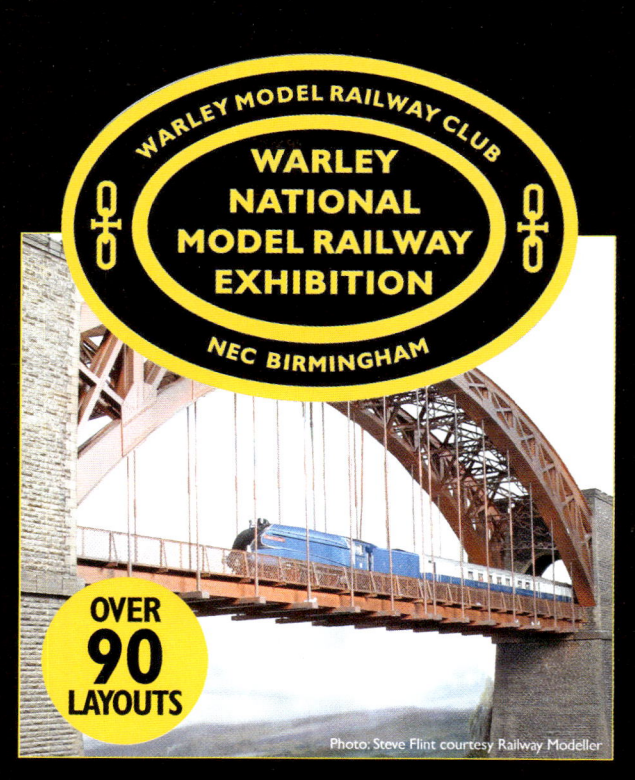

Sounds to blow you away

329-331 Holdenhurst Road,
Bournemouth BH8 8BT
01202 309872
sales@slotrail.com

WARLEY MODEL RAILWAY CLUB
WARLEY NATIONAL MODEL RAILWAY EXHIBITION
NEC BIRMINGHAM

OVER 90 LAYOUTS

Photo: Steve Flint courtesy Railway Modeller

WARLEY NATIONAL 2015

NEC BIRMINGHAM
Saturday 28th & Sunday 29th November 2015

Sat 28th 9.45am - 6pm & Sun 29th 9.45am - 5pm
Advance ticket holders from 9.15am Saturday & Sunday

Over 90 Model Railway Layouts
Gauges Z to 1 and Bigger
Over 150 Specialist Trade Stands
Modelling Demonstrations
Most Major Scale & Gauge Societies
Preservation & Specialist Interest Societies
Full Size Centrepiece Locomotive Display

See our website or Model Press for more details
www.thewarleyshow.co.uk

The UK's Premier Model Railway Event

THE BRM GUIDE TO BUILDING YOUR FIRST MODEL RAILWAY

HOW TO MAKE...
A METCALFE GOODS SHED

TOOLS FOR THE JOB
- Craft knife
- Steel rule
- Cutting mat
- Tweezers
- Bulldog clips
- Small screwdriver
- Pile of magazines

Glues
- Pritt Stick
- Roket Card glue
- UHU glue

■ **Kit**
Metcalfe Models PO232 OO/HO Gauge Goods Shed, £13.99
W www.metcalfemodels.com

One completed goods shed. You too can build one of these easily in a day, no matter what your experience in kit building.

Goods sheds date from the era before most freight travelled in containers. If you model the period up to the 1970s, the chances are that you need a building where items can be unloaded and transferred to road transport for the final leg of their journey. While the railway companies might not have minded the staff getting wet, goods in transit might be damaged by the rain and that means compensation claims from angry customers.

Larger sheds would have provided some temporary storage facilities while goods awaited collection, but for most stations, facilities were modest and in keeping with the amount of traffic they could expect to deal with.

While we don't have space for a goods shed on 'Edgeworth', if the baseboard was about 4" wider, it would be possible to squeeze one on to the front siding. Mind you, this Metcalfe Models kit is so much fun to build, it's tempting to assemble it and then try to work out a use for the model later.

The kit produces a model 237mm long and 110mm wide, enough for a couple of wagons to shelter inside and ideal for a country station. If a little more space is needed then a platform can be attached to one end of the shed. Larger structures could be made by joining two or more kits together.

Since the building is very open with loading doors for both road traffic and the vital space for railway track to pass though, the model includes quite a bit of internal detail. This makes construction a bit more complicated than a simple box but the instructions are excellent and even a beginner could build the kit in a few evenings.

Once complete, there is plenty of detailing scope. Inside the building, sacks and boxes would be found on the platform. Outside, lorries would be backed up to the doors for loading. There were usually plenty of staff on hand to perform all the work too. A crane on the outside platform would help to move the larger items.

Before placing the model on your layout, draw around the building with a pencil to mark its position. The track that runs through will need to be ballasted, something that's much easier to do if you aren't trying to reach inside the shed. Ideally, it needs to be in the middle of a siding so that trains can be moved back and forth to position each wagon under cover.

Modern image modellers don't need to feel left out. These were good solid buildings that found many uses after the railways had abandoned wagonload freight and no longer needed them. Many had their doors bricked up and became the base for small firms or simply storage units. **BRM**

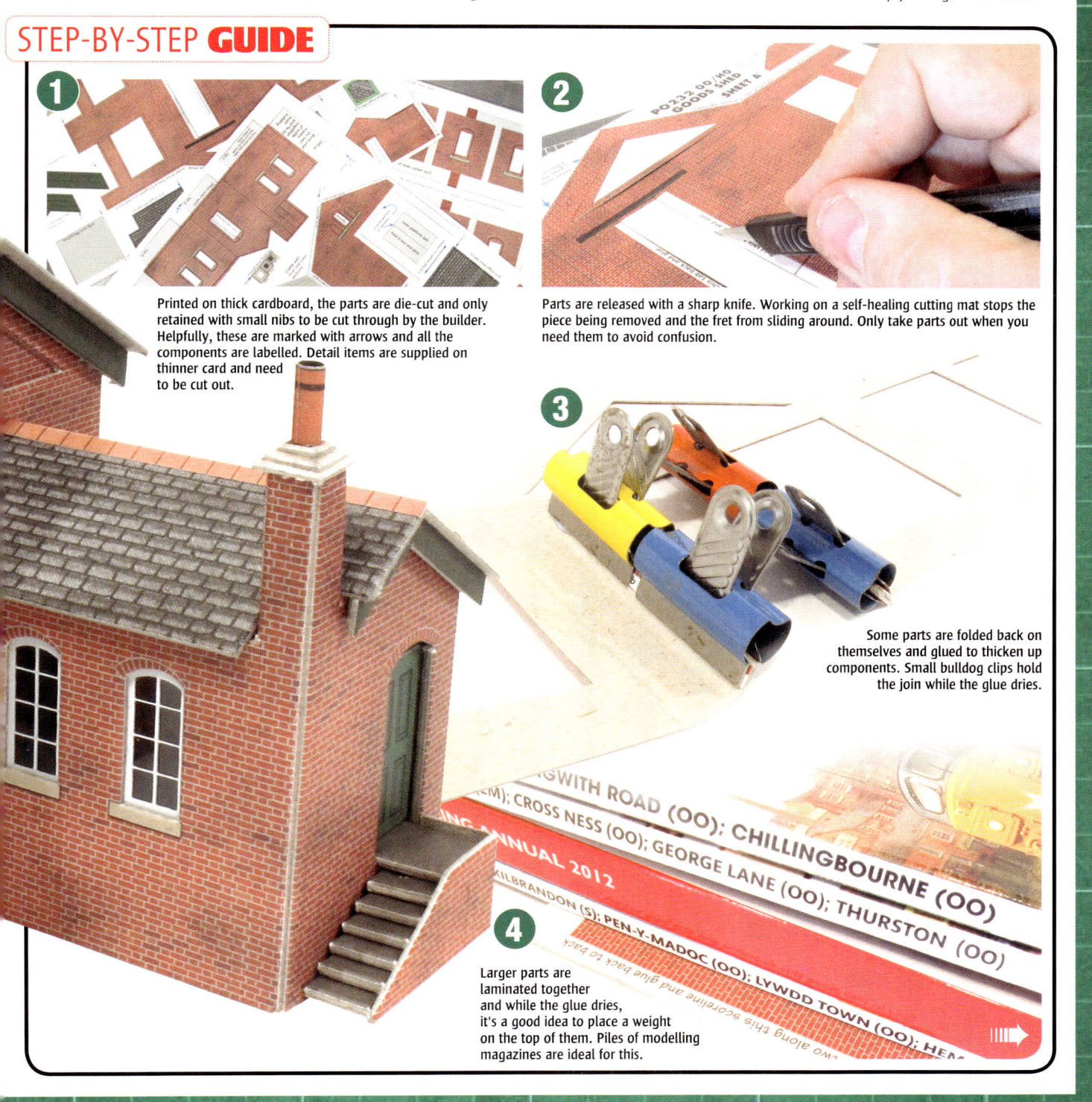

STEP-BY-STEP GUIDE

1 Printed on thick cardboard, the parts are die-cut and only retained with small nibs to be cut through by the builder. Helpfully, these are marked with arrows and all the components are labelled. Detail items are supplied on thinner card and need to be cut out.

2 Parts are released with a sharp knife. Working on a self-healing cutting mat stops the piece being removed and the fret from sliding around. Only take parts out when you need them to avoid confusion.

3 Some parts are folded back on themselves and glued to thicken up components. Small bulldog clips hold the join while the glue dries.

4 Larger parts are laminated together and while the glue dries, it's a good idea to place a weight on the top of them. Piles of modelling magazines are ideal for this.

THE BRM GUIDE TO BUILDING YOUR FIRST MODEL RAILWAY

5 Side walls are thickened up with plain grey pre-cut card pieces and then glazed with printed plastic windows. The later are best fixed in place with an all-purpose glue such as UHU.

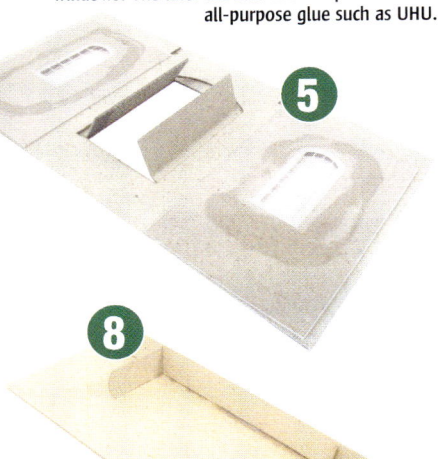

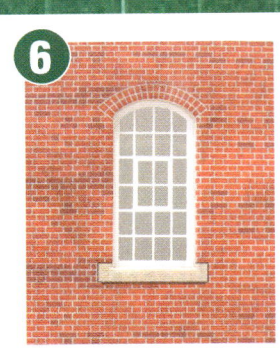

6 By using an all-purpose glue, the setting time allows accurate positioning of the frame within the hole in the wall. This is easier to do from the opposite side to the one the glazing is stuck but be careful not to get glue on the 'glass' as you move it around.

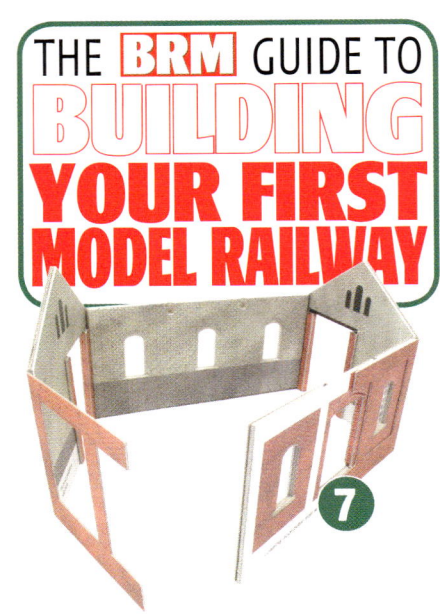

7 An unusual design feature is that the end walls wrap around the sides, the joins being made in the middle of the wall. Assemble the parts on a flat surface, a kitchen worktop is ideal, it'll help to conceal the joins.

8 Some of the leftover bits of card from inside the windows are used to brace the platform edge. It's worth keeping a small stock of these as they are ideal for this sort of job.

9 The platform slots inside and is held with spacers. Glue is run around the hidden edges underneath. The sliding doors are glued in place and can be set as desired.

10 Roof trusses are made up from self-adhesive card parts. We found the glue didn't hold very well and needed a bit of help with some UHU.

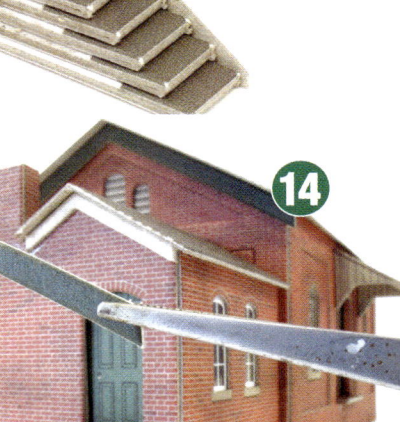

11 The office chimney is formed around a core made up around five layers of grey card. These need to be laminated accurately or the chimney will be an odd shape.

12 Steps are made from layers of card folded back on themselves, then piled up to make the treads. The top step is part of the office floor that sticks out of the door.

13 The office can be attached to either end of the shed but you have to put the piece of brickwork that came out of the shed wall back in first, so don't throw anything away until you've finished the model.

14 Barge boards are spaced from the walls with more grey parts. Place some glue on the back and top of the board so that the roof is well secured. Use tweezers to handle the card to avoid picking up glue on your fingers and transferring it to the printed walls.

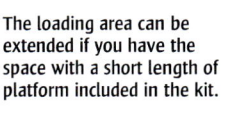

15 The ridge tiles are supplied on printed paper in two colours so you can personalise the model.

16 Chimney pots are paper which has to be rolled around a 3mm rod – a small screwdriver worked well for us. Pritt-Stick on the inside of the roll stuck the paper together. Leaving the first centimetre clear meant it didn't stick to the screwdriver.

17 To complete your goods yard, a weighbridge and hut is also included.

18 The loading area can be extended if you have the space with a short length of platform included in the kit.

METCALFE
Card Construction Kits

A beautiful country station.

Easy to Build

Made easy with these four great buildings kits.

Scenery not included.

00/H0 Goods Shed
Code PO232 £13.99

Includes small weighbridge office.

Also in N Code PN112 £7.25
Does not include weighbridge office.

00/H0 Signal Box
Code PO233 £9.00

An LNWR style signal box with small lamp hut and platelayers shelter.

Also in N Code PN133 £9.00

00/H0 Country Station
Code PO237 £13.75

Also in N Code PN109 £6.75
Does not include platform shelter below.

Nicely detailed brick station includes platform shelter for opposite platform.

00/H0 Platform Kit
Code PO216 £10.75
Also in N Code PN110 £8.25

A versatile custom build style platform that can be easily constructed to any shape required, straight or curved, island or bay. Fully illustrated instructions, as with all our other kits.

Mail Orders to:
Metcalfe Models & Toys Ltd.
Bell Busk, Skipton. BD23 4DU
Tel: 01729 830072
POSTAGE (UK ONLY)
Up to £19.99 £2.50   Thereafter £4.50

Phone or write for free brochure.

See the rest of our range of N & 00 scale kits at:
metcalfemodels.com

THE BRM GUIDE TO BUILDING YOUR FIRST MODEL RAILWAY

HOW TO BUILD... A STONE BUILT LOCOMOTIVE SHED IN PLASTIC

It's time to build a home for your locomotives. Here's a guide to using the Ratio kit.

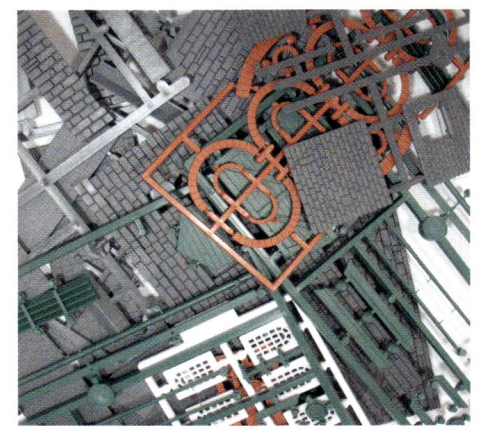

Looking at the main buildings required for 'Edgeworth', the locomotive shed appeared to be the simplest kit to assemble. It only has four walls and a roof after all, so makes a good starting point. I also needed to build it so that the track alignment through the door could be ascertained, thus it was the first kit to appear on the workbench.

Ratio's kit (Ref: 522, RRP £27.50) isn't difficult to build and if you've never put a plastic building together, it's a good choice. There is a lot more potential in the box than you might realise however. While one kit will produce a single road shed suitable for one modest locomotive, extra kits can be used to produce wider and longer structures. Extra parts are included to join the kits together making this an easy job.

Even in its simplest form, there are options to consider. I've built the shed as a dead-end, but if you prefer, the track can emerge from the back so locomotives can run straight through. There's also a lean-to office for the back if your miniature engine crews need somewhere to brew up. We've not used this yet but it might make an appearance later on if I can find a use for it.

All these extra parts come in very handy if you wish to experiment with the paint finish. The moulded stones are incredibly regular, almost like chunky breezeblocks with rounded edges rather than anything hewn from a quarry. To add some texture, I painted the walls cream (Humbrol 103) and then dusted them with ordinary talcum powder. The powder settles into the paint and provides a little texture.

After this, some pale stone (Humbrol 121) was splodged on the surface using a small piece of foam rubber. The trick is to put some paint on a piece of plastic and dip the sponge into this. Dab it a couple of times on the plastic before doing the same on the model. This won't dry perfectly flat either, so we get a bit more texture. As long as the foam isn't dripping with paint, the lighter colour will only appear on the surface of the stonework.

This probably sounds more complicated than it is but that's why the spare wall sections are handy. Paint these first because if you ruin them, it doesn't matter. **BRM**

The kit arrives in a big card box filled with multi-coloured plastic parts. Quite a few are duplicates to provide plenty of options for different sheds.

TOOLS FOR THE JOB

All the plastic kits on 'Edgeworth' were assembled using the same basic set of tools:

- Knife
- Steel rule
- Flush wire cutters
- Abrasive sticks
- Plastic cement
- Liquid plastic glue

STEP-BY-STEP GUIDE

1 On the back of the sides are a lot of moulding stubs that should be removed. A knife would work but a pair of flush wire cutters is quicker. These are also good for removing parts from sprues.

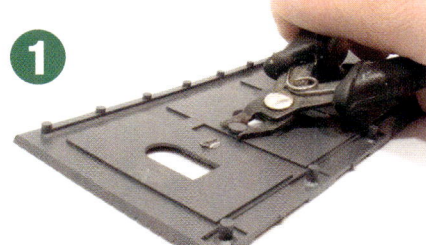

2 Assembly is straightforward enough with plastic cement. The arches above the windows needed a tiny amount of trimming to fit but otherwise everything went together well.

> **Practice painting on a spare bit of wall before working on the model. That way you can throw away any mistakes.**

SUPPLIES
Ratio 522 engine shed - £27.50

Dusting the model with Humbrol dark brown and smoke weathering powders provides just the right finish for a steam era engine shed.

SEE HOW WE DEVELOPED THE SHED AREA ON PAGE 100

③ The roof as a large hole in the top for the vent to be fitted. This is best made as a separate unit and allowed to dry before gluing in place.

④ Before details such as the drainpipes, doors or windows were fitted, all the stone received a coat of Humbrol 103 cream. This was allowed to dry for a couple of hours, then dusted with talcum powder. Finally, some Humbrol 121 was dabbed over the top with a piece of sponge. This leaves a slightly mottled effect and a little texture on the surface of the stones.

⑤ With the paint dry, doors and other details were fitted and painted.

www.model-railways-live.co.uk 73

THE BRM GUIDE TO BUILDING YOUR FIRST MODEL RAILWAY

HOW TO... MODEL THE STATION BUILDING

Edgeworth's station will be familiar to those who've travelled by train to Glastonbury Festival. Here's how we made it.

There's a reasonable chance that some readers will be familiar with the prototype for 'Edgeworth' station building. The Ratio kit (Ref: 504, £27.50) is based on the GWR's Castle Cary station which every year sees a huge influx of traffic during the Glastonbury Festival weekend.

The kit is one of the more complex, or at least fiddly, in the range. There are an awful lot of parts and you need to take care to line things up and keep them square. If you take your time the resulting model is an attractive and pretty classic GWR station.

I'm assuming that passenger traffic is modest at the end of our branch line, but should your expectations be greater, then the kit can be extended with extra canopies by purchasing the separate canopy kit that also serves for island platforms. **BRM**

> Take your time and the resulting model is an attractive and pretty classic GWR station.

GREAT WESTERN RAILWAY COLOURS FOR BUILDINGS

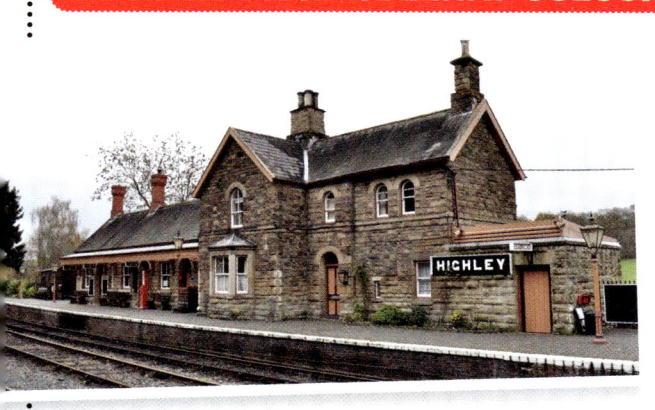

The GWR management laid down strict rules for painting buildings. Essentially there were two colours to be used; 'Light Stone' and 'Dark Stone', both shades of brown.

Dark Stone was to be used on roof girders, ironwork, skylights, window frames, valances, awnings and the raised panel work on doors.

Light Stone was used on the underside of awnings and the sunken sections of door panels.

Having said this, the rules weren't applied vigorously and local variations did occur. Modern preserved railways aren't always a good guide to the colours. Highley on the Severn Valley Railway uses what appears to be too dark a shade of Dark Stone although this could partly be the winter light.

Dark Stone canopy valances also appeared and as I think this looks nicer, that's what 'Edgeworth' received. Mind you, being so close to the locomotive chimneys, it would have become grubby very quickly so the point is probably moot anyway.

For modelling purposes, several people include Dark and Light stone in their paint selections. I've use some from the Railmatch range for all the models on the layout.

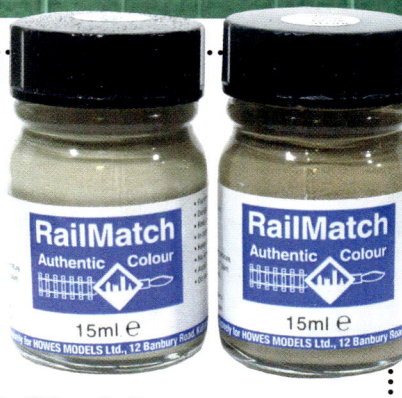

Useful websites:
- www.gwr.org.uk
- www.stationcolours.info

WHAT IS A QUOIN?

Quoins are the large stone blocks at the corner of the wall. Normally they are purely decorative features and on modern buildings are sometimes added as overlays once the building is completed.

To quote the box: 'This kit contains sufficient parts to make the model illustrated without the scenic effect'. I'm not sure how many parts this is, but there are certainly a lot of them.

The model was painted to match the engine shed with Humbrol 103 followed by 121. Once dry, Humbrol dark brown weathering powder was worked over the surface. The chimneys needed a coat of hairspray to encourage the 'Smoke' weathering powder to stick properly.

STEP-BY-STEP GUIDE

1 Before fixing the walls together, the quoins must be fitted to the ends. If you make up the walls first, the quoins won't fit afterwards.

2 With so many sections to each wall, care must be taken to ensure they are square or in-line. Corner braces are included to help with this. The roof sides are supplied in two parts which must be joined before fixing in place.

3 Gaps around the edges of the quoins should be filled with PVA glue applied with a small brush. It's an unusual technique that works surprisingly well.

THE BRM GUIDE TO BUILDING YOUR FIRST MODEL RAILWAY

STEP-BY-STEP GUIDE ▶

4 The corners should be filled if required. I deepened the lines between quoin stones with an Olfa cutter then rounded the sharp corners off with a fine sanding stick.

5 Nine parts are required for the larger chimney and ten for the smaller one. Care is required to keep everything square as wonky chimneys stand out a mile on a model. The joins on the sides and corners of the base both needed some attention, nothing major, but model roofs tend to be very prominent from normal viewing angles so it's worth taking time over this.

6 A little cheating here. Whilst a full set of girders is provided to fit under the canopy, they are fiddly to build and you can't really see them unless your head is underneath it, so I left them out. If you do fit them, remember to glaze the skylights first as you can't afterwards.

7 Valances hang from the lower canopy edge of the canopy. With a pretty small area for the glue to grab on the long front section, I fitted them with plastic cement which allowed for adjustment. This was followed by a wash of solvent which sets the joint quickly.

8 Inside, glazing can be cut pretty roughly as it's just glued over the back of the windows. The skylights are a different matter as no provision is made for the clear plastic to extend beyond the openings.

REALISTIC WHITE PAINT

Although we have white windowframes on some of the buildings, rather than use pure white paint (Humbrol 34), I've chosen a pale grey (Humbrol 147). This probably sounds like an odd decision but when you see the effect on a model, the eye thinks it sees white, but a softer and less glaring colour. It's a subtle change but looks more realistic, especially once any weathering is carried out.

WHAT WE USED
▶ Ratio 504 Station building - £27.50

FINISHED MODEL

www.themodelcentre.com

TMC
The MODEL CENTRE

A huge range of standard and Custom Finish models in both OO and N gauge.

Visit our showroom located in Beck Hole near Whitby - alternatively you can visit our website which boasts a huge variety of both standard and professionally weathered/ enhanced models.

TMC is a one stop shop catering for all of your modeling needs, whether you're a complete beginner or a more experienced modeller - you can even send us your models to be expertly enhanced.

We stock the full Woodland Scenics range, as well as Metcalfe, Oxford Diecast, Peco, Ratio, Wills, Gaugemaster, Humbrol, Noch and more! Our TMC Price Match* ensures you the best possible quality and value.

*subject to T&C's (available online)

Re-creating History with Every Model

Choose from the following options...

- Custom weathering - light, medium or heavy
- Renaming & renumbering
- Crest & shed code changes
- DCC & DCC sound fitting service

- Screw link couplings
- Cab tarpaulin
- Fit parts pack
- Lamps
- Real coal

- Tool carrier
- Fire irons
- Gloss finish
- Cab crew

come & see our NEW! SHOWROOM

METCALFE | Humbrol | HELJAN | WILLS KITS | RATIO | GAUGEMASTER | OXFORD | NOCH ...wie im Original

HORNBY | GRAHAM FARISH by BACHMANN | BACHMANN BRANCH-LINE | SCENECRAFT by Bachmann | dapol | PECO | WOODLAND SCENICS

TMC, Hill Farm, Beck Hole, Whitby, YO22 5LF | T: 01947 899125 | E: websales@tmc-direct.com

THE BRM GUIDE TO BUILDING YOUR FIRST MODEL RAILWAY

HOW TO MODEL A... SIGNAL BOX

Follow this step-by-step guide to building a signalbox kit for your layout.

A lovely looking building but watch out for the finials on the roof. I've stuck mine back on half-a-dozen times already

If there's a structure likely to be scrutinised on a model, it's going to be the signalbox. Railway signalling is a very complicated subject, the study of it can easily turn into a fascinating hobby in it's own right.

Having said this, signalboxes are very charismatic structures and unless it is tiny, a steam-age station would look bare without one. We've used the Ratio kit based on the prototype at Highley station - now part of the Severn Valley Railway - because it looks typically Great Western, although it isn't a standard GWR design. It's also a very attractive model.

Construction is more complicated than most plastic kits as the model has been moulded in different coloured plastic to match the paint scheme of the prototype. This sort of thing was popular years ago but most people realised that unpainted plastic looks just like plastic that hasn't been painted - it's far too shiny and smooth for the wood or brickwork we are modelling here. Still, at least the colours are a good guide for painting.

Of course, once you've built the model someone is going to point out that the layout doesn't have any signals or wires that connected them tho the box, or point rodding.
I told you it was complicated.
BRM

DO YOU NEED A SIGNALBOX?

Not every point is controlled from a 'box. In goods yards it was common to see a lever beside each point for the shunter to operate. Plastic and whitemetal versions are available and you can extend the sleepers using leftover sleepers from tracklaying. The cover over the operating rod can be made from thin card or plastic.

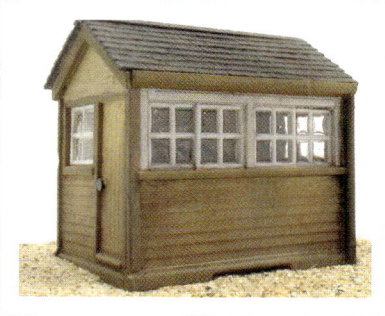

Not all were as big as the one we've used. Wills make a kit for the tiny Staverton 'box which only had four levers.

The box contents are certainly colourful. Most parts are moulded in self-coloured plastic so you could almost get away without painting them, although you shouldn't.

PROTOTYPE INSPIRATION

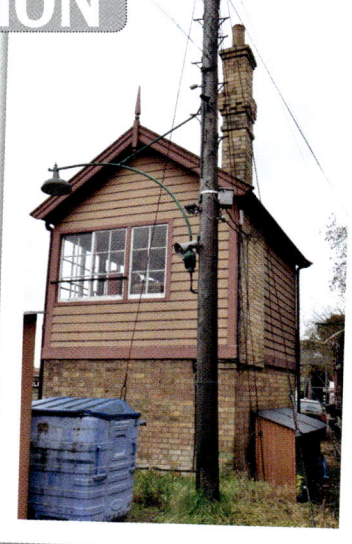

Ratio's kit is a model of the preserved signalbox at Highley on the Severn Valley Railway. The prototype, built in 1883, is a standard design from signalling firm Mackenzie & Holland so it's suitable for use in different locations. It remained in operation until May 1970 when Alveley Colliery closed, marking the end of freight traffic. Preservationists quickly restored it to use and the site remains largely unchanged apart from the fencing between the road along the front of the box and railway lines.

STEP-BY-STEP GUIDE

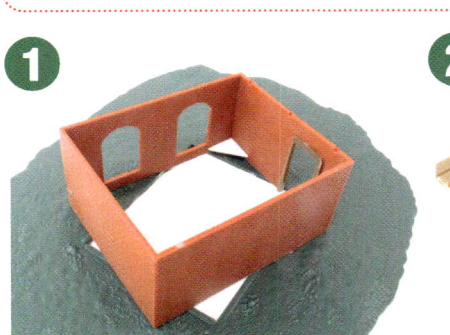

1 A green baseplate is included, but we're not using this as the box will be bedded in on the layout. Assembling the bottom half of the model, I added some plastic card off-cuts in the corners to brace them while they joined.

2 The balcony pokes through the top of one wall. Notches are moulded into the back of the brickwork but have to be opened out so the joists can fit through. The tops of these should be level with the top of the wall. Once the floor is fitted it will stop them drooping.

3 Using plastic cement, all the treads were fitted to one side of the steps. This holds them and allows the second side to be added. Do this before they dry so you can make adjustments. Put the completed assembly somewhere safe while it hardens.

www.model-railways-live.co.uk 79

THE BRM GUIDE TO BUILDING YOUR FIRST MODEL RAILWAY

STEP-BY-STEP GUIDE ▶

4 Each cabin wall is made up and then they are brought together around the floor. The windows need care as there are two different mouldings – parts 19 and 20. Make sure you know which is which. In real life, the windows slide behind each other so they should look like they can on the model.

5 The mitred corners required a little gap filling as the real things are single pieces of wood. Only tiny amounts of filler were required – Deluxe Materials Plastic Putty seems to be stickier than other fillers making it ideal for this job.

6 Cardboard interior walls were cut to fit and stuck in place with UHU. The chimney breast is folded to shape and can be used as a conduit for wires if you plan to add internal lighting. No other fittings are supplied and as this box faces away from the viewer I didn't worry about this.

7  Clear glazing material has to be cut to fit and then glued in place. Humbrol Clearfix is easier to use than plastic solvent or superglue, both of which can fog the glazing.

INTERIORS

Highley 'box has a 14 lever frame. If your model faces the audience or you just fancy fitting a full interior, several companies can supply parts:

▶ **Wills** – Whitemetal kit – SSAM103 – £16.50
▶ **Springside Models** – Whitemetal kit – DA72 – £6.25
▶ **SmartModels.co.uk** – Downloadable kit – RAIL05 – £0.99

8

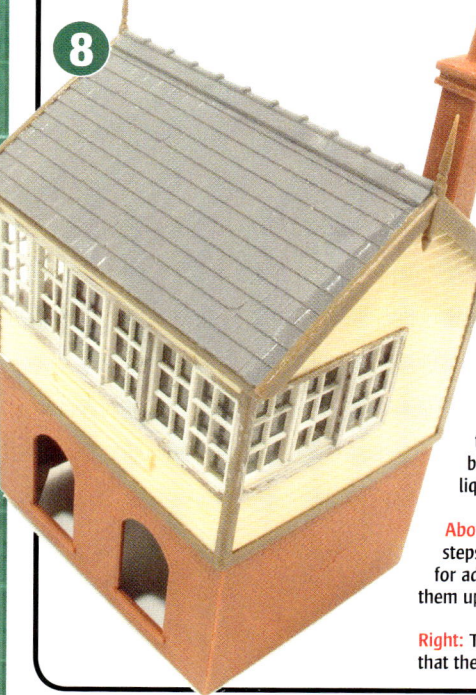

9  **Left:** Fitting the roof requires the beams at the top of the front and back walls to be chamfered so the tiled part sits properly on the sides. You can tell if they are right because the bargeboards will fit. Watch those finials - I've broken both off my model, good job they can be stuck back on with liquid plastic glue!

Above: Balcony handrails fit into notches on the floor with the steps filling the gap. Assemble with plastic cement to allow for adjustment and then wash solvent over the joins to harden them up.

10 **Right:** The guttering appears to fit into holes in the model, except that there aren't any! I just cut off the pegs and glued it in place.

GAUGEMASTER Spotlight
DCC Decoders

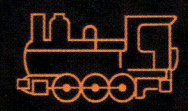

OMNI Series Decoders

The OMNI range of decoders are the follow up to our popular range of OPTI DCC decoders. With the need for a 21 pin decoder (for use in Bachmann and Heljan locomotives, and some Dapol diesel locomotives) we took the opportunity to refresh the whole range and source a new family of decoders that can solve most scenarios in just three items.

The OMNI range have the ability to do so much more than the leading manufacturer's basic decoder, but they have more features included which are not proportional to the difference in price.

You get so much more for just a few pounds more.
- Back EMF for perfect low speed running
- Consisting (double-heading)
- Special lighting effects (firebox lights, flashing)
- On track programming
- Address locking
- Full Technical Support

All three OMNI decoders are also available in handy bulk packs of five, giving you the versatility to install decoders into several locomotives at once at a reduced price - digitise your collection for less!

DCC27 OMNI 21 & 8 Pin Decoder
(BPDCC27 five pack)
Most Suited to OO/HO Gauge Locomotives

A really versatile decoder for use with locomotives that have 8 Pin or 21 Pin sockets.

Dimensions: Length 22mm Width 16mm Depth 5mm
Harness Length: 75mm

BEST FOR OO Versatility

DCC28 OMNI 8 & 6 Pin Decoder
(BPDCC28 five pack)
Most Suited to OO/HO Gauge & N Gauge Locomotives

6 Pin decoder with plugable 8 pin harness. This very versatile 2 function decoder is very small so it can fit in most locomotives regardless of space.

Dimensions: Length 15mm Width 8mm Depth 2mm
Harness Length: 55mm

BEST FOR Multi Scale

DCC29 OMNI Direct Plug Decoder
(BPDCC29 five pack)
Most Suited to OO/HO Gauge Locomotives

A 4 function decoder suitable for direct plug fitting into suitable OO and HO Locomotives.

Dimensions: Length 15mm Width 12mm Depth 10mm

BEST FOR Small Spaces

Other Decoders

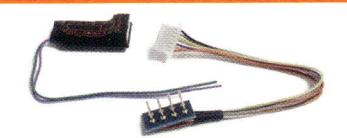

DCC22 Very Small 8 Pin Decoder
Most Suited to OO/HO Gauge Locomotives

Key features of this standard decoder include smooth operation, 14/28 speed steps, plug and play, transponder id-equipped, all mode programming, decoder reset CV, motor isolation protection, advanced consisting, 2 and 4 digit addressing and DCC compatability. this decoder is rated at 1 amp (2 amp peak) with 2 functions at 0.5 amps.

Dimensions: Length 11mm Width 9mm Depth 3mm
Length with Harness: 65mm

BEST FOR Size

DCC23 2 Function 6 Pin Decoder
Most Suited to N Gauge Locomotives

Key features of this standard decoder include smooth operation, 14/28 speed steps, plug and play, transponder id-equipped, all mode programming, decoder reset CV, motor isolation protection, advanced consisting, 2 and 4 digit addressing and DCC compatability. this decoder is rated at 1 amp (2 amp peak) with 2 functions at 0.5 amps.

Dimensions: Length 11mm Width 9mm Depth 3mm

BEST FOR N Scale

DCC26 Standard 8 Pin Decoder
Most Suited to OO/HO Gauge Locomotives

Fantastic value decoder from our original OPTI Range, available again. 4 function, 1.1 amp decoder with adjustable CVs for motor control, Back EMF, built in lighting effects, supports consisting. It is compatible with DC running, and has a full factory reset function. The decoder can be set with any address from 0-9999.

Dimensions: Length 19mm Width 11mm Depth 5mm
Harness Length: 90mm

BEST FOR Tight Budgets

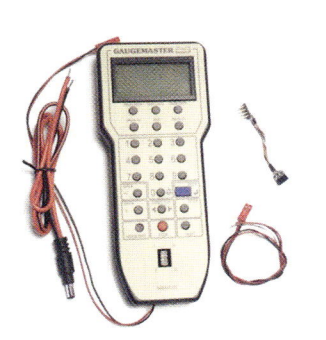

Decoder Doctor

DCC15 Prodigy Decoder Doctor

Makes programming and reading back your decoders easy! This device allows you to test decoders before or after installation.

There is a built-in 8 Pin socket, and the Decoder Doctor also comes supplied with an adaptor harness allowing you to also test 6 Pin decoders.

You can also attach it to a test track for testing already fitted decoders.

Power comes from either a 15V power supply (DCC65) or your DCC Main Track output.

PRICES

Code	Description	RRP
DCC15	Prodigy Decoder Doctor	£79.95
DCC22	Very Small 8 Pin Decoder	£24.95
DCC23	2 Function 6 Pin Decoder	£24.95
DCC26	Standard 8 Pin Decoder	£13.95
DCC27	OMNI 21 & 8 Pin Decoder	£18.95
BPDCC27	OMNI 21 & 8 Pin Decoder (Five Pack)	£89.95
DCC28	OMNI 8 & 6 Pin Decoder	£20.95
BPDCC28	OMNI 8 & 6 Pin Decoder (Five Pack)	£99.95
DCC29	OMNI Direct Plug Decoder	£19.95
BPDCC29	OMNI Direct Plug Decoder (Five Pack)	£94.95

GAUGEMASTER products are availble from your local Model Shop or, in case of difficulty, direct from ourselves.

GAUGEMASTER Controls Ltd, Gaugemaster House, Ford Road, Arundel, West Sussex, BN18 0BN, United Kingdom

THE BRM GUIDE TO BUILDING YOUR FIRST MODEL RAILWAY

HOW TO... SCRATCH-BUILD A GOODS OFFICE

This Goods Office is a great introduction to scratch-building and the perfect way to model on the cheap.

This booklet is a beginners guide and I'm suggesting you have a go at building a model from scratch, not even using a kit? Am I mad?

Not really. There's nothing to be scared of. The materials are cheap enough, you don't need any special tools and best of all, it's great fun.

I could have suggested we save some money by building one of the larger buildings from raw materials, but in truth, the humble hut has many things to commend it as a first subject.

The first is size. Construction won't take very long. You don't need much material and if you make a mistake cutting a part out, it's cheap enough to throw it away and make a new one. Do this a few times and you'll quickly become adept at the process. A good piece of advice when making models from scratch is not to accept something nearly right. It will always annoy you. Do it again, you'll be much happier with the result.

Possibly more important though, small huts were many and varied on the railway. Model railways tend to use the same kits or ready-built versions and so everyone's layout looks the same. The real huts were often in a slightly ramshackle condition so less than perfect modelling is perfectly appropriate for a miniature version.

My model is a simple weatherboarded hut. If you preferred, it could be covered with either brick paper or plastic card.

The materials used are essentially two thicknesses of cardboard. The main shell is 2mm thick artists' mounting board sold by art shops and

STEP-BY-STEP GUIDE

1 Mark out the 2mm thick cardboard for the walls. Window and door sizes will depend on the ones you have chosen but you can draw around them. I marked horizontal lines for the planking to follow as well.

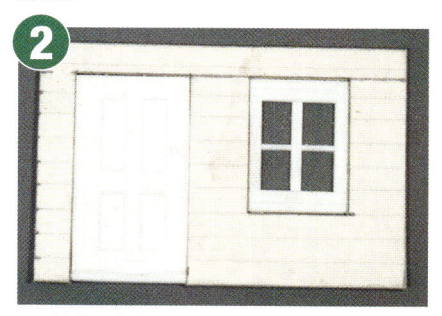

All dimensions in mm — 50, 30, 45, 30

2 Test fit the window and door, but don't glue them in place at this stage.

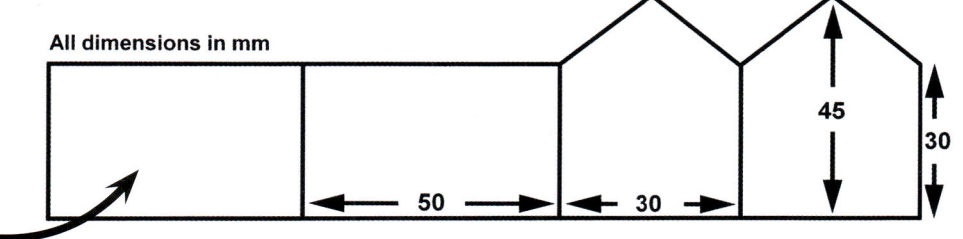

SCORING CARD

If you want a piece of card to bend along a straight line, gently draw a knife along the back of where you want the crease. Your aim is to mark the surface but not cut through it. This is an ideal job for a slightly blunt knife. When you come to bend the card, it should form a nice sharp corner. Practise on a piece of scrap first though.

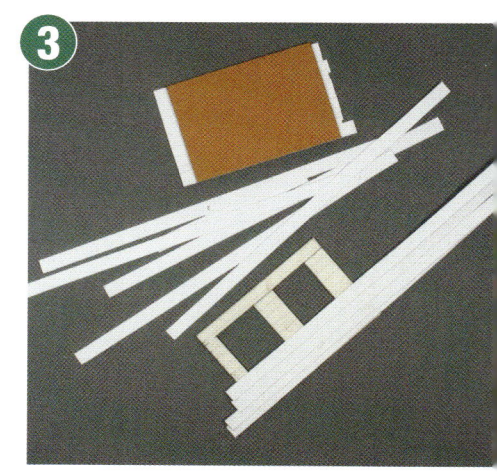

3 The weatherboard planks are cut from thin card 4mm wide. These are glued to the walls with PVA with a 1mm overlap.

TOOLS AND MATERIALS

■ Pencil ■ 6" steel rule
■ Craft knife ■ Wire cutters
■ PVA glue ■ All Purpose glue
■ 2mm thick card (Daler board)
■ Thin card ■ 2mm thick plastic card ■ Thin wire
■ Wills (SS86) Windows and doors pack ■ Small brass or plastic tube

larger stationers under the trade name Daler Board. A single sheet will cost around a fiver and give enough material for over 100 huts.

The weatherboard covering is 160gsm weight card sold as suitable for printers and photocopiers. Each sheet is slightly thicker than a piece of paper, but not much. You could use printer paper, but card is easier to work with.

A window and door are required and although these can be made from card too, commercial plastic versions are easier to use for first attempts. Mine came from a Wills building parts set, but several firms sell spare parts from kits or you could even recycle them from the sort of battered plastic kit found underneath the table at a model railway show second hand stall, priced at a few pence. **BRM**

IF YOU PREFER A KIT...

If you prefer building a kit, there are many suitable models. Ratio's Yard Office is available for £3.50 and goes together very easily.

4 To ensure the planks line up at the corners, I stuck the walls together and worked my way around from one end to the other using the already planked front as a guide.

5 The window and door holes are cut out of the planking. A scrap of card glued over the back of the door will hold the plastic part. The corners are tidied up with 4mm wide strip, scored along the middle and folded to a right angle to cover the join.

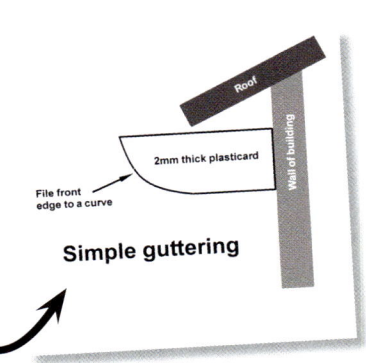

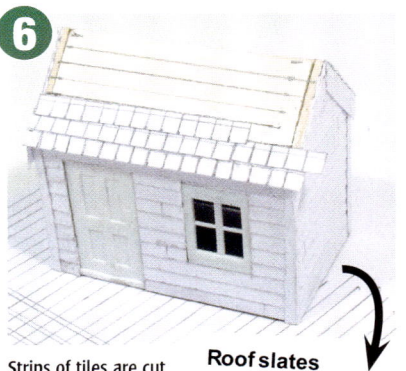

6 Strips of tiles are cut from thin card and overlapped by 1mm.

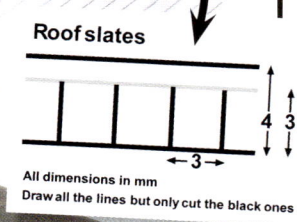

Roof slates

4 3
← 3 →

All dimensions in mm
Draw all the lines but only cut the black ones

7 Simple guttering from 2mm plastic sheet is fitted to the front and a drainpipe made from thin plastic coated wire.

Roof
2mm thick plasticard
Wall of building
File front edge to a curve

Simple guttering

8 A chimney is made from a length of plastic or brass tube poking out from a hole in the roof.

THE BRM GUIDE TO BUILDING YOUR FIRST MODEL RAILWAY

HOW TO MODEL...
THE ROAD BRIDGE

One final structure is needed for the layout - a road bridge. These are commonly used to conceal an exit.

TOOLS FOR THE JOB
- Knife
- Steel rule
- Flush wire cutters
- Abrasive sticks
- Plastic cement
- Liquid plastic glue

Over the previous pages, we've assembled all the main structures with the exception of the road bridge that covers the entrance to the layout. I could suggest that this was part of a grand plan but the truth was, this proved to be the hardest structure to find.

While there are a few ready-to-plant models available, some of these looked too modern for a 1930s branch line. Others just didn't seem to fit with the rest of the buildings and would have stood out on the model. I had hoped for a stone structure to match the station, but the best option I could find was a vacuum-formed plastic Peco model and that requires quite a bit of work to complete.

In the end I've plumped for the Wills plastic kit, part of its 'Craftsman' range. It might be brick rather than stone but that's OK. It's a very nice model and designed to be flexible enough, at the cost of ease of construction It'll fit any site where you need to take a road over a single track railway line.

The model can be built as a standalone structure, but here I'm using it to hide the exit to the fiddleyard so I've only used half the parts. The rest will find themselves bagged up and stashed away in my spares box awaiting another project.

One trick worth remembering with this model is that a layout will look a lot more natural if you don't allow anything to follow the edge of the baseboard. As it crosses my bridge, the road is 10mm narrower at the edge nearest the viewer than it is at the back. The idea is that tricks like this will fool the viewers eye into ignoring the rectangular overall shape. Of course this isn't always possible, but where you can do it, it's worth the effort. **BRM**

> *Since I only needed one half of the kit, replacement parts would have been available had anything gone wrong.*

WHAT WE USED
Wills Kits OO Brick Arch Bridge (SS53): **£12.25** from all good model shops
Geoscenics' Pothole road kit: **£7.00**
W www.geoscenics.com

1 The Wills kit is unconventional in that you don't just stick the bits together and then drop it into place. The parts are designed to allow the modeller to produce a bridge that fits the space rather than trying to adjust the landscape to fit the bridge.

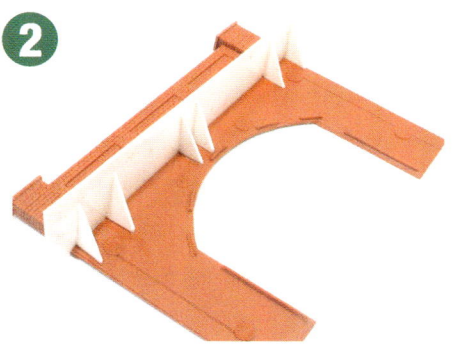

2 I started by fixing the road, cut from 2mm plastic card, in place. By making this 5mm narrower at one end than the other, my bridge would be at a slight angle to the backscene. It's not clear from the diagram but the road fits on top of the arched part with the parapet walls fitting on top of this.

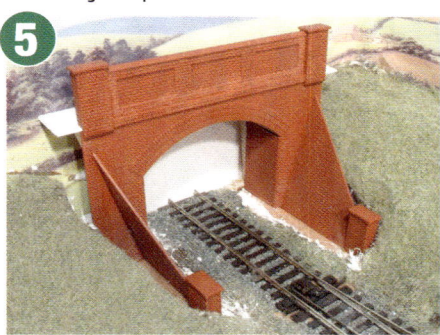

3 The ends of the parapet and pillars for the end of the wing walls are made up. These are ingenious, all being taken from identical sprues. You just pick the correct combination for the part you wish to build.

4 Under the arch, supplied sheet is cut to length and fixed inside. Make sure the walls are parallel to the track. In my case this meant they weren't at right angles to the arch. The curved roof is from Slater's brick Plastikard which is much easier to bend than the Wills version.

5 With a sharp knife, I cut away the scenery around the tunnel mouth to allow the bridge to sit in place. The plaster bandage cuts reasonably cleanly leaving just the polystyrene inside to be hollowed out a bit. The wing walls have to be trimmed and then glued to the bridge face once you've worked out their final positions.

6 Once I was happy with the fit, the brickwork was painted with Humbrol 121 for the mortar and then rubbed the brick faces with crayons to colour them.

7 Some polystyrene packaging was trimmed to provide a road surface either side of the bridge and then the whole lot was bedded in place with household wall filler. Masking the track would have been a good idea. As it is, I had to remove a few plaster spots with a wet cotton bud.

8 Since I didn't want a tarmac road surface, some Geoscenics powder was sprinkled in place, fixed with watered down PVA and tamped reasonably flat with a wet finger. It's only a few millimetres wide and will be hidden by roadside hedges so it's not perfect, but then neither were country roads of the time. Chinchilla Dust or even sawdust would also be suitable for this task.

WOULDN'T IT HAVE BEEN EASIER TO FIT THE BRIDGE AND *THEN* BUILD THE HILLSIDES?
Yes it would, but then every layout plan evolves as you build it. That's part of the fun!

9 Humbrol Dark Earth weathering powder was dusted into all the corners and lightly over the surface of the bricks. At the top of the arch, where steam locomotives would blast out muck, a thick coat of Smoke colour powder was brushed on. To build up the effect, a light spray of hair lacquer helped the powder to stick.

www.model-railways-live.co.uk

Golden Valley Hobbies

www.goldenvalleyhobbies.com

OUR GUIDE TO MODEL TREES

Take a leaf out of our book…

We have a range of products that can be used to represent trees. We can offer trees for any modellers scale from Z scale to G scale model railways (1:220 to 1:45). In varying shade, height and quality. Here are a few…

Two important points to remember when adding trees: Unlike many objects on your model, trees can be virtually any size, so you can create perspective by using smaller scales towards the back of your model and larger scale trees at the front.

Secondly, use low cost and bulk packs to fill large areas of forest, with a front to each area of better quality trees. While picking out individual locations with high quality specimen trees.

BUS 6492 35 OO/HO scale Dark Pine Trees £16.30
BUS 6592 35 N/Z scale Dark Pine Trees...............£10.90
BUS 6499 100 OO/HO Dark Pine trees, no foot.......£35.20
BUS 6476 20 OO/HO Light Pine Trees £13.20
BUS 6576 20 N/Z Light Pine Trees.........................£8.30
BUS 6472 60 OO/HO Light Pine, no foot............£32.40
BUS 6487 25 OO/HO scale Deciduous Trees £17.60
BUS 6489 30 OO/HO scale Mixed Trees..............£22.00
BUS 6466 20 OO/HO Snow Covered Trees..........£15.00
BUS 6566 20 N/Z Snow Covered Trees £8.70
BUS 6587 25 N scale Deciduous Trees £9.60
BUS 6589 30 N scale Mixed Trees £11.40
BUS 6484 16 OO/HO scale Trees in blossom £12.70
BUS 6584 18 N/Z Trees in blossom..........................£7.40
BUS 6333 N/Z 204 Asst Trees Mega Box £338.00

Specimen trees

Although you can use these for your entire layout the cost would be quite high, for many modellers just a few used a key locations is normally enough, without breaking the bank.

These trees feature stems designed to match the real specimen, branch patterns modelled on real trees, and a unique scatter shaped like real leaves. Combined with the variety of colours you can expect visitors to be able to identify each specimen of tree on your model.

They are suitable for HO, OO, O and TT scales. We round this section off with the essential kits to form ground cover and the smaller plants.

BUS 6968 Copper Beech 180mm...................... 6.00
BUS 6967 Ash Tree 180mm 7.20
BUS 6961 Chestnut Tree 180mm 7.20
BUS 6966 Birch 180mm 7.20
BUS 6969 Beech 180mm 7.20
BUS 6943 2 Poplars 115mm 6.00
BUS 6650 2 Weeping Willows 11.50
BUS 6229 10 Silver Poplars 95mm 8.70
BUS 6144 2 Scotch Pines 175 & 210mm 14.50
BUS 6134 2 Fir trees 90 & 120mm 12
BUS 1308 Edge of forest grass set 20.60
BUS 6043 Forest soil and undergrowth starter set....... 18.40
BUS 1203 48 Ferns and Mushrooms 6.90
BUS 6801 Seafoam box for tree construction...... 15.80
BUS 6740 Fall foliage trees 150mm (2) 8.70

Colored Bottle Brushes?

No doubt the Model industry is the largest consumer of these kitchen items - with green fibres the bottle brush can be transformed into a basic Fir tree!

However we have chosen the Busch range as it features a reasonably realistic branch and leaf structure, plus a good plastic 'foot'.

Busch produce bulk packs of these items, with 25 trees of similar sizes sorted for various scales. Typical size ranges are: OO/HO = 50-135mm N/Z = 30-60mm.

The trees are available in four 'varieties' Dark Green, Lighter Green, Snow Covered & Blossom covered.

Fruit from the Orchard

And we have not forgotten where to find some Apples, and Pears! So here are a few trees bearing fruit or blossom. All are OO, HO and TT suitable. We have N and Z scale alternatives.

BUS 6848 2 Apple Trees with fruit 75mm....£5.30
BUS 6843 2 Fruit trees in bloom 75mm....£5.30
BUS 6649 Apple and Plum trees 75mm....£6.10
BUS 6651 Fruit Orchard (3 trees) 95mm....£13.99
BUS 1215 Hops 60mm high....................£13.20
BUS 6331 64 Fruit trees – Ass Value Pk....£155.00
BUS 1204 Wheat field approx. 100cm2....£11.30
BUS 1216 Barleyfield approx. 100cm2...@£11.40

01981 241237
www.goldenvalleyhobbies.com | info@goldenvalleyhobbies.com

PETITE PROPERTIES

NEW KITS!!

1:76

Tel 01526 328 738

www.petite-properties.com

GIFTS FOR THE RAIL ENTHUSIAST

Personalised Railway Totems made to order from **£12.95** + p&p

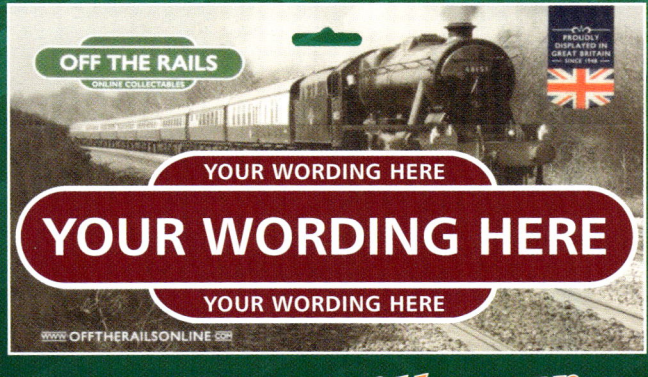

OFF THE RAILS
ONLINE COLLECTABLES
PROUDLY DISPLAYED IN GREAT BRITAIN SINCE 1948

YOUR WORDING HERE
YOUR WORDING HERE
YOUR WORDING HERE

www.offtherailsonline.com

Where will your journey take you...?

www.offtherailsonline.com
Tel: 01903 751700

MAIL ORDER ADDRESS
Dept. R.M.1
39 HIGH STREET
CHELTENHAM, GL50 1DX
Shop Open 9am to 5.30pm
Monday - Saturday
Email sales@cheltenhammodelcentre.co.uk

CHELTENHAM MODEL CENTRE

UK Standard Postage Rate £4.00 per shipment Registered 24hr delivery (Mon to Fri) UK mainland only £7.00. Worldwide postage at cost. PLEASE WRITE CLEARLY, SAE with all enquiries. THESE OFFERS ARE SUBJECT TO AVAILABILITY AND MAY BE WITHDRAWN WITHOUT PRIOR NOTICE. Payment may be made by phone

TELEPHONE ORDER LINES 01242 523117 01242 234644 **FAX AND ANSWER M/C WHEN CLOSED** 01242 226050

www.cheltenhammodelcentre.com

YOUR FIRST STEP INTO MODEL RAILWAY START HERE

CHRISTMAS IS COMING

HORNBY TRAIN SETS OO SCALE
R1151	Calyedion Train Set	£50.00
R1167	Flying Scotsman	£99.99
R1171	Flight of the Mallard	£159.00
R1173	Western Master Train Set	£154.99
R1071	Eurostar Train Set	£169.99
R1155	Pendolion Set	£139.99

BACHMANN OO TRAIN SETS
30-048	Highlander Digital Set	£250.70
30-080	Western Wanderer Set	£84.95
30-105	Midland Marvel Train Set	£106.20

GRAHAM FARISH N GAUGE TRAIN SETS
370-070	Cornish Riviera Digital Set	£157.20
370-080	Countryside Digital Set	£140.20
370-140	Steel Worker Train Set	£96.99

PECO SET TRACK OO
STP00	Setrack Plan Book	£2.95
ST100	Starter Track Set	£54.00
ST200	Standard Straight	£1.30
ST201	Double Straight	£2.05
ST202	Short Straight	£1.10
ST203	Extra Short Straight	£1.10
ST204	Peco Long Straight	£3.45
	Same as Hornby R603	
	12 for £38.40	
ST205	Isolating Track inc. Switch	£3.15
ST220	1st Radius Standard Curve	£1.75
ST221	1st Radius Double Curve	£2.20
ST222	1st Radius Half Curve	£1.25
ST225	2nd Radius Standard Curve	£1.85
ST226	2nd Radius Double Curve	£2.35
ST227	2nd Radius Half Curve	£1.25
ST230	3rd Radius Standard Curve	£2.00
ST231	3rd Radius Double Curve	£2.55
ST235	4 Radius Std Curve	£2.10
ST238	Curve for Y Point	£1.85
ST240	R/H 2nd Radius Point	£8.65
ST241	L/H 2nd Raidus Point	£8.65
ST244	R/H Curved Point	£13.25
ST245	L/H Curved Point	£13.25
ST247	Medium Radius Y Point	£10.60
ST250	Medium Crossing	£8.85
ST266	Curved Level Crossing Set	£8.70
ST269	Curved Crossing add on	£4.65
ST270	Sleeper Built Buffer	£1.65
ST271	Decoupling Unit	£1.60
ST273	Twin Power Clips	£2.80
ST280	Track Fixing Nails	£2.00
ST290	Straight Brick Platforms	£4.75
LK35	Yard Crane	£10.85

PECO 'OO' TRACK
SL100	12yds only Nickel Silver	£32.40
SL100	25yds pack Nickel Silver	£64.00
SL102	12yds only Nickel Silver	£36.00
SL102	25yds concrete Nickel Silver	£70.00
SL80	Single Slip	£28.85
SL86	R/H Curved Point	£12.00
SL87	L/H Curved Point	£12.00
SL88	R/H Large Radius Point	£11.00
SL89	L/H Large Radius Point	£11.00
SL90	Double Slip	£30.95
SL91	Small R/H Radius Point	£9.00
SL92	L/H Small Radius Point	£9.00
SL93	Short Crossing	£8.30
SL94	Long Crossing	£9.65
SL95	R/H Medium Radius Point	£10.00
SL96	L/H Medium Radius Point	£10.00
SL97	Small Y Point	£9.15
SL98	Large Y Point	£10.60
SL99	3-way Point	£24.80
SL50	Roll of Underlay	£8.40
Point of Underlay (per pack of 2)		£5.25

OO STREAMLINE ELECTROFROG POINTS
SLE97	Y Point Small Radius	£9.20
SLE98	Y Point Large Radius	£10.70
SLE91	Small Radius Point R/H	£9.15
SLE92	Small Radius Point L/H	£9.15
SLE95	Medium Radius Point R/H	£10.05
SLE96	Medium Radius Point L/H	£10.05
SLE88	Large Radius Point R/H	£11.48
SLE89	Large Radius Point L/H	£11.48
SLE86	Curved Radius Point R/H	£12.28
SLE87	Curved Radius Point L/H	£12.28
SLE99	3 Way Medium Radius Point	£24.88

CORK SHEETING
THE BEST UNDERLAY MATERIAL
1/32 Sheet 36" x 24" **£4.00**
2 for **£7.00**
1/8 Sheet 36" x 24" **£6.75**
2 for **£12.00**
3/16 Sheet 36" x 24" **£10.00**
2 sheets of 3/16 for **£17.00**
CORK SHEETING

PECO CODE N GAUGE TRACK

SL300	Wooden Sleeper 12 yds only	£32.64
SL300	Wooden Sleeper 25 yds box	£64.00

INSULFROG
SL395	Medium R/H Point	£8.80
SL396	Medium L/H Point	£8.80
SL388	Large R/H Point	£10.00
SL389	Large L/H Point	£10.00
SL386	Curved Large R/H Point	£10.00
SL387	Curved Large L/H Point	£10.00
SL397	Y Point	£8.80
SL393	Short Crossing	£8.40
SL394	Long Crossing	£9.10
SL350	Roll of underlay	£5.50
Point of underlay Pkt of 2		£3.85

ELECTROFROG POINTS
SLE395	Medium R/H Point	£8.90
SLE396	Medium L/H Point	£8.90
SLE388	Large R/H Point	£10.08
SLE389	Large L/H Point	£10.08
SLE386	Curves R/H Point	£10.08
SLE387	Curves L/H Point	£10.08
SLE397	Y Medium Point	£8.90
SL310	Railjoiners n Gauge	£2.10
SL311	Insulated railjoiners	£1.85
SL330	Decouplers	£1.85
SL340	Railbuilt Buffer Stop x 2	£1.60

CODE 80 N SET TRACK
ST300	Starter Set	£44.00
ST1	Std Straight	£1.10
ST2	Straight	95p
ST3	No 1 Rad Std Curve	£1.10
ST4	No 1 Rad 1/8 Std Curve	95p
ST5	R/H Setrack Point	£8.35
ST6	L/H Setrack Point	£8.35
ST50	R/H Setrack crossing	£8.40
ST51	L/H Setrack Crossing	£8.40
ST8	Sleeperbuilt Buffer Stop	£1.85
ST9	Power Clip	£2.80
ST11	Double Straight	£1.50
ST12	Double Curve	£1.40
ST14	2nd std curve	£1.40
ST15	2nd DI Curve	£1.50
ST17	3 Radi Double curve	£1.85
ST18	N 4 Radi curve ½	£1.95
ST19	N 4 Radi Curve full	£2.25
ST20	Level Crossing	£8.15

SUNDEALA BOARD
600mm x 1200mm Approx 4' x 2'
SINGLE SHEETS £10.50 SHOP ONLY
6 SHEETS £55.50 + £9.00 P/P UK Only
12 SHEETS £103.80 + £16.00 P/P UK Only
EXTRA POSTAGE MAY BE REQUIRED IF OTHER ITEMS ARE ORDERED WITH **SUNDEALA**

HORNBY OO TRACK SYSTEM
R606	Curve 2nd Radius	£1.75
R607	Double Curve 2nd Radius	£2.20
R608	Curve 3rd Radius	£1.90
R609	Double Curve 3rd Radius	£2.60
R610	Quarter Straight	£1.30
R614	Diamond Crossing L/H	£9.99
R615	Diamond Crossing R/H	£9.99
R618	Double isolating track	£7.45
R620	Railer / Uncoupler	£4.99
R628	1/2 Curve Large Radius (33")	£2.05
R643	1/2 Curve 2nd Radius	£1.60
R645	Single Track Level Crossing	£13.20
R8072	L/H Point	£9.50
R8073	R/H Point	£9.50
R8074	L/H Curved Point	£14.85
R8075	R/H Curved Point	£14.85
R8076	Y Point	£10.50
R8077	L/H Express Point	£14.85
R8078	R/H Express Point	£14.85
R8221	Extension Point A	£13.30
R8222	Extension Point B	£23.99
R8223	Extension Point C	£22.99
R8224	Extension Point D	£32.00
R8225	Extension Point E	£17.95
R8226	Extension Point F	£21.00
R8244	Uncoupler Unit	£1.90
R8261	4th Radius Curve Small	£1.90
R8262	Double 4th Radius Curve Large	£2.85
R8909	Track Supports	£10.20
R910	Fishplates (Pack 12)	£2.60

STOCK BOXES FOR 'OP' SIZE LOCOS/CARRIAGES
to store your spare locomotives/coaches etc
LARGE SIZE Tender Loco size boxes 330mm L x 48mm D x 62mm W BLUE / RED / GREEN / BROWN / BLACK £3.50 each
ANY 4 LARGE BOXES FOR £12.00
MEDIUM SIZE 2-6-4 Tank size boxes 220mm L x 48mm D x 62mm W BLUE / RED / GREEN / BROWN / BLACK £3.00 each
SMALL SIZE 08 or Saddle Tank size boxes 157mm L x 48mm D x 62mm W BLUE / RED / GREEN / BROWN / BLACK £3.00 each
ANY 4 SMALL OR MEDIUM BOXES FOR £10.00
LOCO DISPLAY BOXES
Will take tender locomotives.
Internal Dimensions: 340mm L x 92mm D x 75mm W.
Mounted on a MDF base virtually dust free
£12.00 each - 2 for £22.00 - 3 for £30.00
All sizes are approximate

BUILD YOUR FIRST MODEL RAILWAY

THE BRM GUIDE TO BUILDING YOUR FIRST MODEL RAILWAY

HOW TO MODEL...
HEDGES AND FENCES

USEFUL TOOL

Although you can cut wood with a sharp knife, if a large number of identical lengths are required, a small guillotine is a useful addition to the workshop. The NWSL Chopper II available from EDM Models isn't cheap at £48.00 but with a cast metal base and arm it feels like it should give many years service.

British law states that railway lines have to be fenced, so we'd better build some fences and hedging. Here's our simple, step-by-step guide.

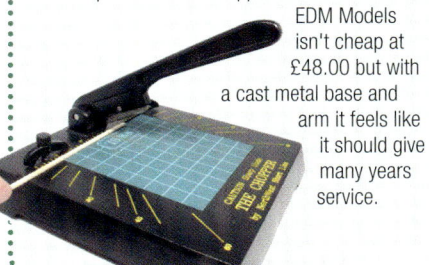

British law requires railway lines to be fenced off to stop people and livestock finding their way onto the track. Because of this, our locomotives weren't normally fitted with cowcatchers, unlike American locomotives where the huge distances prevent fencing off the entire railway.

There were exceptions though. A few minor lines built under light railway regulations had some leeway in this respect, but generally, alongside any railway line you'll find some sort of fencing.

Within station areas, railway companies used distinctive and decorative fencing, but out in the countryside, wooden five-bar or wire and post fencing was more common. The latter is available in model form, but threading the wires through posts is fiddly, so we've tried to keep things as simple as possible.

For variety, I've modelled some hedges as well. These are a lot easier in miniature than wooden fences as some rubberised horsehair covered in flock powder will produce a good looking model and they can follow the ground contours.

At the back of the layout, I like to use fences to hide the join between 3-D groundwork and the flat backscene. This is fine in the countryside, but around the locomotive shed area there isn't enough space. Here, we've built a wooden panel fence that would both frustrate train spotters and make the transition from model to painting easier on the eye. **BRM**

HEDGES

1 Cut a strip of rubberised horsehair about 20mm tall and 12mm wide. Liberally coat the sides and top with PVA, then sprinkle scatter material over the glue.

2 Glue in place with PVA. You might need to place a little weight on top of the hedge to hold it down as the horsehair is pretty springy. It's very flexible, so will follow ground contours well.

3 One hedge complete.

WHAT WE USED
Rubberised horsehair
4D Models 100 X 150 X 25mm - **£2.40**
W www.modelshop.co.uk
You can also buy horsehair from upholstery suppliers in large sheets.

5-BAR WOODEN FENCE

1 Ratio Lineside (Ref: 323) fencing is supplied in 216mm lengths moulded in either white or black plastic. Before use, I painted it with Humbrol No. 173, Track colour, to represent creosoted wood.

2 Fence posts should always be vertical, its the rails that follow the ground contours. For small variations, the fence can be gently manipulated with fingers to make the bends. PVA on the bottom of the main posts and on the back of any that touch the backscene hold it in place.

3 Steep contours require more effort. Here the fence was cut into posts and rails then re-assembled with plastic glue to match a cardboard template I'd made to match the ground profile.

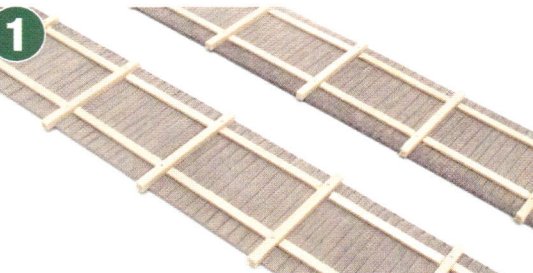

WHAT WE USED
Ratio Lineside Fencing (No.323)
£3.80 for 860mm

PANELLED FENCE

1 Strips 24mm tall of 3mm thick plywood are scribed with a knife to show individual planks. This is given a coat of wood weathering stain before the posts and rails are glued on with PVA. After this, the whole fence received three more coats of stain to finish it off.

2

WHAT WE USED
EILEENS EMPORIUM
Birch Plywood 600mm x 300mm x 1/8" (PLY108M) - **£4.50**
Bass Wood Strip 3/32" x 3/32" x 12" (WS0303G) 3 Pieces - **£1.20**
Bass Wood Strip 1/16" x 1/16" x 12" (WS0202G) 3 Pieces - **£1.00**
W www.eileensemporium.com

NG TRAINS
Weathered Wood Stain - **£7.90**
W www.ngtrains.com

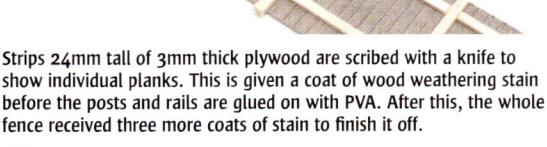

TREES

The simplest way to fill your layout with trees is to use ready-made models. This example comes from Hornby but there are many specialist suppliers who can produce identifiable species.

If you need a forest then Hornby's tree kits are worth a look. They consist of a plastic covered armature which is bent to shape, then covered with a foliage mat teased out to make it see-through.

Whilst not perfect, and probably best not used in the foreground, these look suitable when planted in clumps.

Seafoam is a natural product that looks a lot like miniature real trees. It has to be trimmed to size and large leaves pulled away before spraying with grey or brown paint.

Spray the 'branches' with hair lacquer and then sprinkle with flock powder. Seafoam is too delicate to apply foliage matting but has enough support for flock alone to work.

THE BRM GUIDE TO BUILDING YOUR FIRST MODEL RAILWAY

HOW TO MODEL...
FIELDS & UNDERGROWTH

It's time for 'Edgeworth' to go all green as we set about modelling the surrounding fields and undergrowth.

If you read most model railway magazines, you might gain the impression that electrostatic grass is pretty much the be-all and end-all of model scenery nowadays. Once the hills have been blasted with nylon strands, that's all the work done.

While the fibrous grass is much more realistic than flock powder used on its own, the overall texture can be a bit monotonous. 'Edgeworth's' fields had some texture but they were all the same colour and unlike real life, the undergrowth was all the same length.

Taking scenic effects one stage further isn't difficult and for little effort and with a small selection of materials, you can really bring your hillsides to life. Even if you haven't gone down the static grass route and stuck purely with flock, building up layers of ground cover is worth the effort.

With limited space, I've avoided recreating cornfields or complicated crops. If you want these then a specific book on scenery is going to be your best guide. I'm just going for a variety of textures here.

Apart from flock powder and static grass, the main requirement for all this is a can of cheap hairspray. If, like the **BRM** team, you don't use this day-to-day, then you'll need to buy some specifically for the job. A cheap can will cost

STEP-BY-STEP GUIDE

1 On page 50, if the ground wasn't ballasted, I'd attacked it with the static grass tool. The result has texture and the mix of green and wild honey (beige) isn't a bad colour. It's just a bit uniform.

2 Rather than try to follow every ground contour, I left some of the fencing floating in mid air, so the first job was to hide this gap. A line of PVA glue was run along the top edge of the embankment and around the bottom of the fence posts.

3 Lumps of coarse ground cover were pushed into the PVA. The idea is to apply the flock in clumps. Thicker ones hide the flying fence, smaller bits just add texture.

4 Masking tape covers the track and ballast and a piece of card protects the backscene from copious amounts of extra strong hold hair lacquer applied over the greenery.

5 Fine flock is sprinkled over the hairspray before it dries. I started with a little dark green fine scatter and topped this with some mid-green. There's no clever way to do this, just chuck the stuff around until it looks right. A final spray should stick everything down permanently.

6 One of the front fields receives a good dose of hairspray, it looks a bit like early morning dew in this photograph.

under a couple of quid, so it's probably not with pinching anyone else's either. Your layout is worth it.

Hair lacquer is simply a weak spray glue. Although not intended for our purposes, it works well, especially if you pick something labelled 'Extra hold'. The trees on my layout, 'The Hellingly Hospital Railway' haven't shed their leaves after many years so I'm happy with the results. If the idea of using hair products worries you, matt varnish works just as well but costs more and doesn't smell as nice.

My method is simply to spray the scenery with lacquer then sprinkle flock or static grass. For really deep ground cover, just repeat the steps until you are happy with the result. Be a bit careful with the vacuum cleaner until everything has dried. I built one field up to half a centimetre and then created some interesting effects by vacuuming too closely. Mind you, they did look like convincing areas of flattened crops where vehicles had been driven so perhaps I've discovered another useful trick by accident! **BRM**

DO YOU WANT MORE OF THE SAME?

Then, why not subscribe to the **BRM Digital Edition?** Subscribe for a year for just £32.99, that's just £2.75 an issue!

www.brmm.ag/BRMdigi

7

WHAT WE USED
- Hornby R8881 - Burnt Grass Coarse scatter
- Hornby R8882 - Moss Green Fine scatter
- Woodland Scenics T49 Green Blend Fine Turf
- Woodland Scenics Medium Green poly fibre
- Woodland Scenics Wild Honey poly fibre
- Greenscene Flower Pastel Pack GS137
- PVA Glue
- Hairspray (the cheaper the better)

Another coat of static grass adds depth to the vegetation. I repeated the spray and grass steps a couple of times to really build depth and then finished with a sprinkle of yellow flock for extra colour.

8

The other field was also sprayed but this time I puffer a pure beige mix of grass over the surface to represent grass turning to hay.

STORING FLOCK POWDER

Flock can be horribly messy if the bag containing it bursts or isn't sealed properly. I found the resealable plastic trays supplied full of rice by my local Chinese restaurant ideal containers for it. As a guide, a large bag of Woodland Scenics flock requires the eating of two portions of rice – but do wash the trays before refilling them!

I've no doubt that a quick search through the kitchen section of your local supermarket will yield something equally suitable.

Label the boxes or cut out the packet headers and put them inside to remind you what is in each tub.

BUY SIX ISSUES OF BRM AND GET SIX FREE!

That's right, you get 12 issues of **BRM** (each with a free DVD!) for just **£25.50***!

SUBSCRIBE TODAY!

2 WAYS TO SUBSCRIBE

Call our hotline
01778 392002
and quote BRM/GUIDE15
(please have your bank details to hand)

Complete the form opposite and send to
FREEPOST WARNERS GROUP (BRM)

*Payment is by Direct Debit only and your first payment will be £25.50. After you have received 12 issues, your direct debit will step up to just £22.50 every six months. You will not receive a renewal reminder and your Direct Debit will continue unless we are told otherwise. Offer closes on 31st August, 2016.

Direct Debit Subscription Order Form

Please complete these instructions to pay by Direct Debit.

☐ **YES!** I would like to subscribe to BRM for just **£25.50** by direct debit. *(BRM/GUIDE15)*

Title _____ Forname _____
Surname _____
Address _____
_____
_____
_____
Postcode _____
Email _____

Name(s) of account holder(s)
_____

Name of Bank or Building Society
_____

Account No. ☐☐☐☐☐☐☐☐ Sort code: ☐☐ ☐☐ ☐☐

Reference No. *(Office use only)*   Identification No. 942240

Banks and Building Societies may not accept Direct Debit Instructions for some types of account

Instruction to your Bank or Building Society
Please pay Warners Group Publications Plc Direct Debits from the account detailed in this instruction subject to the safeguards assured by the Direct Debit Guarantee. I understand that this instruction may remain with Warners Group Publications Plc and, if so, details will be passed electronically to my Bank/Building Society.

Signature(s): _____   Date: _____

SETTING THE SCENE

THE BRM GUIDE TO BUILDING YOUR FIRST MODEL RAILWAY

The location of many good model railways is obvious before you see any trains. Here's a brief guide to capturing that unique atmosphere.

It's said that you should be able to guess the location where any model railway is set without looking at any of the trains. How do we achieve this?

To be honest, I had no idea when I started out. Over the years though, I think I've picked up a few ideas. The key is to model what you see and not what you think you see. That's easy to say, but much harder to do, especially if you are building a fictitious location but one area that might not occur immediately is what the buildings are made of.

Not whether they are made from brick or stone, but what type or brick or stone? This varies by location and getting it right can make a big difference to your model. After all, just because the instructions say you should use particular paints on the model doesn't mean you have to do what you are told. It's your model railway after all.

Here are a few photographs that hopefully explain what I mean. **BRM**

> *One area that might not occur immediately is what the buildings are made of.*

STONE

Stone is grey isn't it? Sadly not. Stone isn't even used in the same way across the country when building. People become very attached to the way their buildings are constructed and a surprisingly large number really can tell the difference between different areas and the materials used.

A quick look at prototype buildings shows the variety of colours and finishes. Beware though, high status buildings can often be built of imported stone. Witness the huge amount the Isle of Portland dug up and shipped around the country (often by train) and then used in preference to the local material.

A better guide to local stone is often older buildings such as castles. Moving great lumps of rock wasn't easy when they were built, they often used what was to hand.

Right Aberdeen, or 'Granite City' as it's nickname implies, has stone that is properly grey, just like most of us imagine stone to be. Whilst this is the Town Hall, and could have used stone imported from a distance, the city fathers were proud of their rock and built this fine structure using it. Try Humbrol 64, dry highlighted with 147, both greys, to represent this.

Left Caernarfon is home to the Welsh Highland Railway and sandstone walls. While a grey base coat would be a good start, you'll need to add pale yellows, browns and ochres to the mix to properly model this. Mind you, with WHR Garratts running past several times a day, some of the stone will pretty quickly gain a coating of soot!

www.model-railways-live.co.uk 93

THE BRM GUIDE TO BUILDING YOUR FIRST MODEL RAILWAY

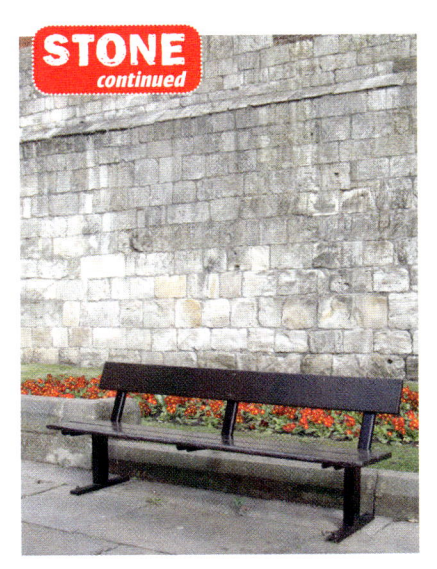

STONE continued

York stone is classic and often exported around the country. The city walls are off-white (Try Humbrol 147 with a touch of cream) with ochre highlights. The faces weather to a greyer colour which has a touch of green in it.

Sheffield's sandstone isn't very different to York but here there's a lot more yellow in the colour. Humbrol's 121, Pale stone, would be a good starting point here with some 72, pale Khaki. Notice also how neat the mortar lines are. Even for a building in a canal basin, the work is very high quality and surface finish almost flush.

Left Welshpool: A much darker stone with greys and rust colours in the rock. It's possible that years of accumulated muck have affected the appearance but that's what we're concerned with then it's what we have to model. Start with Humbrol 121 pale stone and then highlight with 66 and 67. For the rust bit, possibly 25 mat Khaki or 62 matt leather, but you'll need to experiment as it's quite an orange shade which would need to be toned down in miniature.

BRICK

Just like stone isn't always grey, bricks aren't always red. Even when they are, it's rarely the same shade of red. Local bricks are less common than local stone. Most brick buildings you see date from a time when railways had a thriving trade moving building materials around. Despite this, you wouldn't normally ship bricks huge distances, so the colours were often determined by the reasonably local clay supplies available to the brickworks.

In modern times, there is an opportunity for the keen 'brick spotter' to see lots of different varieties. Find a local architectural salvage yard and see what they have in stock. This has often been sourced from a wide area so should present quite a variety.

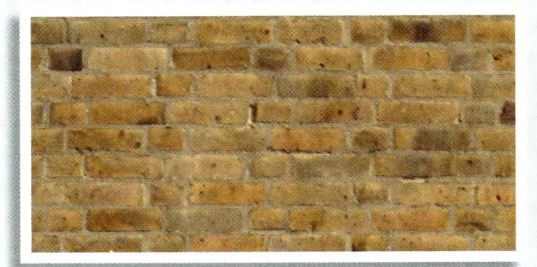

Right In York, Bile Beans might keep you healthy, bright eyed and slim but the bricks are almost white on the surface. Reproducing this in model form would be a real challenge but I'd think that dry-brushing a red brick wall with Humbrol 147 would be a start. On the end wall, mortar has seeped out over the lower portions of the wall.

Below These old stables in Worcester are a pretty standard example of red brick. Even so, if you look closely, there's a huge variety of colours in here and quite a few blackened ones too.

Easily the most yellow bricks I've been able to find, these are from central London. The brickworks of Yiewsley, Starveall in Middlesex and Kent churned out the colours in the early part of the 20th Century. Being a soft clay, the faces discoloured quickly and the vivid colour, almost a Cotswold Stone shade, faded and during the days before the Clean Air Act, turned black with soot.

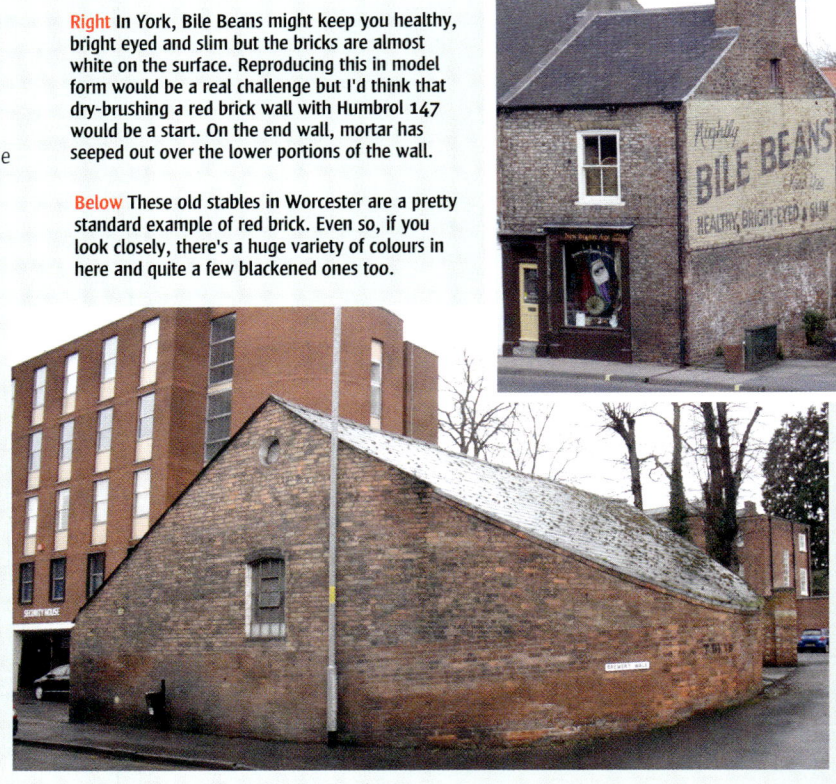

The most northerly model shop on the mainland, Durran's in Thurso. Considering the location, the stone looks the same colours as Cotswold stone but not as yellow. Humbrol 83 ochre is a good starting point with 121 pale stone for the brighter bits around the windows.

You can see the effect of Phoenix Precision paints Cotswold stone colours on this repainted resin building. It's based on a new build, so for an older building you might want to mix in a little cream to tone them down a bit or wash over the model with a weak dark brown.

TOP TIP

When painting stonework, let the paint dry until it's tacky and then sprinkle talcum powder onto the surface. As well as adding texture, it unifies the colours and tones them down a little. Work the powder in with a soft brush. Finally, dust the excess off with a larger brush. Any talcum powder will do, that stuff lurking at the back of the bathroom cupboard you received as a present from your Granny will be fine. The smell will die down reasonably quickly!

TOP TIP

The easiest way to colour brick faces in my experience is to paint the entire wall a mortar colour such as Humbrol 121, let it dry and then use a selection of pencil crayons rubbed on the surface for the final colours. In my pencil case are a huge number of browns and I'll usually colour each wall in three different ones to provide a variety of colours.

Dark brown or purple Staffordshire 'blue' engineering bricks were popular with the railways because of their high strength and resistance to moisture. Many of the viaducts and bridges like the one shown here in Birmingham, are approaching their 100th birthday but apart from dirt and the occasional plant growing in the mortar, look as good as new.

www.model-railways-live.co.uk 95

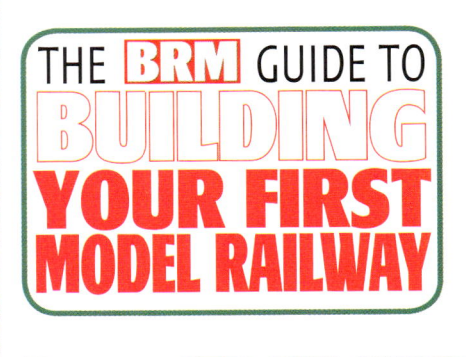

THE BRM GUIDE TO BUILDING YOUR FIRST MODEL RAILWAY

HOW TO... HIDE THE JOIN

With the layout taking shape, it's a shame to leave unsightly gaps around the base of buildings.

The experts at bedding in a building are the people creating the Vale Scene at Pendon Museum. Every building, from the smallest privy to substantial structures such as the Duck's Stores, has foundations just like the real thing. All the walls are carried well below ground level and are then set into holes created in the landscape. While this might be the perfect solution to floating buildings, it isn't practical for most of us, not least because we don't want to make a hole in the baseboard every time we put a building in place.
Andy York

I once found myself exhibiting next to a P4 layout. The builder was justly proud of the finescale trackwork. His locomotives featured beautiful valve gear and operated with silky smoothness.

Sadly, the whole effect was spoilt, for me at least, because several of the buildings were floating in mid-air. Some of the gaps would have allowed a 4mm scale dog to walk under the walls. It was a great shame as all the work on the rolling stock went largely unnoticed because of this *faux pas*.

Put simply, real buildings, at least those made of brick or stone, don't float. Most have substantial foundations below the ground and in paved areas you can see a clean line between the tarmac or paving and the base of the wall.

Avoiding a gap around the bottom of the walls isn't always easy. Preparation is the key – your building will usually have a flat bottom to the wall so the surface it sits on needs to be flat as well. If this is difficult to arrange, such as in rural locations, then it's not a problem, the prototype provides us with a bodge, simply allow some grass or weeds to grow and that will hide the join. **BRM**

Writers in model magazines have been telling readers to avoid gaps under buildings for over 50 years. Don't let your layout down with this simple mistake

STEP-BY-STEP GUIDE

Ballasting in the shed area had deliberately left space for the building to sit in position. Once fixed, the ballast is brushed up to the edge of the walls, trying to keep as thin a layer as possible. The same method works if your building is sat in a field, where flock can be brushed up to the base of the walls.

The first step to avoiding a gap along the base of any wall is to make sure the building is firmly fixed in position. Try to create as level an area for it to sit in as possible and then glue the model down (I use UHU) using a bit of weight to hold it in place. The hammer shown here has been carefully positioned as I wanted to fix the shed, not make a hole in the roof.

If adding a building to a completed area of the layout, scrape away the surface to level it. Ballast fixed with PVA is easy to clear with a screwdriver used as a chisel. If you use a chisel, the granite won't do the cutting edge any favours.

With a bit of work, the undergrowth becomes a feature in its own right. Here we have some waste ground with a build-up of scenic material including bristles dipped in coloured flock to produce foxgloves.

USEFUL PRODUCTS

The ultimate gap cover is either electrostatic grass or coarse flock powder. A puffer bottle is the perfect way to add static grass here as you can really blast it into the corners. Flock takes a little more delicacy. Place clumps with a pair of tweezers as these are easier to get into the nooks and crannies than your fingers.

Any corner will attract rubbish which will gradually disappear into the plant life. An old Coopercraft wheelbarrow with a missing wheel, is buried under static grass.

www.model-railways-live.co.uk 97

THE BRM GUIDE TO BUILDING YOUR FIRST MODEL RAILWAY

HOW TO FIND... THE CORRECT STATION FURNITURE

No steam-era station is complete without the correct furniture, so this is a summary of what should be 'cluttering up' our platforms.

It's tempting to title this section 'Platform Clutter' as it's about all the stuff you find on a steam era station platform. Nowadays, platforms are kept clear to stop us tripping over things but years ago, we were apparently better at looking where we were going so there were a variety of machines along the walls and trolleys of all descriptions.

Rural areas would often see lines of milk churns at the end of the platform to be loaded on to fast services. Newspapers, mailbags and parcels also moved by rail and found themselves stacked up under the canopy. Luggage would also be stored out in the open, often large travelling trunks or piles of suitcases.

If this seems like a different world, it was. But take a look at photographs from the era and you'll soon be piling all sorts of detail up on the platform.
BRM

BENCHES

Classic GWR seats on Leamington Spa station with the 'Shirtbutton' monogram cast in the uprights and picked out in cream, contrasting nicely against the dark brown paintwork. These aren't original benches though, they are replicas cast from originals and available from: www.coxsarchitectural.co.uk

Many railway companies took great pride in their station benches. Cast iron supports included company crests or coats initials. Many of them have survived into the current era either in preservation or occasionally on the real railway.

Right We used a set of etched benches from Dart Castings' Shire Scenes range. Three benches cost £4.50, and can be assembled with solder or superglue.

Make sure you get the back and seat facing the correct way (The seat has two slats the same width) and assembly is easy. Presumably people have become heavier since steam days as you only get two uprights per bench in the kit.

TROLLEYS

Platform trolleys have largely disappeared from the railway today. Large stations might have some metal items for passenger use, but even this is rare. Thirty years ago, even a modest station platform would be home to a couple of large flat trolleys that provided seats for trainspotters or assistance for staff moving newspapers, parcels and mailbags on and off trains.

For £5.00, Wills Platform furniture kit provides benches, noticeboards and four generic trolleys suitable for use both on the platform and in the goods yard.

Wheelbarrow type trolleys were ideal for moving luggage, especially travelling trunks. Most preserved railways have a selection on display or if you really want to do your research, the Warehouse Gallery at the National Railway Museum is full of them.

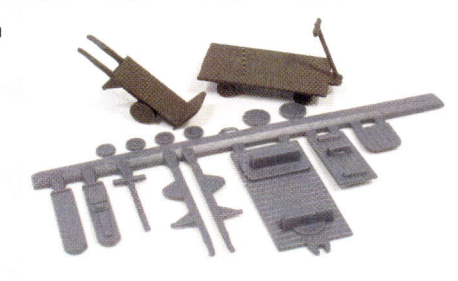

Cooper Craft produces a really accurate plastic kit for a GWR platform trolley for £2.50. Each kit contains three trolleys. They are a little fiddly to put together, and you need to be careful when attaching the handle. It should be upright when stationary as this operates the brakes and ensures they are on and the trolley won't roll off the platform.

POSTERS

Stations are often covered with both advertising posters and the railways' own notices. A little thought is required when choosing them. For a start, make sure you have the correct company, no LMS posters on LNER stations for example. Also, think about the destinations offered. Railways would tend to try to sell trips well out of the local area.

Trackside Signs produces a nice set of station signs for £5.99. Each one is die-cut and printed on self-adhesive paper for ease of use.

I stuck each sign to a noticeboard or piece of 0.5mm thick plastic card and then superglued them to the building. As the signs have a gloss finish, they need a coat of matt varnish to tone them down.

MACHINES

Dart Castings set of whitemetal machines just require a coat of paint before glueing to the platform. Be careful not to bend the scales, although they'll straighten if required with gentle finger pressure.

Today we only see vending machines on platforms, but years ago passengers would be tempted with weighing scales for people or their luggage, devices to stamp metal tags for their bags and of course, chocolate vending machines.

SIGNS

Every station has a sign, often several signs, so passengers know where they are. On a model, this is one of the first things people look at and I'm afraid to say, it's the one that has currently got me beaten. I'm sure there is a supplier of the correct design of signboard out there, so if **BRM** readers know of one, drop us a line and you'll see the platform correctly adorned in a future issue.

Great Western station signs have a standard design, a pair of round pillars with conical caps support a black and white nameboard between them.

For the moment, I've made signs using the Cooper Craft nameboards set. It contains blank boards, surrounds, supports and letters. Paint the board with liquid glue and place each letter on it. Once the name is made up, cut the board to length and then adjust the surround to fit.

Right Painting is fiddly. I find filling the black background in and then scraping or sanding the front produces the neatest results.

Useful Websites
- **Cooper Craft:** www.cooper-craft.co.uk
- **Dart Castings:** www.dartcastings.co.uk
- **Trackside Signs:** www.tracksidesigns.co.uk

THE BRM GUIDE TO BUILDING YOUR FIRST MODEL RAILWAY

HOW TO...
CREATE THE ENGINE SHED AREA

Maybe not the neatest area in a railway environment, but a small servicing shed is vital to 'Edgeworth'. Here's how to make it realistic.

Stations are normally very neat and ordered places. They are after all, a passenger's first contact with the railway and an advert for the company. Look outside the public areas to where locomotives were fed and watered and things change radically - organised chaos was the order of the day with little huts and stores springing up as required with no consideration for aesthetics.

For modellers, this makes for interesting detailing. The space will be dirty and full of life. Just as in real life, the finished model should be allowed to evolve with details being added over a period of time. It's certainly one of those spots on a layout that can never be finished. Having said this, there are certain basic requirements that must be fulfilled. A steam locomotive needs coal and water to operate, so facilities for these must be provided. At the end of the day, vast quantities of ash will be raked out of the locomotive and need to be disposed of.

All this requires tools which will find natural homes where they are easy for the staff to find. The traditional steam railway was much less tidy in this respect than today's heath and safety orientated system. Despite this, a modern depot will provide just as much interest even if it will be a bit cleaner. **BRM**

WHAT WE USED
Wills SS-22 2 x GWR Lamp Huts: **£4.20**
Ratio 511 2 x Wooden Lineside Huts: **£4.85**
Cooper Craft 2005 3 x Workmen's Set of Tools: **£2.50**
Hornby Skaledale GWR Water Column and Crane: **£13.99**

ONE TO AVOID
A set of locomotive driving wheels cluttering up the back of the shed area is a model railway cliché seen on many layouts but almost never in real life. A GWR Pannier Tank weighs almost 50 tons so you don't lift it without substantial equipment.

For this reason, repairs normally took place at major works or in a small number of suitably equipped sheds. Even these didn't have lines of driving wheels stood around, they were far too valuable.

THE SHED

1

You can't really go wrong with a classic GWR corrugated iron lamp hut. The Wills model isn't a typical example thanks to the roof vent and fire bucket rack, but it's a nice, crisp, well-moulded kit that assembles well. A dusting of rust colour weathering powder brings the colours to life and accentuates the corrugations.

3

The basic model needs to be painted to represent creosoted wood. I start this with a thin coat of Humbrol No. 64 pale grey.

5

If there is one thing a steam railway has a lot of, it's ash. The stuff gets everywhere around the area where fires are dropped. Pale grey weathering powder worked into the ballast with a stiff brush simulates this nicely. Watered down PVA will fix the powder permanently.

7

Detailing inside locomotive sheds can be great fun but you need to make sure the visible surface of the walls is correct. Our Ratio kit needs stonework adding as the kit is plain inside, but in this Airfix shed, I've added brick plastic card and then hung some tools from the Cooper Craft range.

2

Our crew need a bothy in which to relax between shifts. Although a stone lean-to is included with the locomotive shed kit, I didn't have space to attach it to the main building. Instead, the Ratio wooden hut will provide a suitably ramshackle accommodation.

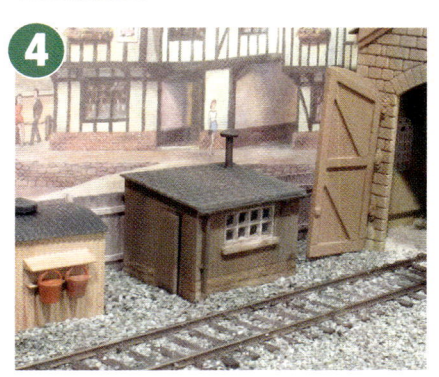

4

Once fully dry, dark earth weathering powder is working into the surface to give the appearance of wood that has been treated, but not for a long time.

6

Inside the shed, track is normally set into concrete or brick. Replicating this in model form is fiddly and since the view into the shed is limited on 'Edgeworth', I cheated and used some Hornby fine ballast instead. The colour contrast with the normal ballast helps to fool the eye.

8

Cooper Craft produces some nice workman's tools moulded in plastic. With a little painting they are a quick way to add a bit of detail.

WATER TOWER

While not actually in the shed area, water supply is crucial to operate steam locomotives and facilities would be provided at the end of a branch and at some stations along the line.

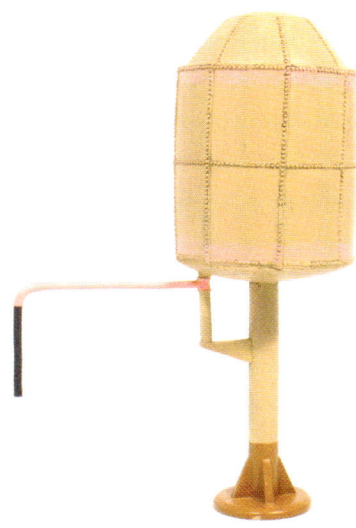

Hornby's Skaledale GWR water column is a nice model and the only ready-to-plant building we've used on 'Edgeworth'. I'm not convinced about some of the colours the model is painted in though. The pink parts seem far too pink.

One thing I am certain of is that a top-heavy structure needs to be firmly fixed to the baseboard to survive transport, so a hole was drilled in the base to take a short length of plastic tube. This was glued into a matching hole in the baseboard. Make sure the arm will reach to the middle of the track, about 45mm away, when you fix the column.

Fixed in position, repainted and dusted with weathering powders, the model looks the part. I'll need to add some drainage under the outlet pipe in the future - a simple grating would suffice but I'll need to find a suitable etched part for this.

THE BRM GUIDE TO BUILDING YOUR FIRST MODEL RAILWAY

HOW TO MODEL...
PEOPLE AND ANIMALS

A layout needs people and animals, but they need to look realistic. Here we offer some top tips to ensure results with a large degree of realism.

TOOLS AND MATERIALS

- You'll need small brushes with a decent point on them. Humbrol's Detail Brush fits the bill with the added benefit of an ergonomic triangular handle. At £12.99 a pack, you'll want to look after them carefully, but good brushes make a difference when painting small objects.

- As far as the main enamel paint ranges go, currently only Caucasian flesh colours are available. Humbrol's version is darker and more suited to the ruddy-faced outdoor worker than Revell's paler equivalent.

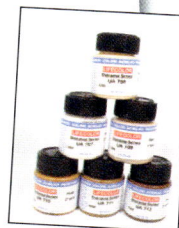

- Lifecolors Flesh paint set contains six acrylic paints aimed at military modellers and specialist figure painters. As well as the basic colours, you get some darker tones to create shadows in the skin. This is probably a bit too much for 4mm scale work but if you start to enjoy figure painting, you might want to take your efforts further.

There's not much point in a railway if there aren't many people around. On our stations we'll see staff and hopefully plenty of passengers. In the cabs of locomotives there will be drivers and firemen. Around the yard, shunters and signalmen.

You can buy some of these ready-painted but that's quite expensive and can limit the selection available to you. At some point, most modellers decide to buy little people in bulk and paint them themselves.

Painting figures isn't difficult. You need some reasonable quality brushes and plenty of different colours. It's a job that is best carried out as an occasional break from other jobs - stick some figures to a bit of wood and have them handy around the workbench. Then while you're waiting for some paint or glue to dry or just fancy a quick job, you can paint a few more bits of clothing. Just blackening all the boots, the work of a few minutes, can seem like satisfying progress sometimes.

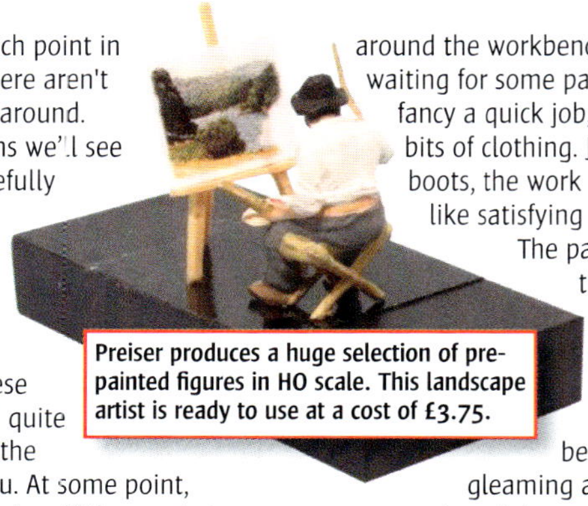

The palette of colours suitable for the era in which 'Edgeworth' is set is pretty limited. Most people wore a selection of browns, greys and beige. Shirts would be white, but probably not as gleaming as anything washed with modern detergents. Humbrol 147 (Pale grey) looks better than pure white in the same way that Railmatch 'Weathered Black' looks more natural than a pure black. If you're modelling the modern era then of course anything goes so you can indulge your love of neon pink if you really must! **BRM**

Preiser produces a huge selection of pre-painted figures in HO scale. This landscape artist is ready to use at a cost of £3.75.

A selection of 4mm scale people. From left to right: Two Merit ready-painted figures (plastic), a pair of Slater's Huminiatures, one ready-painted, the other plain (plastic), Linka sandwich board man (whitemetal), Monty's Models Gentleman (whitemetal), Dapol track worker (plastic)

PAINTING FIGURES

1 Remove all mould lines and flash with a sharp knife. Scraping along the lines with the blade is particularly effective and easier than using a file or abrasive.

2 If the figure isn't attached to a sprue, fix it to a piece of wood. Hopefully there is a spigot on one leg that can be push in to a hole. If not, use a drop of superglue, the joint will be easy to break when you are ready to remove it.

3 Start with your flesh colour paint. Be generous with this as a coat of paint makes seeing the detail a lot easier. If you have a lot of figures to paint and an airbrush, it's probably worth spraying the whole lot in one go.

4 Work from the centre outwards with the detailed parts, painting until complete. I usually start with shirts and anything inside the coat or jacket. This way you can avoid over-painting parts by error. If you make a mistake, a brush dipped in thinners and worked around the area should work a treat.

5 Remove the paving slab attached to the figures' feet with a sharp knife. Only Mafia victims wear concrete shoes, not people on model railways layouts!

6 Rub the feet on fine sandpaper or a file so the bottoms are level. Ideally the figure should stand up on its own. This makes glueing it to the layout easier and should stop it leaning over. If you are really worried about it standing up, drill a hole in the bottom of the leg and put a bit of wire in there that can then stick into the layout surface.

TOP TIPS

1. Use figures in static poses - avoid running men frozen in action
2. Look at how real people stand and try to copy those sort of groups
3. Remember the weather. If it's summer try to avoid figures wearing thick coats.

PAINTING ANIMALS

Painting animals isn't very different from people except that there's not as much detail to deal with. The biggest problem is working out exactly which colours your animals should be. We tend to think of cows being black and white but before the Second World War, there were far more local breeds to be seen such as a the Lincoln Red or Welsh Black. Even today, if you are modelling a Scottish layout, can you be without a few Highland Longhorn cattle? For more information on traditional animal breeds, take a look at the Rare Breeds Survival Trust Website - *www.rbst.org.uk*

SHINE A LIGHT

As we get older, our eyes don't work as well. For some tasks, the average 60-year-old person needs at least three times the amount of light compared with the average 20-year-old.

The solution is simple, stop relying on the bulb in the middle of your ceiling to light your work and buy a proper desk lamp and shine the light straight on to whatever you're working on. Better still, a lamp with a built in magnifying lens will really make life easier.

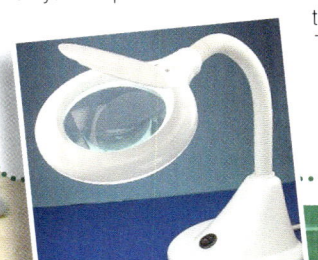

I can't see to paint things that small

www.model-railways-live.co.uk

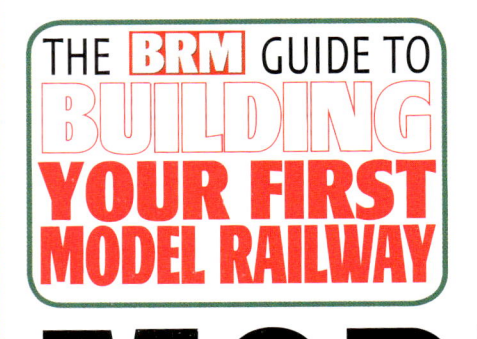

THE BRM GUIDE TO BUILDING YOUR FIRST MODEL RAILWAY

BUYING MODEL TRAINS

If you're new to the hobby and spoilt for choice, here are a few tips for smart model buying and the best places to get what you need.

YOUR LOCAL SHOP

Most towns and cities of any size have a model railway and/or hobby shop that will stock many of the staple items required to build a model railway. The chances are, it will also have a selection of new and secondhand models for you to peruse (such as Classic Train & Motor Bus in Leamington Spa, pictured left). They provide a good opportunity to take a look at any models you want before making the purchase. The quality and quantity of the selection varies wildly between shops, as does the customer service experience. However, traditional model shops are a vital resource for the new modeller and a good way to meet like-minded folk who can answer your questions and provide solutions to problems you might encounter. Some shops also undertake repairs, DCC decoder fitting and other useful services to help the novice modeller. Once you get to know them well, you might be able to get a good deal or two, especially if you're paying cash (smaller retailers often have to pay high credit card charges), but remember that they've got to make a living and pay the bills too!

A quick look in the Yellow Pages or online will reveal where your local model shop is, but if you don't have anything within easy reach, there are plenty of other options...

FOR: Convenience, try before you buy, extra services, local

AGAINST: Quality and product range varies considerably, prices can be higher (although there's no P&P cost), not every town/city has a model shop

ONLINE SHOPPING

The majority of locomotive and rolling stock purchases are made by mail order. These used to be done by telephone but most are now made through retailer websites, which offer a much wider range of products (both new and secondhand) than is usually available in 'brick and mortar' shops. Shop around for the best prices (but remember that, in most cases, postage and packing costs extra). Study the advertisements in magazines such as **BRM** for special offers and those hard-to-get items. The big mail order houses usually take pages and pages of adverts in magazines, making it easy to find what you want. However, if you can't find a particular product, there are alternate sources...

FOR: Convenience of online shopping, extensive range, special offers, lower prices, secure payment, exclusive products from certain suppliers

AGAINST: P&P costs, not possible to check model before it's posted, parcels can be damaged in post

AUCTION SITES

Internet auction sites such as eBay and www.rmweb-buyandsell.co.uk are used by private individuals, retailers and secondhand specialists to sell a huge quantity and variety of model railway items. Type in the name of the product you want and, in many cases, a huge number of options will be revealed, ranging from unboxed damaged models for spares to brand-new pristine items fresh from the factory. Prices can vary widely and highly sought-after or collectable items can sell for greatly inflated prices. Set yourself a realistic limit and don't be tempted to keep chasing it. Another good tip is to wait until the last few minutes of an auction before placing your bid; this will avoid bumping up the price too early. Check the rating of the vendor and the postage costs as they too vary considerably. As it's an auction, you might lose out on popular items, but there will usually be another one along soon after!

FOR: Convenience of online shopping, endless range, worldwide, secure payment, some real bargains to be had.

AGAINST: P&P costs, not possible to check model before it's posted, parcels can be damaged in post, some vendors will not take returns, too easy to pay 'over the odds' for sought-after items.

PAUL BIGLAND

EXHIBITIONS

If you want to see, handle and maybe even run a model before you buy, exhibitions are the next best thing to a local model shop. In fact, with traders often attending from all over the country, the range of items for sale will usually be much greater than any single shop could manage. There's also a mix of traders, from those dedicated to RTR models to secondhand dealers and specialists in scenery, tools, accessories, books and much more. It's easy to go to a show with money burning a hole in your pocket, spend too much and buy the wrong things, so do your research first, compile a shopping list and try to stick to it. That's easier said than done though and you'll always find something you weren't planning for. If the trader is unable to test your purchase, it's worth asking a nearby layout, politely, if they can give it a run before you leave. If there's a problem, you can return it for exchange without the bother of having to post it.

You might be able to get a good deal or two, especially if you're paying cash (not everyone takes cards and mobile card machines are not always working at some venues), but remember that they've got to make a living too! Look out for local and major regional/national exhibitions in the diary section in model railway magazines such as **BRM**.

FOR: Convenience, if it's local, supports clubs, huge range at bigger shows, hunting bargains is part of the fun, no P&P costs.

AGAINST: Not always possible to try before you buy, easy to spend too much!

4 GOOD QUESTIONS TO ASK BEFORE YOU BUY
1 Has it been test run?
2 How old is it?
3 Is it DCC Ready?
4 Can I return it if it doesn't work?

TOYFAIRS/SWAPMEETS

Like exhibitions, toyfairs and swapmeets bring together an eclectic mix of traders from all over your region and further afield. Aimed more at collectors than layout builders, they can nevertheless be a good source of secondhand and new models, die-cast road vehicles and accessories. Held on weekends or weekday evenings in leisure centres and event venues such as racecourses, details of your local and major regional/national exhibitions can be found in the diary section in model railway magazines such as **BRM**.

FOR: Convenience if local, huge range at bigger events, looking for bargains is part of the fun, no P&P costs.

AGAINST: Not always possible to try before you buy, easy to spend too much!

THE BRM GUIDE TO BUILDING YOUR FIRST MODEL RAILWAY

HOW TO... CHOOSE A LOCOMOTIVE

They're the stars of our show, so picking the right machines is vital!

'Railway modelling is such an expensive hobby."

It's true. Spending a fortune buying models is easy. Just get in touch with any of the advertisers in **BRM** and they will happily lighten your wallet if you ask nicely. As most modellers will tell you though, it doesn't have to be that way.

The single most expensive item you will buy is probably a locomotive. Shopping around can help a little but the best way to save money is to be realistic with your purchase. For our branch line we don't need a big express locomotive. It would look ridiculous and be unprototypical for day-to-day operation. Far better to take the same money and buy a couple of modest locomotives that while less glamorous, can perform all the duties we need.

To keep the costs down further, your models could come from the secondhand market.

There are lots to chose from and if you fancy trying to personalise your model with some weathering, real coal in the bunker and a crew, as long as the model runs well it doesn't need to be new.

With this in mind, we've picked a couple of locomotives that will be suitable for both passenger and goods work. Obviously you'll gradually want to add to your roster with other models, we all do, but it's a start. **BRM**

57XX PANNIER TANK

Pannier Tank: Ex-works No. 8791 at Swindon in 1935. COLLING TURNER/RAIL ARCHIVE STEPHENSON

One of the most numerous types of locomotive in Britain, the 0-6-0 pannier tank is synonymous with the Great Western Railway. Used for passenger, goods and shunting duties, unless you are modelling a very strange location on the Great Western system, you will need at least one example in your fleet.

The first '57XX' locomotive appeared in 1929 as a development of an earlier class. Subsequent batches were built by the GWR and outside contractors for the railway. In total, 863 engines had been produced by the time the last emerged in 1949.

Examples lasted through the BR period becoming some of the last steam locomotives operating in the UK on the London Underground system.

With such a large class, there were variations between individual locomotives. A small group was fitted with the equipment required to work with autotrailers.

When I started looking for a typical GWR 0-6-0PT, I was shocked to discover that at the time, there were no models listed as current in the OO gauge ranges. As a result I headed to the secondhand market and picked up a Bachmann 'Blue Riband' model for £60. When it arrived, the locomotive was new in its box albeit a bit dusty.

Bachmann introduced this model in 2005, replacing a version originally manufactured by Mainline. Buyers should be wary of this older model if they are planning to fit DCC though, as its split chassis design makes installation more difficult. If this doesn't worry you, check the running (some examples were better than others) and it's possible to pick up a bargain.

Hornby has included an older half-cab Pannier Tank in its range for many years, but it was based on an incorrect chassis and is very basic compared to modern models.

14XX TANK LOCOMOTIVE

Designed by Charles Collett, the first 14XX class was introduced in 1932 for light branch line work. The first 75 locomotives were fitted with push-pull equipment for working auto-trains. Twenty further locomotives followed without these fittings. The class survived into British Railways days with the last being withdrawn in 1965. Four are preserved.

Introduced by Airfix in 1978, the model found its way to Dapol before joining the Hornby range. It eventually updated the chassis under the model to improve running. Earlier examples could be poor runners due to the inherent limitations of the 0-4-2 wheel arrangement and difficulties in trying to get the weight distribution right.

In the 1980s, many modellers found themselves cutting their teeth on brass chassis kits to try and make their 14XX run smoothly without sitting down at the back when the power was turned on. An all-new 14XX has been announced by Hatton's/DJModels for release in 2016. This should finally give GWR modellers a decent representation of this key class.

The prototype gained a degree of fame outside the railway enthusiast community with the appearance of two locomotives in the Ealing Comedy *The Titfield Thunderbolt,* although the sharp eyed will notice that one was a fake body fitted on a lorry chassis allowing it to take a trip through the town of Mallingford! Hornby released a train pack to celebrate the film in 2013, complete with a 14XX with the GWR letters painted over.

No. 1451 at Hemyock with the 1.42pm branch train from Tiverton Junction on 8th August 1962. M.J. FOX/RAIL ARCHIVE STEPHENSON

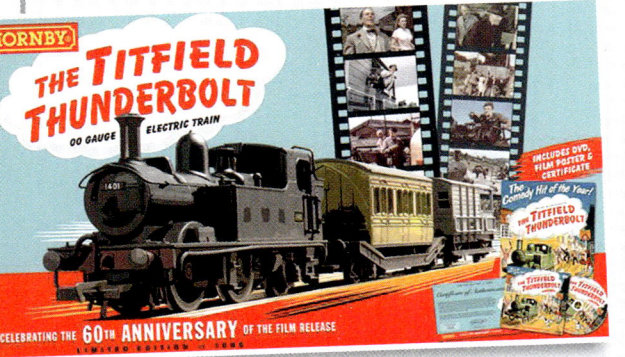

GWR 57xxs appeared with a number of different features throughout their lives - the Bachmann model here has a top feed unlike the prototype on the left.

If you model the Great Western, you must have a Pannier Tank!

www.model-railways-live.co.uk 107

ARMOURFAST™

Extensive range of military 1/72 models including US, British, German and Russian Armour

Great new models now available

SU 100

M18 Hellcat F

Sherman M4A3 76mm

Sherman Firefly

Range now includes Farmhouse and our Stone Walls and Gate

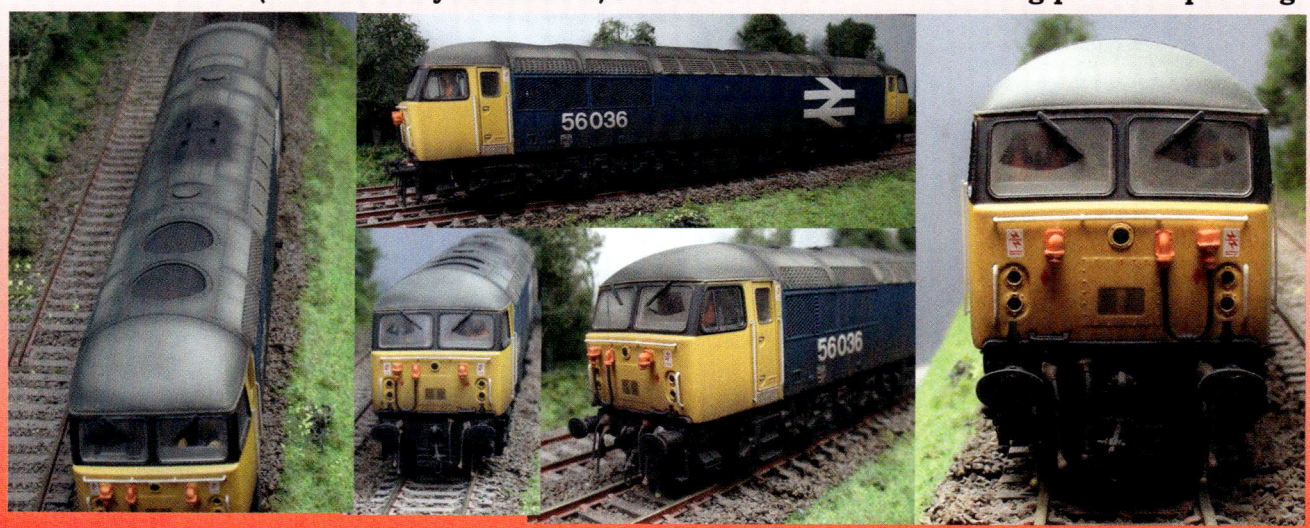

Shop online at:
www.armourfast.com
Join in online at: www.armourfast.com/forum

HORNBY

TELEPHONE: 01244 400930

CHESTER MODEL CENTRE

71 - 73 BRIDGE STREET ROW (East) CH1 1NW

GC WEATHERING "It's the little things we do"

OPEN 7 DAYS A WEEK Mon - Saturday 10:00am - 17:30pm Sunday 11:00am -17:00pm

From GC Weathering exclusively for Chester Model Centre
Complete respray and custom weathered finish including driver and detailed front end.
Brand new loco (ex R2692 Oystermouth). Order now for £175 including post and packing.

The Model Shop For The North West and North Wales - www.chestermodelcentre.com

PARKSIDE DUNDAS
QUALITY MODEL RAILWAY KITS FOR THE ENTHUSIAST

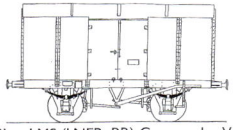

'0' LMS (LNER, BR) Gunpowder Van 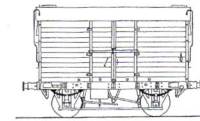   '00' GWR 6 Ton Insulated Van (Diag. X7)

We manufacture and supply a wide range of accurate well designed plastic rolling stock kits in all the main scales.
OUR MAIL ORDER SHOP IS ALWAYS AT YOUR SERVICE
Catalogues for '0', '009' and 'N'. Send £2.00 per catalogue, £1.00 for 'N' catalogue
Mastercard, Visa, Amex and PayPal welcome.

PARKSIDE DUNDAS, MILLIE STREET,
KIRKCALDY FIFE, SCOTLAND KY1 2NL
Tel/Fax: 01592 640896 (24 hour)
sales@parksidedundas.co.uk • www.parksidedundas.co.uk

Visit ➔ Scalescenes.com
Download ➔ Print ➔ Build

The home of quality downloadable card model railway kits since 2005

Arrange structures to suit your layout

NEW Industrial Series
ONLY £2.99 each

Card kits that pass closer inspection

Industrial A - Warehouse
Industrial B - Boilerhouse
Industrial C - Workshop
Industrial D - Water Tower

View our large range of N and 00 kits and texture sheets

Buy once - unlimited prints

scalescenes.com

MARCWAY
51 YEARS

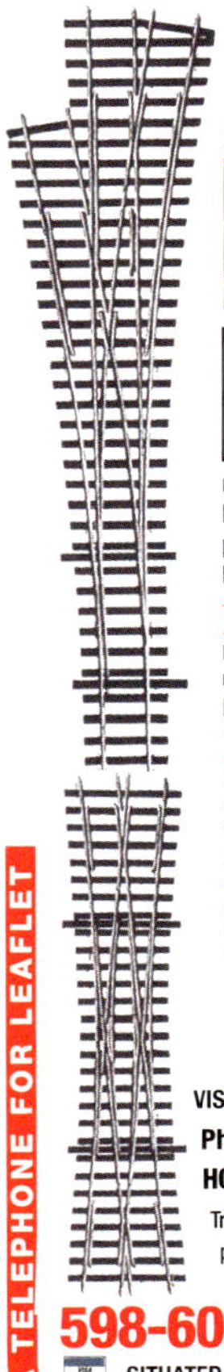

POINTWORK
RENOWN FOR QUALITY

Ranges available in gauges 1, 0, SM32, 00, EM, HO 0-16.5. All are ready to run and spray finished. SAE or phone for leaflet

Custom Pointwork
We construct custom pointwork & junctions in any gauge to your required specifications.
All gauges from G to 009 including Dual Gauge & American O & Narrow Gauges.
PHONE MARC ON 01709 542951 (not always maned)
TECHNICAL & CUSTOM POINTWORK

MARCWAY Flexible Tracks 
Injection moulded plastic based flexible track. Very finely detailed moulding with fine chair detail & bullhead N/S Rail. Available in O, OO, EM & P4. Beautifully proportioned to capture trackwork of the British steam era.

MARCWAY O Gauge Pointwork
Handcrafted with code 125 bullhead nickle silver rail matching Marcway, Peco etc. Extensive standard range including 3 ways, slips, crossings, curve points etc. L & R point start at £43.95.
Introduction offer 4x72" or 48" points £159.00

MARCWAY OO & EM Pointwork
Handcrafted in either OO or EM gauges with code 75 nickle silver Bullhead rail and to match to SMP Scaleway track. Range includes slips, 3 ways, curve points etc. Construction & finish as per O. Prices start at £25.50 for L or R.
Introductory offer 4 x L or R, hand 36" or 48" points for £90.00

MARCWAY TRACK MATERIALS
For all gauges: Rails, sleeper strips, cut sleepers, track gauges, point levers & motors, switches, planners, metal track templates, point kits, frog units etc

POSTAGE EXTRA AT COST

MARCWAY SCALE MODELS   ☎ 0114 2449170

VISIT OUR SPACIOUS SHOP - 1200sq ft Sales Area • SHOP OPEN 10am–5pm 6 days a week
Phone, Fax or Post your order. marcway.net has full Marcway Pointwork list
HORNBY & SCALEXTRIC MAIN AGENTS Peco - Farish - Gaugemaster - Bachmann etc. Sets, Train Packs, Locos & Rolling Stock, Track Controls & Acessories etc. Also modellers tools, airbrushes, paints, plastic, metal and wood section and sheet. *Secondhand equipment bought and sold.* Vast selection combined with helpful & friendly service - Free technical advice by phone or in store

598-600 ATTERCLIFFE RD, SHEFFIELD S9 3QS
SITUATED 2 MILES FROM M1 JUNC 34 (Meadowhall Exit) 200yds from Attercliffe Tram Stop

PROFESSIONAL POINTMAKERS FOR FIFTY ONE YEARS - GAUGES 1, O (Fine & Coarse) Scales SM32, OO, EM, NARROW GAUGES ETC. - SAE OR TELEPHONE FOR LEAFLET

Book Law Publications
Santona / Foxline & Runpast Publishing.
382 Carlton Hill, Nottingham. NG4 1JA.
Tele 0115 961 1066 /Fax 01623 792704
Secure online orders - www.booklaw.co.uk
SHOP OPEN :- Mon-Sat :- 10-30-15-30

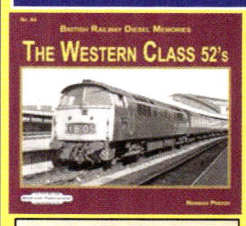

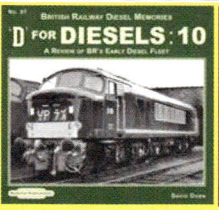

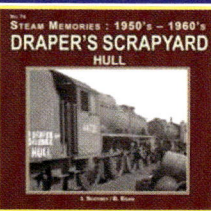

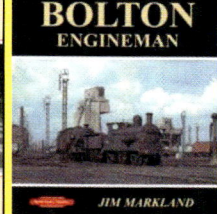

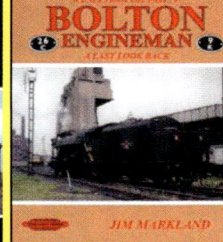

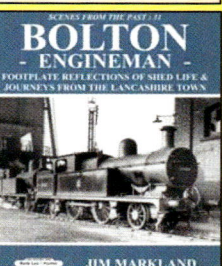

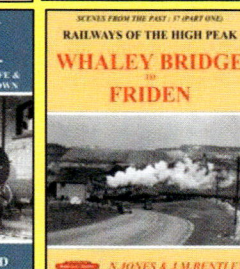

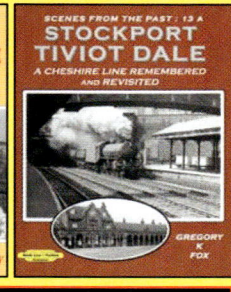

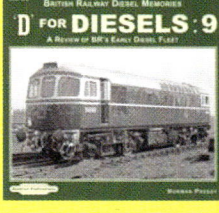

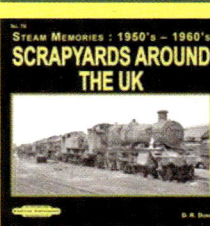

Title	Price
Drapers Scrapyard	£9.99
D For Diesels Part 10	£9.99
The Western Class 52's	£9.99
Scrapyards Around The UK	£9.99
East Coast Main Line Part 7	£9.99
Bolton Engineman Recollections	£19.99
Bolton Engineman A Last Look Back	£17.99
Bolton Engineman ; Reflections	£17.99
Whaley Bridge To Friden	£15.99
Stockport Tiviot Dale	£14.99
Railways In & Around Stafford	£19.99
Royal Scots / LMS Patriots (Each)	£9.99
Class 50's To The Cornish Riviera	£12.50
Manchester – Crewe Part 2	£23.99
Forward To Nottingham Victoria	£19.99
D For Diesels Part 9	£9.99

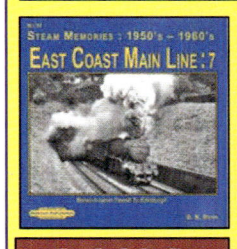

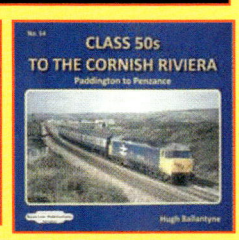

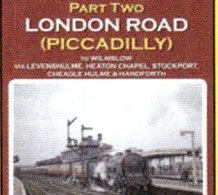

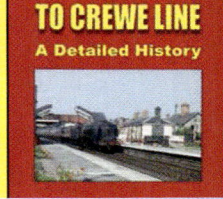

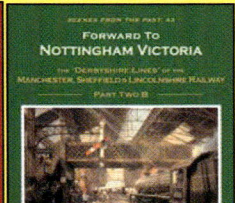

ALL ITEMS SENT POST FREE.   Quote - BRM

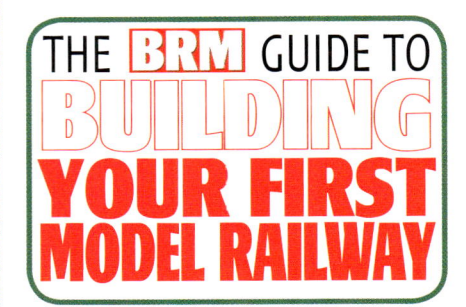

THE BRM GUIDE TO BUILDING YOUR FIRST MODEL RAILWAY

HOW TO... DECIDE ON

Every railway line needs appropriate wagons and coaches, so let's see what is suitable for 'Edgeworth'.

COACHES

If there is an area that I'm afraid to claim any sort of expertise on, it's railway coaching stock. All of my layouts have been goods only, apart from a set of workmen's vehicles and a couple of BR Mk 1s. If the subject interests you, there are many books to read, websites to surf and finally, specialist suppliers who will help you build the models you need for your layout.

Fortunately, for a GWR branch line we can stick to RTR models, at least to start with. There are a couple of iconic designs in the carriage shed, so if we include them in our stock box then we'll be off to a good start.

One of the reasons that the Great Western is so popular with space-starved modellers is that it ran a lot of short trains on country lines and these trick the eye into thinking the model is longer than it really is. Try to squeeze a prototypical six or eight coaches into 'Edgeworth' and as well as running out of platform space you'll find that one end of the train pokes into the fiddleyard. Run a realistic two-coach train or even a single autocoach and the models seem more at home.

As well as coaching stock, the GWR was an early adopter of railcars, powered first by steam and then diesel motors. Both passenger and parcels diesel railcars were produced years ago by Lima and appear intermittently in the Hornby range. Dapol has announced the earlier streamlined version although a date for delivery isn't available yet. All of these would be ideal for 'Edgeworth' if you can track them down.

BR 74XX 0-6-0PT No. 7442 waits to leave Barmouth with a local for Dolgelly in September 1961.
A W Croughton/Rail Archive Stephenson

GWR ESSENTIAL 1: 'B SET' COACHES

Permanently coupled Brake Composite coaches, known as 'B Sets' were two-coach trains mainly used on branch lines. There were several Third Class and one First Class compartment in each coach as well as a guard's compartment and a luggage area, but no corridor or gangways. Built from 1924 until 1936, they survived into BR days as you can see from the photograph. Beware if you decide to renumber your coaches. There were 11 different diagrams with lengths varying from 57' to 61' so make sure you pick the right batch.

Hornby's model began life as part of the Airfix Railways range. This means excellent availability

'TOAD' BRAKE VAN

Goods trains not fitted with either vacuum or air brakes should have a brake van at the end in which the guard rides. They can maintain control of the train using the brakes fitted in his vehicle.

If you model the GWR then you definitely need a classic single-ended, open verandah 'Toad'. The nickname derives from the GWR's telegraphic codes and just means brake van.

The prototype first appeared late in the 19th century and continued to be built after Nationalisation. Not all 'Toads' are the same, those built after the First World War being 4' longer than their predecessors. There were also special versions for specific trains or areas. 'Toads' were often allocated to specific lines, areas or workings and had their home station painted on the van sides.

Both Hornby and Bachmann currently produce 20 Ton 'Toads' or if you fancy building a kit, Ratio can supply a plastic one.

WAGONS

Another area for research is the wagons used for moving goods on your line. The types you own will say a lot about the local area. For example, in rural locations, at certain times of year, vast numbers of vans would be made available to move the harvest from field to market.

If you have included a cattle dock on your model, you'll need suitable rolling stock to move the beasts to market. Don't try and put horses in one though, they had their own rather more salubrious accommodation and if your model is set in the vicinity of a racecourse, you'll need horseboxes too. While there are many books on the subject, this is really an area where careful study of photographs will pay dividends. Try to identify the types of wagons in stations similar to your model, work out what they are loaded with and how this has been loaded.

No. 1450 leaves Tiverton Junction with a brake van for Hemyock on December 21 1963. M J Fox/Rail Archive Stephenson

ROLLING STOCK

the steam locomotive to run around the train at each end of the line. For busier lines, it was possible to run a train with up to three autocoaches and in this instance the locomotive would often be marshalled inbetween.

In normal operation, where the coach is leading, the driver sits in the end fitted with the gong. It must have been an interesting experience for men used to peering along a boiler to have such a clear view of the track ahead.

on the secondhand market as well as the current range. Both GWR and BR colours have been produced over time as well as different running numbers.

GWR ESSENTIAL 2: AUTOCOACH
An autocoach is the passenger accommodation in a push-pull train. Coupled to a suitable locomotive, described as auto-fitted, a set of driving controls was provided at one end removing the need for

Above Our model can trace its ancestry back to 1978 when it was introduced by Palitoy. The moulds passed through Airfix, Mainline, Dapol and currently reside with Hornby. A quick search on eBay allowed us to pick this one up for under £20 in respectable condition. Eventually we'll treat it to some detailing work using Dart Castings parts and perhaps even some new glazing from the Shawplan Laserglaze range.

Ex-GWR 14XX No. 1409 waits to leave Cinderford with a train for Newnham on September 7 1949. *A.W. Croughton/Rail Archive Stephenson*

Left If there is a single type of wagon you will definitely need on a steam era line, it's coal wagons. Coal was the lifeblood of the railways with more of this moved than any other commodity.

COAL WAGONS
'Edgeworth' is set in the 1930s and this gives one pleasant benefit. Unlike BR models, not all of our coal trucks need to be grey or brown. Wagons were owned by many private companies, some of which painted them in brightly coloured and attractive liveries to advertise their wares.

There is a pitfall for the unwary modeller. You shouldn't really choose your stock based on the colours that appeal. PO wagons often had quite small spheres of operation, not venturing far from the home town or colliery painted on the side. This makes it easy to set the location of your line by choosing local traders or firms selling limited edition wagons as they often provide suitable models for specific areas.

Alternatively, you can say, "It's my model, I'll run what I like" and select models that appeal to you. I'll admit that the wagons shown from my modelling of the Hellingly Hospital railway in Sussex, are wildly inappropriate as they appear to originate from my home town or have my surname on the side. I normally have stock liveried with appropriate local coal merchant names, but every so often it's nice to be able to have a change.

www.model-railways-live.co.uk 111

THE BRM GUIDE TO BUILDING YOUR FIRST MODEL RAILWAY

HOW TO GO ABOUT...
BASIC MAINTENANCE

Once a layout is built there are one or two things that you'll still need to do to ensure that your trains keep running smoothly, especially at exhibitions. Here, you'll find the most important of them.

Keeping a model railway working isn't a difficult task, but there are a few simple jobs that can transform operation from a frustrating session of poking errant locomotives into a pleasurable pastime.

The amount of work depends more than anything else on where the layout lives. If it's in a dirty and damp room then keeping things working will be harder than a nice dry and clean location. Those who take a layout out on the road will experience all sorts of atmospheres from air-conditioned perfection to air filled with smoke and steam from a nearby model engineers' layout.

The most important task is to maintain the flow of electricity to motors. Dirt between the wheels and rails is the biggest impediment to this. Happily, simply cleaning both of these makes the biggest improvement to running possible. As a guide, I clean both at the start of every day at an exhibition and if your layout lives at home, a quick clean before each operating session is a good idea. Having built your layout, you'll have a pretty good idea what to do to fix any problems. Again, dirt and dust are your enemies. If the model lives in a dusty environment, consider some plastic covers to protect the scenery. Thin polythene sheets from a DIY store are usually sufficient for this and have the advantage of being light enough not to damage any models they rest on. **BRM**

LOCOMOTIVE MAINTENANCE

The No.1 cause of poor running is dirt on locomotive wheels. Whenever someone mentions they have a problem with a model, the first thing I do is to take a look underneath and see how mucky the treads are. Normally the wheels have thick, black bands of muck around them and the owner is amazed at the improvement when these are removed. Cleaning is best carried out with the model supported in a cradle such as the Peco foam version seen here. Using some fly leads powered from the track, set the wheels spinning and then hold a fibreglass pencil to the treads. Work on one wheel at a time and you'll soon see the dirt disappear and the colour return back to shiny metal.

Don't forget to clean the back of the wheels where the pick-ups are touching

LAYOUT MAINTENANCE

Just as you need to keep the locomotive wheels clean, the track also has to be nice and shiny if electricity is to flow. A bewildering range of options is available to help, but I prefer a simple track rubber on the rail tops to polish them. The one shown is from the Double O Gauge Association, but both Peco and Hornby manufacture examples.

Do not use emery paper or any hard abrasive. These produce microscopic scratches in the metal which attract dirt – exactly the opposite of what you need. If there is a particularly stubborn piece of muck or even paint, rub at it with an old lollipop stick as it'll work without scratching.

Ballast can cause problems if it finds its way into the wrong places. The sides of rails, in between check rails and around point tiebars all seem to be magnets for tiny stones which will then make rolling stock jump as it passes over. A small screwdriver is ideal for removing errant lumps, especially on freshly ballasted track where the effects of glue can stick the stuff to the inside faces of rails.

If your layout lives in a damp room then an occasional spray of WD-40 on any point motors will protect them from corrosion and restore free movement. Just like oiling a locomotive, there's no need to flood the area, just a quick blast from the side. This isn't magic however, so if the point is stick, look closely for dirt or ballast that has worked it's way under the tiebar.

the metal. Any muck here is as bad as that on the treads, although dirt build-up tends to be slower so you don't normally need to do this as often.

While poking around underneath, check there isn't any fluff or hair between pick-ups and wheel backs. Even a tiny amount will stop the electricity flowing. Watch out for stray track pins too as these can short out a model and damage it.

Modern locomotives are normally supplied ready-lubricated and adding more oil can actually cause problems. Dirt and fluff becomes stuck in the liquid, exactly where you don't want it to be. If you really must add oil, use tiny amounts of very thin machine oil applied from a dropper. The instructions supplied with the model will suggest where these should be. If you don't have the instruction sheet, look online as the servicing details can often be found with a quick search.

Normally the axles are worth attending to every year and if the model has been stored, any lubricant is likely to have dried up, so the gears will also benefit from a drop. Valve gear can be oiled too, but unless you can hear it squeaking leave it alone as dirt here can cause parts to wear quickly.

USEFUL TOOLS

Spinning locomotive wheels under power for cleaning can be achieved with a couple of wires but holding them and a fibreglass pencil is a job that seems to need three hands. A piece of copper-clad sheet with a couple of brass strips soldered to it makes the job a lot easier.

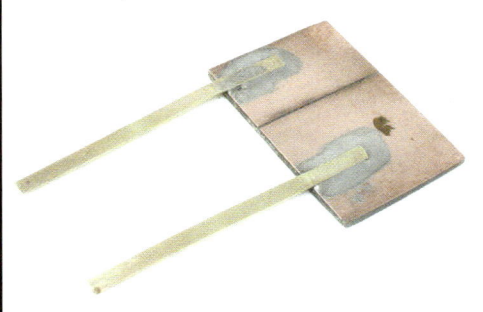

Flyleads are useful for both maintenance and wiring a layout. These are flexible instrument wires with a crocodile clip at each end - simple to make but invaluable, especially as they are two metres long.

www.model-railways-live.co.uk 113

THE BRM GUIDE TO BUILDING YOUR FIRST MODEL RAILWAY

HOW TO... EXHIBIT YOUR LAYOUT

So, you've been to a model railway exhibition, looked at the people behind the barriers and thought, 'I could do that'. You're right, you probably could. Allow me to take you through a typical weekend show and explain how it works.

DAY 1: FRIDAY

Firstly, pack the layout and everything else you need to take into a vehicle, ideally your own car. Exhibition managers prefer this as you'll only need to claim for petrol and not van-hire on expenses.

Don't forget cables, transformers, electrics, curtains and any other accoutrements to make a good looking display. A checklist of essential items is a good idea if you tend to the forgetful. I was with a layout that arrived at a Scottish show only to realise that our 12V transformers were still at home – six hours away! Fortunately the local club members rallied around and we lashed something up, but it made for a fraught setting up.

Having checked the location, collect your other operators and set off. After fighting your way through Friday rush-hour traffic the fun really begins when you find the hall.

On arrival, find someone in charge to show you where you need to go. Unload the contents of the vehicle into your spot. Most shows will provide floor space, a socket and if you've asked for it, a table.

I like to put the layout up as quickly as possible and then test all the trackwork with a short wheelbase locomotive as this shows up problems better than a long wheelbase one. Once you're satisfied it will all work, head off to your accommodation and possibly even a pub.

Make sure the layout fits in the car before you offer to take it to a show, and don't forget all the electrical bits, curtain and other stuff!

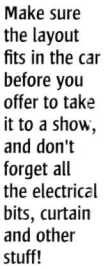

HOW DO I GET INVITED TO SHOW MY LAYOUT?

This is the million dollar question. The simple answer is that someone will see your layout at a show, like what you've done and invite you. Getting that first invitation is the difficult part. Your best bet is to join your local model railway club. Assuming it organises a show then you'll normally be invited to exhibit. This is partly because you are a member, but mostly because you will be cheap. Don't knock it, this works.

The other method is to go out with someone else's layout and talk to other exhibitors. A couple of good photographs showing your model waved under noses can also get you started. The more shows you attend, the better known you'll be on the circuit.

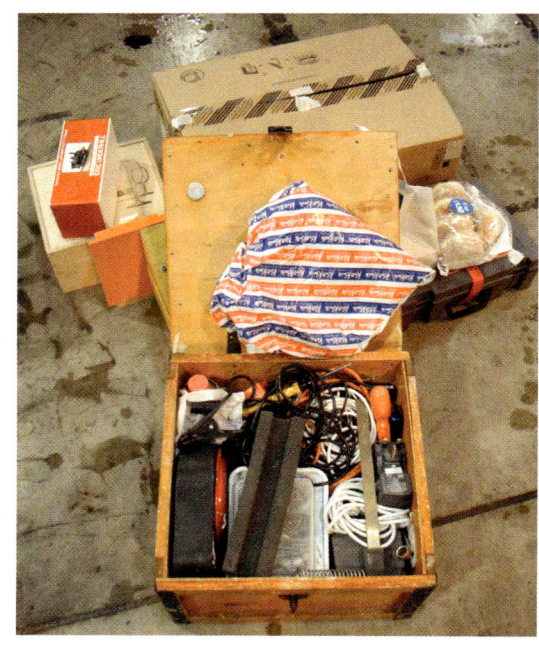

> **THE VOICE OF EXPERIENCE**
> Remember to take plenty of cold drinks. Most shows provide tea and coffee but escaping from the layout to go and get it can be difficult when the show is busy. We always take bottled soft drinks as dehydration can be a real problem when you spend the day chatting in a warm hall.

Exhibition floors can be hard. A small piece of carpet stops your feet and legs getting tired from standing all day.

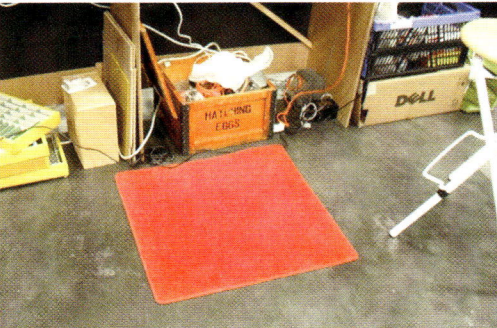

Setting up 'Melbridge Dock'.

DAY 2: SATURDAY

Grab the best breakfast you can this morning. You don't know when you'll find time to eat again.

Back at the layout, clean the track and put the stock out. Assuming everything still works there is normally time for a stroll around the show before the crowds arrive.

The first visitors will head for the trade, but soon there will be a line of faces in front of your layout. The Saturday morning crowd always look very serious and aren't very chatty. Just keep things moving and you might get a grunt of approval.

Things lighten up as the day progresses. Lunch will be provided in some form and at this point you'll be glad you brought spare operators so you can get away from the stand. Don't rely on the organising club lending you someone to help out - they probably don't have the manpower. During the afternoon you'll be asked many questions about the model. This is my favourite part of exhibiting. Some of the questions will seem horribly basic, but remember, we were all beginners once.

Soon enough though, the show will close and everyone will be shepherded out of the building. The evening usually involves a trip to the pub but not always. We've taken trips into London to see the Christmas lights and enjoyed dog racing in Walthamstow in the past.

'Melbridge Dock', operated by Parker Senior, in full exhibition setup. Note the curtain hiding the jumble of wires and boxes underneath.

The view from inside the barrier on a busy Sunday morning.

DAY 3: SUNDAY

Day two of a show is very much like day one. A more relaxed start means that if any running repairs are required, it's an ideal time to do them.

Sunday traditionally sees 40% of the total visitor numbers. It's traditionally the day for families, so fewer grumpy faces and more children. It's a good day for touring the trade stands and the exhibition manager will distribute expenses. Sensible layout owners will tuck this away to cover fuel costs, but many of us spend it on new stuff for the layout. At least it keeps the trade happy!

The end of the day arrives and everything goes into reverse. Layouts are loaded back into cars and vans with the added fun that everyone wants to leave at the same time. Eventually you arrive home, unload the layout and relax. Another show done.

www.rmweb-buyandsell.co.uk

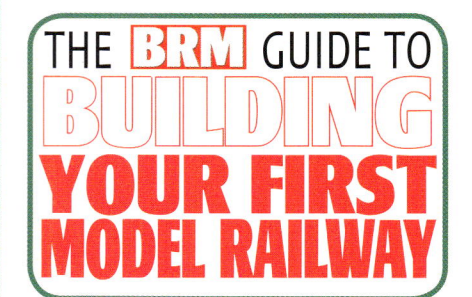

THE BRM GUIDE TO BUILDING YOUR FIRST MODEL RAILWAY

HOW TO...
PREPARE YOUR LAYOUT FOR EXHIBITION

Not everyone wants to take their model railway out to exhibitions but 'Edgeworth' needed to appear in public, so we thought it would be useful to show what's involved in making it presentable.

All together and just needing paint or varnish.

Not everyone wants to take their model railway out to exhibitions. There's nothing wrong with screwing the model firmly to the wall and only showing it to your friends and family. 'Edgeworth' needed to appear in public, so we thought it would be useful to show what's involved beyond simply building the model.

Successful exhibiting involves a bit of planning. The first question to be answered is: "How am I going to move the layout?"

If you have built an enormous model that can justify a lorry to lug it around, then that's great. On the other hand, you probably aren't in need of advice on building your first layout. For most of us, moving the model means packing it in the back of the family car. So, everything, including a spare operator, ought to fit in it.

At an exhibition, you will be allocated space based on the size of your model and left to fill it. You could stick the layout on a table but it's not ideal. For most visitors, it will be too low for comfortable viewing. You're also at the mercy of whatever tables the show can provide. These can be wobbly and of varying heights, so it's far better to bring your own legs.

Most people start by building (or buying) folding trestles. The trouble with these is that they are bulky, not particularly stable and use a lot of wood. For 'Melbridge Dock' we developed a simple leg system that is essentially a pair of goalposts separated by folding sides. These take up next to no space in the car and have proved very stable. Best of all, they don't require much carpentry skill.

One problem with this is that the measurements will vary depending on the size of your model and the car it has to fit in. I've included the dimensions we used in the captions but you'll need to vary them to suit your needs.

As well as supporting the model, you really need to provide illumination. The light available in exhibition halls ranges from a dim orange glow in the NEC to bright sunlight in some schools. Your model will look 100% better if you bring some lights of your own. Simple bulbs will work, there's no need for sophisticated set-ups unless you want to experiment.

You might feel that this is a lot of work, but don't skimp on it. If you plan to show your model, a bit of effort now will be appreciated the moment you come to unpack after a long drive early one morning to a show.

We'd like to thank the Leamington & Warwick Model Railway Society for letting us use their clubrooms for this article. **BRM**

READY TO GO

'Edgeworth' packed up and ready to go to a show.

> Not everyone wants to take their layout on the road, but if you do, here's a 'to-do' list to get mobile.

PACKING THE MODEL FOR STORAGE AND TRANSPORT

Above Mark all the board ends and transport boards so you can locate the right board on the right holes quickly. In fact, mark every bit of wood so you know where each part goes. You might think you'll remember but you won't and neither will anyone helping you set up.

Left To protect the scenery, the baseboards are transported facing each other. To hold them in place, we've used nothing more sophisticated than some rectangles of 9mm thick plywood.

HOW BIG ARE THOSE BOLTS?

M8 bolts might look like they're over-engineered - one could support the model on its own and we need 12 to hold the layout in its carrying boards, but there is a good reason why I didn't chose anything smaller.

At the end of a weekend exhibiting, you're tired and just want to pack up and get on the road. Fiddling with small nuts and bolts isn't going to improve your temper, especially when you drop them and they roll away. These bolts have big, chunky threads that are easier on tired fingers.

We've chosen wing nuts too as it saves finding a spanner - none of the bolts needs to be more than finger tight.

www.model-railways-live.co.uk 117

THE BRM GUIDE TO BUILDING YOUR FIRST MODEL RAILWAY

LEGS

The leg system is simple, a pair of goalposts are joined with hinged ends that concertina flat for transit or can be locked with a connecting block. Dimensions will need to be altered to suit individual models but 'Edgeworth's' are one metre tall, 130cm long and the beams are separated by the baseboard width.

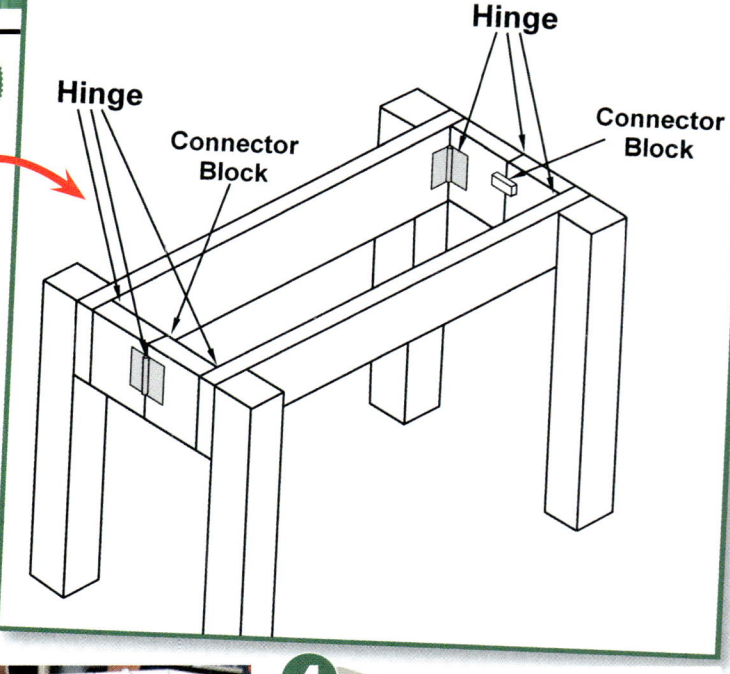

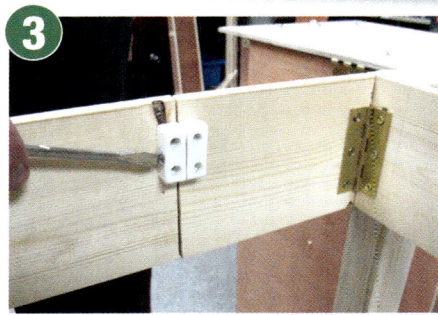

1 The length of the legs is determined by the space available in the vehicle you'll be using to transport them. We designed ours to fit in the back of a Citroen Berlingo. As you can see, most of the floor space is available.

2 The layout fits between the legs when in the back of the car. The lighting rig sits on the side of the legs leaving space for stock boxes, travel bags and any goodies bought from traders over the weekend.

3 Once it's standing up, the first job is to tighten the bolts in the connector blocks. As the legs aren't very wide we'll need to add a short screwdriver to the exhibition tool kit.

4 Along the back of the beams are some wooden blocks to stop the layout being pushed forward. The lighting poles will stop it sliding back so it will be clamped in place.

5 With the legs set up, the layout is placed on the beams and the connecting pins inserted in the hinges.

6 The fiddleyard legs are a simple frame that plugs in to pockets under the baseboard. The weight of the layout holds these in place, no need for bolts or screws.

7 Although the system is pretty stable, I screw the packing boards to the end. This makes everything even more solid and also stops us tripping over the things during the show.

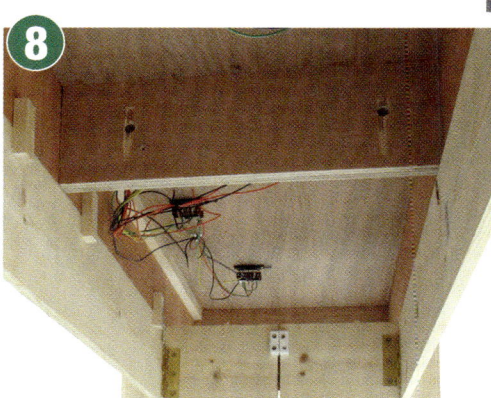

8 Access to the underside of the baseboard is excellent so if anything goes wrong, there's no problem getting to either point motors or wiring.

SAFETY FIRST

If any of the screws stick through the woodwork, file the points off straight away. Don't leave the job until later as you will get a reminder when the setting the layout up. Blood looks terrible on a model; guess how I know...

118 www.RMweb.co.uk

LIGHTING RIG

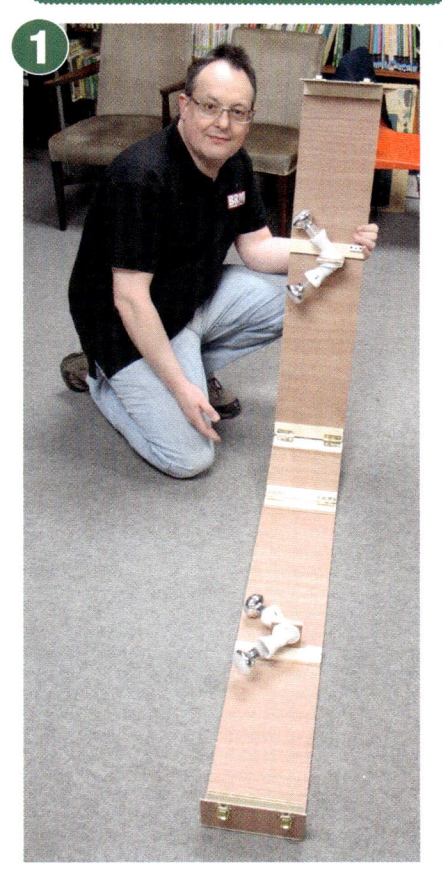

1

To keep the weight down, 'Edgeworth's' fascia is made from 3mm plywood strengthened with some decorative moulding glued to the front. Since we won't get a single 9' length in the car, it is designed to fold up.

2

By folding back on itself, the woodwork protects the light bulbs in transit. Having used this on my layout 'Flockburgh' for a few years, I know the system works well enough that we've never managed to break a bulb in transit.

3

Supporting the fascia are some simple gallows made from 2" x 1" softwood and screwed to the sides of the legs. They fix to the fascia with furniture connecting blocks. Make sure you can get at the screws easily as at over 6' above the ground, most of us are going to be doing them up while stretching.

WHAT SORT OF LIGHTS SHOULD I USE?

On 'Edgeworth' we will use conventional 60W light bulbs.
The illumination might be slightly yellow but having tried daylight balanced bulbs, I feel that although the results look good in a dark room, there is too much light spill in most halls for the effect to work properly.

The worst case scenario is finding yourself in a room with bright sunlight coming in through the window. I've seen layouts where very sophisticated lighting rigs have been defeated by strong backlighting on a sunny day. At least ours is cheap and if the bulbs break, they can be replaced from a local shop!

WHAT ELSE WILL I NEED?

Layout presentation is massively improved by hiding everything below baseboard level behind a curtain.

My preference is for a polyester based material in a dark colour fixed to the baseboard with either drawing pins or Velcro. This seems to resist creases as they tend to drop out once it's hung up and saves me ironing the thing before every exhibition.

If you don't have someone handy with a sewing machine, use some iron-on webbing to hem the edge of the material and stop it fraying.

At a show, you are provided with space and a 13Amp socket. Everything else has to be brought along by the operators. As well as transformers and leads, don't forget all the screws and bolts to hold the model together, tools, and electrical leads. Some gaffer tape is handy too.

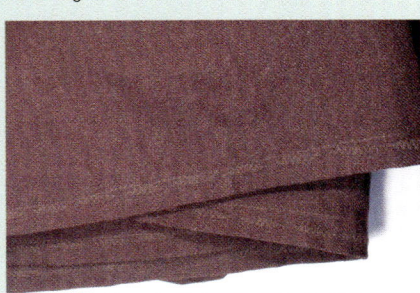

Basically, fill a box with anything you consider useful. I use a wooden crate that I acquired from work many years ago but plastic boxes work just as well. Many of the basics live in here so I can't forget them as it's often a long drive if you need to nip home to retrieve a missing essential.

USEFUL TOOL

Cutting the softwood accurately is a lot easier with a cheap mitre saw from a DIY store. For around £25, you'll find it improves your carpentry no end.

THANKS
We'd like to thank the Leamington & Warwick Model Railway Society for letting us use their clubrooms for this article.

www.model-railways-live.co.uk

THE BRM GUIDE TO BUILDING YOUR FIRST MODEL RAILWAY

HOW TO...
APPLY THE FINISHING TOUCHES

A model railway layout is never complete, but there are some essential finishing touches to make before showing your layout to friends or family.

To be honest, there's a lot of modelling left to do on 'Edgeworth'. They say a model railway is never finished and that's certainly true of this one. I expect to be adding details for some time to come, but then that is one of the great joys of the hobby isn't it? Before we went to press, there were a few tasks completed that didn't fit anywhere else. You can add as many finishing touches as you like, but remember that very often, less is more. **BRM**

IMPROVE THE DISPLAY

If you plan to show your layout to anyone, it needs to look its best. Never mind how perfect your modelling is, if the model is surrounded by tatty bits of woodwork then viewers are going to notice these before they spot you've fitted post-1923 lamp irons to a 1921 locomotive!

I know this stuff isn't glamorous, but even at home it matters. It's a lot easier to persuade your family that railway modelling is a worthwhile hobby if the layout doesn't look like it's been hauled out of a skip!

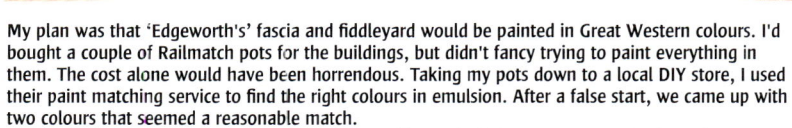

My plan was that 'Edgeworth's' fascia and fiddleyard would be painted in Great Western colours. I'd bought a couple of Railmatch pots for the buildings, but didn't fancy trying to paint everything in them. The cost alone would have been horrendous. Taking my pots down to a local DIY store, I used their paint matching service to find the right colours in emulsion. After a false start, we came up with two colours that seemed a reasonable match.

For the darker areas of stone, I'm using Velvet Truffle 3. The lighter areas use Soft Almond 3. These are from the Dulux range that is mixed in store. A 250ml tester pot of each cost £3.70 and provided more than enough paint for the job, in fact I suspect I'll be bringing the lighting poles into the correct livery at some point. A satin varnish protects the paint a little, as well as brightening it up.

Since I'm no signwriter but wanted the layout name displayed on the fascia, I took a trip to a local company which produces vinyl shop signs. Within ten minutes, they had cut me the word in a white, self-adhesive material. I chose a sans serif font, but there was the sort of selection familiar to anyone with a computer available if I preferred something fancier.

The letters are supplied ready to use on a backing sheet. A semi-transparent front sheet was stuck to the front by the sign shop to aid fixing them in place.

To letter the fascia, the backing sheet is peeled away and the name held roughly in place with masking tape. It's important to position the lettering properly as once it's stuck in place, moving it is practically impossible. I spent quite a bit of time looking along the panel to make sure the bottom of the text was parallel to the edges.

Once I was happy, each letter was firmly rubbed to stick it to the woodwork. Then the front sheet is peeled away leaving the vinyl letters perfectly spaced. The whole job took around 15 minutes and the results look superb.

> **OUR LETTERING CAME FROM**
> SIGNDEPOT
> www.signdepot.co.uk
> 135mm tall vinyl lettering: £18.00 for the word 'Edgeworth'

PROTECT THE FIDDLEYARD

At exhibitions, the fiddleyard needs to be fitted with a front panel to discourage curious onlookers from fiddling with the rolling stock. It's nothing more than a rectangular piece of 9mm thick plywood, but this is enough to keep people out.

At home, when the model is operated from the front, this would get in the way so I've fitted it to the baseboard with furniture connecting blocks. By removing the big bolt from the centre, the panel can be lifted away.

FINISH THE LANDSCAPE

I've smoothed the front edges of the hillsides with household filler and then treated them to a couple of coats of dark grey emulsion paint. This looks far nicer than exposed polystyrene.

WEATHERING TRACK

Steam era trackwork was kept in fine fettle by regular work from the local track gangs. Locomotives of the time didn't make as much mess as diesels do either.

Despite this, the rail sides were never shiny, so I spent some time painting them with Humbrol No.173 Track colour. It's not the most exciting job in the world, but not difficult. A No. 2 size brush seems to be wide enough to cover the rail but not get paint on the ballast. Should you get paint on the stones, a couple of drops of thinners will wash the colour into the ballast so it just looks like dirt.

Of course, it would have been quicker to spray paint the track before ballasting but I like to get something running first. You would also need to mask off the scenery to stop overspray. Finally, the ballast can be very efficient at removing paint from sleepers and rails, so I find I end up repainting most of it anyway.

STATION FORECOURT FENCING

WHAT WE USED
Ratio 422 GWR Station Fencing in black: £3.50 for 4 lengths, 680mm in total

Finally, a little Ratio GWR station fencing will stop people falling into the goods yard. Carefully cutting this from the sprue leaves enough runner attached to the bottom of each post to provide something to push into holes drilled in the raised groundworks. There should be a gate to allow access to the platform for staff but I'm assuming this is on the other end of the building where you can't see it.
I used Ratio 422 GWR Station Fencing, which costs £3.50 for four lengths – 680mm in total.

C&L Finescale Modelling
The Track Specialist
All you need to start you off on the right track

C&L Flexi Track – the place to start
Prototypical **Sleeper spacing & length** for great looking track. **Turnout Kits** include chairs etc.

Carr's modelling products for your Solder and Fluxes, Chemicals, Ballast & Baseboard Fittings

Recent additions to our range
DCC Concepts
- Track & Back to Back Gauges with handles
- Colbalt Motors & Accessories (low prices)
- Colbalt Signal & Point operating levels
- DCC Decoders, Rolling Roads & Wheelsets

Green Scene
- Scenic Scatter (huge range - fine or course)
- 'Ballast Mate' ballast spreader (N, OO, O)

Gaugemaster
- Seep Point Motors, Track Tester & CDUs
- Controllers/Transformers (full range)

Dapol
- Working Signals (N, OO) Ready to use!

PECO Competitive prices
We also stock **Ratio, Metcalfe & Wills** (see website for more)

Sample Prices
'OO' SL100 x 1 (code 100) **£2.95**
SL100 Box (code 100) **£63.95**
SL80 Single slip code 100 **£27.95**
SLE192 Small Radius c.75 **£9.50**
'N' SL300 1 yard (code 80) **£3**
SL300 Box (code 80) **£63.95**
Code 55: SLE380F S/Slip **£33.95**
'O' SL700BH Box (c.124) **£72.95**
SLE791/2 'O' Med t/outs **£38.95**

Build your own plain track?
Use **Exactoscale** 'Fast Track' bases & rail or **C&L** chairs, sleepers & rail.

N Gauge — It's simple to build your own Flexitrack or Turnouts (**Finetrax Range**)
Flexitrack available in metre lengths & Turnout Kits for A5/B6/B8/Diamonds

Visit our **Shop** at:
Aran Lodge, Severn Rd. Hallen, BRISTOL, BS10 7RZ (4 miles M5 Junc 18 Avonmouth)
Mon – Thursday 9am – 4pm

www.finescale.org.uk
Tel: 01179 505 470

---

www.yorkmodelmaking.co.uk
Providers of **architectural detailing** suitable for **scratch builders** and for **upgrading kits**
Precision laser cut plastic components with realistic depth, that won't warp
Affordable and easy to use to create perfect results for all your buildings

Windows, doors, valences, canopy brackets, brick detailing, tiles etc

Alternatively send a large SAE for 0, 00 or N scale price lists to
York Modelmaking, Unit 13, Bull Centre, Stockton-on-Forest, York, YO32 9LE
01904 400358

Trains4U.com
01733 895989 Trains4U@btconnect.com

Peterborough's Model Railway and Slot Car Specialists

HORNBY | HELJAN | GRAHAM FARISH by BACHMANN | DAPOL | PECO | AIRFIX | Revell | TAMIYA | ESU | WILLS KITS | SCALEXTRIC | TCS | RATIO

27 St. David's Square, Fengate,
Peterborough PE1 5QA
Open Tues-Sat 9am-5pm, Sunday-Closed

GraphicAir
Graphic, Design, Art and Modelling Supplies.

NEO for iwata

NEO TRN2 Side-Feed Trigger Airbrush
TRN1 Gravity feed also available

5 YEAR WARRANTY

NEO CN Gravity Feed Airbrush
NEO-BCN Suction Feed also avaialable

Gravity or Suction Feed
Great value airbrushes
Interchangeable colour cups
Small & Large Gravity cups
Trigger action pistol grip
0.35 or 0.5mm set-up

MS 09 SCENIC DETAILS COLOURS
CITY AND SURROUNDINGS
WAR ON THE ROAD

LIFECOLOR ACRYLIC HOBBY COLORS
Great effects from LifeColor Scenic Details Colours. Use straight from the bottle to bring your scenery alive!

GraphicAir online
Unit 1 Levens Hall Park, Lund Lane, Killinghall, Harrogate, HG3 2BG T: + 44 (0)1423 522836 F: + 44 (0)1423 525656 E: info@graphicair.co.uk
W: www.@graphicair.co.uk

HARBURN HAMLET
OO / HO Accessories 'Ready to Place'

Loads & loads for 00 layouts — Just place them in to a place!

TIERED KEGS
FL146 £5.10 | FL147 £5.10 | FL148 £5.95 | FL149 £5.95
FL143 Casks (5) £8.95 | FL141 Ale casks £4.75
FL144 Beer Kegs £5.95
FL140 Barrels £4.75
FL150 Red oil drums £5.95
FL151 Green oil drums £5.95
FL145 Oak casks £9.90
FL154 Rusty drums & cans £5.95
FL160 Brick stacks (3) £5.95
FL168 Coal sacks £5.95
FL126 Coal sack load £5.95
FL131 Scrap load £5.95
FL171 Asstd merchandise £5.95
FL170 Pipes £6.30
FL123 Grey bags £4.75
FL111 Crates £4.75
FL121 Sacks £4.75
FL122 Brown bags £4.75

SLEEPERS
FL102 New wood £4.75
FL104 Concrete £4.75
FL103 Rotten £4.75
FL112 Crates part cov'd £5.95
FL100 Wood beams £4.75
FL120 Covered load £4.75
FL101 Planks £4.75
FL165 Builder's stockpile £6.50
FL161 Tipped bricks £5.95
FL181 Logs £8.35
FL180 OTA timber load £8.95
FL124 Red mailbags £4.75
FL133 Asstd shipment £9.25
FL125 Grey mailbags £4.75
FL132 Crates shipment £9.25
FL117 Coil (2) £6.75
FL115 Steel Plates £5.95
FL116 Coil load £9.50
FL134 Ballast bags £5.95

P&P £3.00 per order

'N' gauge modelling? - See our website for Harburn Hamlet N gauge products
Harburn Hobbies, 67 Elm Row, Edinburgh EH7 4AQ
Order:- by Phone: 0131 556 3233; Online: www.harburns.co.uk; by Post from above address

THE RAILWAY CONDUCTOR

MODEL TRAINS & ACCESSORIES

OO GAUGE • N GAUGE • DIECAST • RADIO CONTROLLED • TOYS ETC

NEW SHOP NOW OPEN

UNIT 2, THE OLD DAIRY FARM, CRAFT CENTRE,
UPPER STOWE, NR. WEEDON, NN7 4SH

OPENING TIMES: MON TO FRI 10AM-5PM, SAT 10AM-5.30PM SUN 11AM-4PM

ebay Visit our ebay shop

- WE DO MAIL ORDER
- WE ACCEPT ALL CARDS AND PAYMENTS

Visit our website: www.therailwayconductor.co.uk
E: jonathan18r@sky.com
T: 01604 830722 M: 07961 757094

Pennine Models at Haworth

HUGE RANGE OF HORNBY - Can't find Hornby? Call us first! Full range of Peco, OO Dapol, Humbrol, Scalextric, Heljan, Oxford Diecast, EFE Buses, Ratio, Wheels & Parkside, Plastic Building Sheets, Javis Scenery Packs, Tillig Track & Busch/Auhagen Building Bits. All at discount prices

SCALEXTRIC • METCALFE • HORNBY • SKALEDALE • AIRFIX

VAST RANGE OF PLASTIC KITS many going back 10 years

33/35 Mill Hey, Haworth, Keighley BD22 8NQ
Tel: 01535 642367
penninemodels@googlemail.com

Wednesday to Sunday 11am-5pm

GRIMY TIMES
WEATHERING SPECIALIST & NOW MUCH MORE

Now known as
Grimy Times Model Railway

Shop now open at 187, Orford Lane, Warrington WA2 7BA
T: 01925 632209   M: 07921 830484   E: grimytimes66@yahoo.co.uk

www.grimytimes.co.uk

We look forward to seeing you!

ALL SCALES CATERED FOR

RE-NUMBERING & RENAMING

EXCEPTIONAL QUALITY & PRICE

TITLED TRAINS

Over 200 different packs of *Quality* signage in a variety of scales covering all periods.
Adding Detail and Realism

MODEL RAILWAY SIGNS

www.sankeyscenics.co.uk
For the Best in Model Railway & Accessories

Sankey Scenics

The ultimate online marketplace

FREE TO REGISTER!

RMweb BUY & SELL

ARE YOU BUYING?
- 1000s of products available to buy
- Search for everything from hard-to-find accessories to brand new locomotives
- Includes major brands like Hornby, Bachmann, Dapol…
- …plus more specialist brands to offer the ultimate one-stop-shop!
- Used by private sellers and reputable retailers

OR, ARE YOU SELLING?
- Sell your unwanted products via 'Buy it Now' or 'Auction'
- Easy to list products with up to six images
- Free to list items worth under £30

PLUS WE DON'T TAKE ANY OF THE FINAL SALE PRICE!

www.rmweb-buyandsell.co.uk

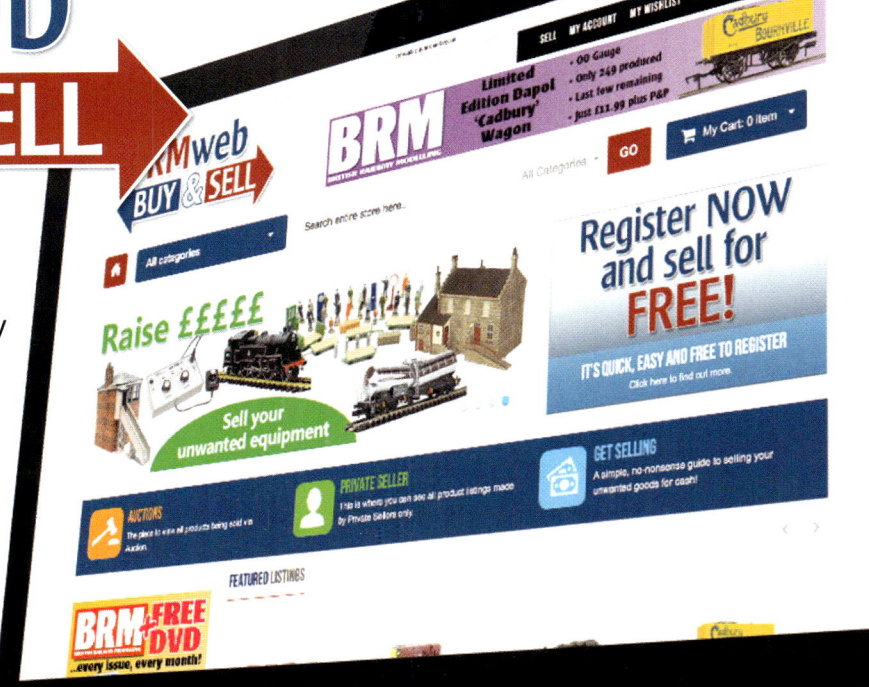

QUALITY BACKSCENES

Fine-art backscenes to add that final professional touch to your layout. Available as standard in a variety of themes and scales plus a bespoke service using your sketches or photographs.

For 'O', 'OO', 'N' and even 'Z' gauge layouts and ...

... for 1:43/50, 1:72/76/87 and 1:144/200/220 scale dioramas and wargaming

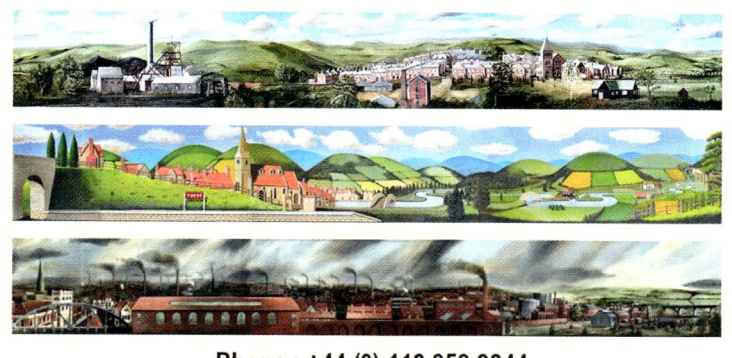

Phone : +44 (0) 118 959 9844
Email : studio@qualitybackscenes.co.uk
Website : www.qualitybackscenes.co.uk

THE HOBBY GOBLIN
STOKE-ON-TRENT
13 Queen Street, Burslem, ST6 3EL

- Hornby • Bachmann • Peco
- Lenz • Dapol • Gaugemaster
- Graham Farish • Metcalfe
- *Plus much more*!

Wide range of scenery

www.thehobbygoblin.co.uk
T: 01782 823818 E: info@thehobbygoblin.co.uk

We support www.iworry.org

THE HOBBY SHOP Est.1988
Tel. 01795 531666
www.hobb-e-mail.com

N° 122 WEST S¹ Faversham, Kent, ME13 7JB
SMS Text no. 07889 818727

120 x 60cm Hobbyboards
Available from stock
£10 per sheet
£55 for 6 sheets
add £8 for Next Day delivery*

sundeala.co.uk

* for UK Mainland deliveries. For deliveries to Highlands & Islands of Scotland, Isle of Man, Channel Islands and Northern Ireland please add £20 for delivery.

see our website or visit us to view current stocks

Peter's Railway
The Great Train Robbery

ISBN 978-1-9088970-53

The Latest Book - The Latest Adventure !

Peter, Harry and Kitty foil a terrible crime and catch the villains. Their methods are brave and unconventional, causing much damage and enjoyable mayhem...   just £4.99

This is the 16th book in the Peter's Railway series, following Peter and Grandpa's adventures building a railway across the farm.

Books for children who love trains and engineering

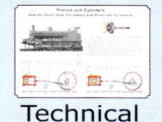

Story   Technical   History   Adventure

For more info & personally signed/dedicated copies see
www.PetersRailway.com
or buy from bookshops, steam railway giftshops or amazon.co.uk

---

Colour-Rail

Visit our redesigned website at www.colour-rail.com to view 60,000 images – steam, modern traction, stations, buses and much more. Nearly every named BR engine featured.

Looking for a good home for your treasured negatives and slides?

Then e-mail colourrail@aol.com or write to 558 Birmingham Road Bromsgrove B61 0HT

Train Times Model Shop
37 Seaside, Eastbourne, BN22 7NB

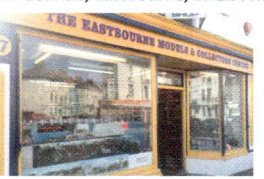

Stocking everything you need to start or improve your model railway from

Airfix, Bachmann, Dapol, Gaugemaster, Hornby, Metcalfe, Peco, Simply Southern, Wills & Ratio, Woodland Scenics and more.

Open 9-5 Tuesday – Saturday
7pm Close on Friday Nights

www.traintimesmodelshop.co.uk
traintimestoo@gmail.com - 01323 722026

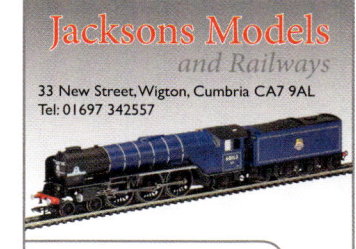

Jacksons Models
and Railways

33 New Street, Wigton, Cumbria CA7 9AL
Tel: 01697 342557

- TRUCKS • CARS • PLANT
- KITS • PLANES • MILITARY
- RAILWAY • BUSES

Stocking Model Railways by Hornby, Bachmann, Farish, Peco, Dapol, Metcalfe, Corgi, Oxford etc. Railway Scenery by Gaugemaster, Woodland Scenics, Javis, Expo etc.

Shop opening hours: Monday - Friday 9am - 5pm; Saturday 10am - 3pm; Closed Sunday and Wednesday; Late night opening Thursday until 7pm

www.jacksonsmodels.co.uk

MORRIS MODELS
NORTH LANCING

80 Manor Road, N Lancing,
West Sussex, BN15 0HD
Tel 01903 754850
www.morris-models..co.uk
info@morrismodels.co.uk

We are between Brighton & Worthing, just off A27 west of Shoreham Airport

BRITISH RAILWAYS
HORNBY, GRAHAM FARISH, PECO, dapol, REDAN
PLUS MANY OTHER RANGES OF SCENIC MATERIALS, BUILDINGS, VEHICLES etc

BICYC-LED
OO/HO & N Cycles & M/cycles with working lights!!
See our webshop for details
Easy free parking!!
Open Mon – Sat
9.30 to 5.00

CONTINENTAL RAILWAYS
FLEISCHMANN, Roco, BRAWA, TRIX, herpa, FALLER, Preiser, BUSCH, NOCH, MINITRAINS

Blackwells Of Hawkwell
Miniatures Specialists
01702 200 036 or 01702 204 210 Sales@blackwells-miniatures.com

Heki Tree's & Scenics
www.blackwells-miniatures.com

Make your layout stand out with Heki Trees & Scenic Materials
Quality at affordable prices

Order Online or just call to find out about the Biggest and Best range of Scenics on the market today.

Heki 2015 Catalogue £6.85 post paid

P.O.Box 2099, Hockley, Essex. SS5 4UY
Tel 01702 200036 e mail sales@blackwells-miniatures.com

Trade Supplied

OSBORNS MODELS
📞 01237 423453

LASER CUT — N GAUGE
EXETER CENTRAL

7 HONESTONE ST, BIDEFORD, N. DEVON, EX39 2DL
WWW.OSBORNSMODELS.COM

CARD KITS FROM THE CARD MODELLING SPECIALISTS
Manufacturers, distributors and retailers of top quality card kits and scenic background sheets at best-value prices
For value, accuracy, and hours of modelling pleasure, card modelling is a sure winner, with plenty to choose from to suit all tastes and modelling standards.

PROTOTYPE MODELS — Victorian Bridge kit
ModelYard
Mainstreet Models
HOWARD SCENICS
TOWNSCENE — BACKGROUNDS OF DISTINCTION
BILT-EEZI
ALPHAGRAPHIX
SUPERQUICK
PLUS: Materials & tools

FREESTONE MODEL ACCESSORIES
Mail Order & Exhibitions
Access / VISA

Tel: 01993 775979
www.freestonemodel.co.uk
e: sales@freestonemodel.co.uk

ADM TURNTABLES – INDEXING DRIVE SYSTEMS

- W www.admturntables.co.uk
- T 01933 411127
- E alastair@admturntables.co.uk

'One of the best quality turntable drive units currently on the market'
BRM Magazine

ADM Indexing Drive Systems for 'N' and 'OO' gauge layouts**
- Based on a commercially available turntable uniquely having the bridge live through 360 degrees, preventing breaks in sound equipped locos
- Is a quiet running system, driven by a toothed belt; powered by a stepper motor with up to 100 programmable indexing positions which we think makes it the ultimate 'indexing' turntable solution

** drive systems also available for other sized layouts

For more information please take a look at our website
www.admturntables.co.uk

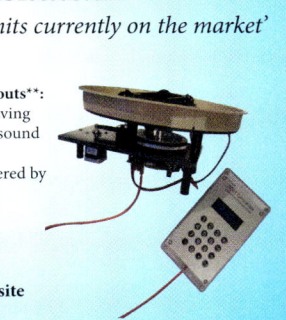

GEE DEE MODELS - NOTTINGHAM
HORNBY LOCO OFFERS

Ref	Description	Price	Ref	Description	Price
R3222	Great Western 42xx 2-8-0 4261	£110.95	R3225	GWR 72xx 2-8-2T 7233	£118.95
R3206	A1 Tornado B.R. Blue	£110.95	R3240A	B.R. K1 Black L/Crest 62027	£120.95
R3229	B.R.(W) Star Class 'British Monarch'	£127.95	R3224	B.R. 42xx 2-8-0T L/crest 5239	£107.95
R3098	A1 Tornado B.R. Green	£112.95	R3305	B.R. K1 Black E/Crest 62059 wthd	£120.95
R3205	B.R.(W) Rood Ashton Hall L/C	£113.95	R3244TTS	Duke of Gloucester TTS Sound	£139.95
R3202	B.R. A3 Flying Scotsman Wthd Grn	£143.95	R3189	LNER L1 2-6-4T Green 9003	£116.95
R3106	GWR 28xx 2-8-0 2807	£139.95	R3194	B.R. Schools 'Epsom' Black E/C	£125.96
R3131	LNER A4 'Great Snipe' Garter Blue	£135.95	R3245TTS	Blue A1 Tornado TTS Sound	£143.95
R3005	B.R.(W) 28xx 2845 weathered	£130.95	R3208	B.R. Schools 'Brighton' Black E/C	£129.95
R3114	B.R. B1 4-6-0 61270 L/Crest	£120.95	R3231	B.R ex GE j15 0-6-0 65356 E/Crest	£98.95
R2916	GWR 28xx 2-8-0 2812 Shirtbutton	£111.95	R2829X	Southern T9 314 Black DCC Fitted	£105.95
R3242	B.R. K1 Black E/Crest 62015	£120.95	R3232	B.R ex GE j15 0-6-0 65445 L/Crest	£98.95

Many other loco's in stock both current & discontinued. Give us a ring for your wanted items
All above prices include VAT. Post £6.00 UK mainland only. Offshore and Overseas at cost.

GEE DEE MODELS - NOTTINGHAM HORNBY COLLECTOR CENTRE
21 HEATHCOAT STREET, NOTTINGHAM. NG1 3AF

www.geedee-modelshop.com   Tel. 0115 9412211

Why not visit the shop with possibly Hampshire's largest stock of model railways, die-cast, books, magazines, scalextric, second hand and much more all under one roof.

DCC equipment from DCC Concepts, ESU, Gaugemaster, Hornby and Bachmann.
Sound decoders from South West Digital

Full range of model railway products from the leading manufacturers including:

Hornby, Bachmann, Graham Farish, Heljan, Peco, Dapol,
Wills, Superquick, Metcalfe, Gaugemaster, DJH
Parkside, South Eastern Finecast, Woodland Scenics and many, many more.

Also stockists of Die cast models including:
Corgi, EFE, Oxford Die-Cast, Base Toys & Classix.

Modelling materials & tools

Wide selection of books, DVDs, videos and magazines

7A Normandy Street, Alton, Hants GU34 1DD
Tel: 01420 542244
altonmodelcentre.co.uk

ALTON MODEL CENTRE

Monday: Closed
Tuesday to Saturday: 9.00am to 5.00pm
Sunday : see website / call

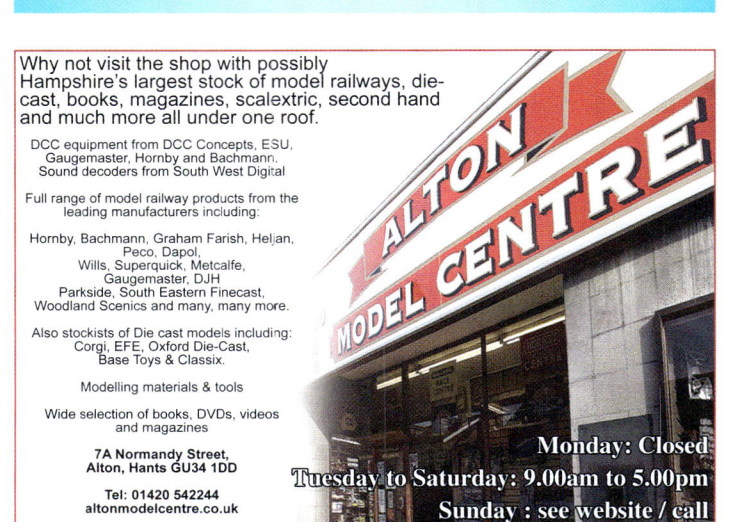

MAD ABOUT TRAINS OF GAINSBOROUGH (K&M MODELS)

For all your Model Railway needs from design to finished layout, scratch built buildings, trees dioramas etc. We carry a vast selection of scenic materials. We carry a comprehensive range of all aspects of Railway Modeling from track pins to finished layouts. DCC Specialist, repairs, weathering etc undertaken in our own workshop.
Hornby, Bachmann, Peco Gaugemaster, Dapol and Knightwing stockists. Large range of scenic materials
We are always looking for second hand collections.
Just give us a call or come and visit our shop.

Tel: 01427 811040
Mobile 07858612716
106 Trinity Street, Gainsborough DN21 1HS
e-mail: sales@madabouttrains.co.uk
www.madabouttrains.co.uk

Model Rail Baseboards

Find us on Facebook

Manufacturers of modular baseboard systems.
Custom made baseboards, helices, storage systems, control panels.
Complete layout service also available.
For more information and to see our gallery go to

www.modelrailbaseboards.com
sales@modelrailbaseboards.com
Tel: 0035387 6555052

MODEL RAILWAY SOLUTIONS

Tel: 01202 798068
Email: info@modelrailwaysolutions.co.uk

Contact us for a quote on all your baseboard and helix requirements, either bespoke or from our own modular range.

Please take a moment to browse our online store or visit us at -
Unit 1, 10-12 Alder Hills, Poole. Dorset. BH12 4AL.

www.modelrailwaysolutions.co.uk

MODEL MASTERS
The Inspirational Model Railway Centre

BACHMANN BRANCH-LINE · METCALFE · GRAHAM FARISH · PECO
DAPOL · BUSCH · HARBURN HOBBIES · HORNBY INTERNATIONAL

NOT Just a model shop for all these products but we also do

- Mail Order • On Line Store • Service and Repairs • Gift Vouchers • Consultancy Service and Advice • Layout Design and Building Service*
- Wiring and Scenics in House and On Site*
Also large stockists of Continental items

Regardless of size or price, to customer's requirements

Why not visit us soon whilst on holiday or passing. With new stocks now arriving and working displays, we are sure you will find some inspiration.

INTERNATIONAL HOUSE, CLIFTON ROAD, WESTON-SUPER-MARE, SOMERSET BS23 1BW
Monday-Saturday 9.00am-5.00pm
Tel: 01934 629717 Email: sales@modelmasters.co.uk
www.modelmasters.co.uk

Model Scenery Supplies

An internet based shop supplying hundreds of items you need to build realistic terrains and landscapes. With fast, reasonably priced postage.
Take a look...

www.modelscenerysupplies.co.uk

Scatter - Grass - Foliage - Trees - Bushes - Turf - Tufts - Plants
Buildings - Figures - Animals - kits - Base Boards - Accessories

We Specialise in N gauge and OO scale, supplying quality, interesting products to enhance and complement the railway scene.

15 North Norfolk Business Centre, Northrepps, Cromer, Norfolk NR27 9RQ

SOUTH EASTERN FINECAST

S.E.C.R. / S.R. / B.R. Wainwright 'H' Class

NEW SECR LOCOMOTIVE TRANFERS and LINING 4mm SCALE
Range of VAC-formed Building Sheets - 4mm, 7mm & 10mm Scales.
English, Flemish and Plain Bond Brickwork available, sheet size 14" x 9"
1/24, 1/43 CAR KITS, 1/32 STEAM TRACTION ENGINE KITS, 4mm LOCOMOTIVE KITS
Full catalogue £3.50 UK, £5.00 Overseas
S.A.E price list only
GLENN HOUSE, HARTFIELD ROAD, FOREST ROW, EAST SUSSEX RH18 5DZ
Tel: 01342 824711 Fax: 01342 822270
Website: www.sefinecast.co.uk

MONK BAR model shop

Find us by Monk Bar
2 Goodramgate
York YO1 7LQ
Tel. 01904 659423
info@monkbarmodelshop.co.uk

Model Railways - Diecast Planes & Vehicles
Plastic Kits & Figures - Scalextric - Jigsaws

Open
Monday - Saturday
9am - 5.30pm
Only 2 minutes
from York Minster

Large selection of
OO & N Gauge

Stockists of Hornby, Bachmann, Peco, Dapol, Gaugemaster, Ratio, Wills
Woodland Scenics, Metcalfe, Oxford Diecasts, Base Toys and many more

www.collectable-models.co.uk

GAS CUPBOARD MODELS — MODEL RAILWAYS

www.gascupboard.co.uk

#1 Fisherman

There are many stranger hobbies than ours...

Gas Cupboard Models
6 St Georges Works, Silver Street,
TROWBRIDGE. BA14 8AA

01225 777888

LIMITED EDITION
Dapol OO Gunpowder Van
Wakefield & Co, Milnthorpe

Crafty Hobbies
01229 820759
www.crafty-hobbies.co.uk

54 Cavendish Street, Barrow-in-Furness,
Cumbria LA14 1PZ

Another Delightful Model At
C&M Models

**N GAUGE SCOTRAIL
'SALTIRE' 156 £109.95**

EXCLUSIVE TO C&M MODELS

1 Crosby Street, Carlisle CA1 1DQ
Tel: 01228 514689
e-mail: sales@candmmodels.co.uk
Website: www.candmmodels.co.uk
Tuesday to Saturday: 10a.m. to 5p.m.
Sorry, but Fay is no longer available

4mm Scale Kits

Code	Description	Price
RC416	LNER/BR Dia 120 4w Gresley 4w full brake BY (1928 to 1970s)	£9.00
RC436	LMS Dia 2115 6T Express Fish van	£9.00
RC442	LNER/BR Loco Coal Wagon (1939-1960's)	£7.50
RC443	BR/GWR Tunny Ballast Wagon Dia P23 (1947-1980's)	£7.50
RC444	SR/BR 20T Ballast Wagon Lamprey (new doors) (1979 to 1990s)	£7.50
RC445	SR/BR 20T Ballast Wagon Crab (1983 to 1990s)	£7.50
RC446	SR/BR 20T Ballast Wagon Lamprey dia1/570 (1951 to 1990s)	£7.50
RC447	SR/BR 20T 2 door Mineral Wagon dia 1386 (1928 to 1960s)	£7.50
RC448	SR/BR 20T Ballast Wagon Tunny dia 1771 (1928 to 1990s)	£7.50
RC449	SR/BR 15T Ballast Wagon Ling dia 1773 (1928 to 1990s)	£7.50
RC463	LMS/BR 27ft Long Low Wagon dia 2069 (1942 to 1960s)	£7.50
RC464	LMS Double Bolster Dia 1674 (1925 to 1960s)	£7.50
RC465	LMS/BR 27ft Tube Wagon dia 1675 (1933 to 1970s)	£7.50
RC473	BR Dia 1/120 MDV 21T Mineral Wagon (1961-1990's)	£7.50

Our kits are injection moulded plastic with cast whitemetal minor parts and designed for standard 26mm axles. Included is a coupler mounting block for Bachmann 36027 Mark 2 Couplings. Wheels are not included. Allow plenty of time for delivery because they are very popular.

www.slimrails.co.uk P&P £3.00 per order Tel: 01772 436829

Slimrails, 51 Mendip Road, Leyland, Lancashire, PR2 5UJ

Chivers Finelines by Slimrails

N Gauge kits

- RC1052 ZCA Seahorse open
- RC1073 OTA Timber wagon
- RC1068 OCA Open wagon
- RC906 LNER Extra long CCT
- RC910 SR CCT utility van plank
- RC960 BR tube wagon
- RC962 GWR Open C
- RC963 LMS Long Low
- RC964 LMS (BR) Bolster
- RC965 LMS Tube wagon
- RC966 Blue spot fish van
- RC967 GWR Python
- RC991 LNER Horse box

All £7.50 each
All require wheels and couplings

MP Middleton Press
EVOLVING THE ULTIMATE RAIL ENCYCLOPEDIA

Published 26 September

BOSTON TO LINCOLN
Including
Horncastle to Louth
£18.95 P&P free (UK) MAIL ORDER

Recently Published
WOLVERHAMPTON TO STAFFORD

www.middletonpress.co.uk
Easebourne Lane, Midhurst. GU29 9AZ
T: 01730 813169 E: sales@middletonpress.co.uk

Please visit our website or telephone for a brochure

ITEMS MAIL ORDER LTD

MAYFIELD, MARSH LANE, SAUNDBY, RETFORD, NOTTS, DN22 9ES

Tel/Fax: 01427 848880

BA SCREWS IN BRASS, STEEL AND STAINLESS. SOCKET SCREWS IN STEEL AND STAINLESS. DRILLS, RIVETS, TAPS, DIES, END MILLS, SLOT DRILLS ETC

BRASS CHEESE SCREWS FROM £2.32/100
BRASS ROUND SCREWS FROM £3.85/100
BRASS CSK SCREWS FROM £4.67/100
SOCKET GRUB SCREWS FROM £1.72/10
STANDARD PACK SIZES 10, 25, 50 AND 100

Special Offer
BRASS CHEESE 12 BA X 7/16" £5.96/100

PHONE FOR FREE LIST

TRAIN TERRAIN
'Specialist Model Shop'
Open: Tues-Sat 10.00am til 3.30pm
European & American Model Railway & Scenery Specialists

We custom build layouts and dioramas to order

We can supply many product ranges including:
Faller • Minitrains • Roco • Inspirescene
Noch • Busch • Acme • Woodland Scenics
Auhagen • Kibri • Vollmer • Oxford • Kato
Bachmann American inc. On30 • Joefix • PIKO
Athearn • Lilliput • Walthers • Tillig • Proses
Gaugemaster • Albion

Workshop & Retail Area
199 Plumstead Road, Norwich, NR1 4AB
'Upstairs at Great Eastern Model Railways'
Trade Enquiries Welcome Telephone: 01603 304379
Email: info@trainterrainmodels.co.uk
www.trainterrainmodels.co.uk

MODELMANIA of BRISTOL

13 CLOUDS HILL ROAD, ST. GEORGE, BRISTOL BS5 7LD

*Junction of A420/A43
(St. George Fountain)
Buses 42 or 43
from City Centre*

BACHMANN • DAPOL • GAUGEMASTER
GRAHAM FARISH • HORNBY • KESTREL • METCALFE
PECO • RATIO • SUPERQUICK • WILLS
WOODLAND SCENICS • RAILMATCH PAINTS
MODELMASTERS TRANSFERS
CAMBRIAN WAGON KITS EFE CORGI
CLASSIX AND OXFORD DIECAST 1:76TH

MAIL ORDER SERVICE - *SORRY NO LISTS*
Open: Tuesday to Friday   9.30 to 17.00
               Saturday   9.00 to 17.00
Tel: **0117 9559819**
Email: modelmaniaemail@aol.com
Ebay Shop: modelmaniabristol

Wellingborough Trains & Models

We are now an outlet of Golden Valley Hobbies

Stockists of:
Bachmann, Hornby, Peco,
Gaugemaster, Humbrol, Airfix,
Fisher-Price Trackmaster,
Woodland Scenics, Expo and many more

Childrens craft corner

Wellingborough Trains and Models
17 Market Street, Wellingborough,
Northamptonshire NN8 1AN
Tel: 01933 274069
Email: trainsandmodels@gmail.com
Web: www.trainsandmodel.com

OPENING HOURS:
Tues, Weds & Thurs 9.30am - 3pm
Sat 9am - 5pm Other times are available by appointment only, please call to arrange

PENDUKE
MODELS & SCENICS

- Printed Backgrounds, Building Materials etc.
- Grass, Flocks, Scatters & Coal
- Litchen & Moss
- Hand Painted Figures & Models
- Model Railway Accessories
- Tools including Static Grass Applicators

www.pendukemodels.co.uk
Safe & Secure Online Ordering, or call us on 0777 552 6112

PAY SAFELY WITH PayPal

Scenics in use on *Starlingford* layout by Gavin Browne

NICK TOZER
RAILWAY BOOKS

RAILWAY BOOKS BOUGHT & SOLD

Free Railway Booksearch Service

155 Church Street, Paddock,
Huddersfield, HD1 4UJ
Shop now open: Tue/Wed/Sat
(non-show dates) 11:00-17:00
+ Thu 14:00-20:00
Tel: 01484 518159 (answer machine)

www.railwaybook.com
email: nick@railwaybook.com

P & D Marsh

Kits, ready painted models and laser cut buildings in N and OO gauge. Selection below:

PAINTED & FINISHED MODELS

	N	OO
Postman, bike & postboxes	£7.60	£8.00
Loco crew (2)	£7.60	£8.00
Belishas, bus stop & post box	£7.60	£7.50
Window cleaner with ladder	£7.60	£6.50
1950's motorbike & rider	£5.50	£7.50
Coalmen & scales	£7.60	£7.50
Benches (4)	£5.80	£6.75
Firebuckets on stand (2)	£6.50	£6.75
Lawnmower, wheelbarrow etc	£7.60	£6.75
Men riding bikes (2)	£7.60	£7.50
Bikes (4)	£7.35	£7.50
Trackside signs (4)	£6.85	£7.50
1950's AA motorcycle patrol	£7.60	£11.95
GWR Home signal	£7.60	£11.00
GWR junction signal LH or RH	£14.50	£18.95

The Stables, Wakes End Farm, MK17 9FB
Tel: 01525 280068
www.pdmarshmodels.com

Tri-angman
specialist in model railways

Tri-ang, Hornby, Wrenn, Bachmann, Minic etc...
buy, sell & repair hard to find items and collectables

Find me on
www.tri-angman.co.uk
or contact:
Tel 07966 333605
laurence@tri-angman.co.uk

Dereks Transport Books
www.derekstransportbooks.com
dereksbooks@btinternet.com
All transport subjects covered
Established 1995 Ringwood

HASLINGTON MODELS
134 Crewe Road, Haslington, Crewe CW1 5RQ
Telephone/Fax 01270 589079
email: haslingtonmodels@live.co.uk

Appointed Stockists of
Bachmann, Farish, Hornby, Peco,
Gaugemaster, Dapol, Vi-Trains, Heljan,
Humbrol, etc etc.
• FREE Parking
OPEN THURS, FRI & SAT ONLY 10.00-16.00

SouthWest digital
Distributor for the UK
ESU Trade welcome

As real as it gets!
Photos: Chris Perkins

ALL products come with a 2 year warranty and FREE return postage

Close your eyes and you're there!

UDRIVE
responsive sound algorithm
The highest quality sounds in all gauges. A wide range of responsive steam and diesel sounds developed for the all new UDRIVE

Crystal clear digital sound

Test drive the latest loco sounds with stunning clarity at SWD – call now for more info

T: 01934 515382 info@swd4esu.co.uk
www.southwestdigital.co.uk

Platform Models

PLATFORM MODELS

Model Railway items both new and second-hand
Also baseboards supplied by Model Railway Solutions

All prices 10% below RRP

We offer a large range of loco's, train sets, coaches, wagons, track, buildings, accessories, kits, vehicles, figures and animals, scenery, tools and glues & paints for both OO Gauge and N Gauge. There is a great range of DCC & electrical stock, including Digitrax dcc systems. All prices are 10% below the RRP and there is plenty of free parking right outside. We also have a second hand section where you can buy items that may be harder to get hold of now-a-days or if you are after a bargain.

Free parking
Opening Hours: Mon-Sat 10-5

10-12 Alder Hills, Poole, Dorset BH12 4AL
Tel: 01202 798068
or shop online at:
www.platformmodelsltd.co.uk

3mm Scale Model Railways
4 Greenwood Drive, Redhill, Surrey, RH1 5PJ. Tel: 01737 761919
40 Page Full Colour Catalogue £4.50
Catering exclusively for TT and 3mm Scale
www.3smr.co.uk
BlackBeetle, BullAnt, Halling, Tenshodo
www.motorbogies.com

CAPTURE THE MAGIC OF IRISH RAILWAYS with ALPHAGRAPHIX
Etched brass locomotive & carriage kits in 7mm scale
Plus full supporting range of Card construction kits for Railway & Street buildings
Send 6x 2nd Class Stamps for CATALOGUE
23 Darris Road, Selly Park, Birmingham B29 7QY

BILL HUDSON BOOKS
Please visit our totally revamped site.
Now with secure online ordering!
www.billhudsontransportbooks.co.uk
Tel/Fax: 01629 580797
Please visit: Matlock Station, Station Yard, Matlock DE4 3NA

DURHAM TRAINS OF STANLEY
MORE THAN JUST A MODEL SHOP
WE STOCK ALL MAJOR BRITISH OUTLINE ROLLING STOCK AND SCENICS AS WELL AS OXFORD DIECAST. WE ALSO OFFER A CHIP FITTING SERVICE RTO READY AND HOME DCC READY LOCOS AND SERVICE MOST MAKES OF LOCOS. JUST CLICK ON OUR WEBSITE FOR MORE INFORMATION. WE ALSO HAVE OVER 3000 ITEMS FOR SALE ONLINE.
6 STATION ROAD, STANLEY, CO.DURHAM, DH8 0JL
SHOP OPEN MON-TUES-FRI-SAT OPEN 0930-1700 • THURS 1100-1900 • CLOSED WEDNESDAY AND SUNDAY
TEL: 01207 232545 • www.durhamtrainsofstanley.co.uk • email: sales@durhamtrainsofstanley.co.uk

JOHN DUTFIELD LLP
Gift Vouchers available
Stockists of many brands inc Bachmann, Hornby, Graham Farish, Dapol, Gaugemaster and Peco.
Secondhand bought and sold.
Selection of kits, glues, tools, paints and accessories.
Wards Yard, 133 Springfield Park Road
(at the junction with Hill Road) Chelmsford CM2 6EE
TEL: 01245 494455. EMAIL: heatherwilkinson@btconnect.com
www.johndutfieldmodelrailways.co.uk
OPENING HOURS: 9.00am-5.30pm Mon, Tues, Thurs, Fri and Saturday Closed Wed, Sun & Bank Holidays All major credit/debit cards accepted.

MANKIM MODELS
213 Shrub End Road, Colchester, Essex CO3 4RN
Tel: 01206 574929
NEW & SECONDHAND DIECAST & RAILWAYS
Major Credit Cards Accepted
Sorry no lists
Ample Parking
HORNBY - PECO
BACHMANN - FARISH
CORGI - OXFORD
EFE - AIRFIX etc
NEW & SECONDHAND RAILWAYS & DIECAST
WARHAMMER
Scalextric

Millennium Models
Hornby, Bachmann, Peco and more.
New and Secondhand stock
Jarvis, Dapol, Metcalfe, Corgi, Oxford
67 Queen Street, Morley, Leeds LS27 8EB
Tel: 0113 2189286 www.milllennium-models.co.uk

Pooleys Puffers
Model Railway Supplies, New & Second Hand Bought & Sold
Proprietor DAVID POOLE
Diecast Models Kits & Accessories
382a Jedburgh Court, Team Valley Trading Estate, Gateshead, Tyne & Wear. NE11 0BQ
Mon - Thurs - 10am - 5pm. Fri - Sat & Bank holidays please telephone for opening times. Sunday Closed
Tele: 0191 4910202/4106386 Mobile: 07976 519178
www.pooleyspuffers.com e-mail: pooleyspuffers@btopenworld.com

Stevenson Carriages & Millholme Models
4mm Coach Kits in LMS TPOs, LNWR, Midland & LY.
Millhome Loco Kits now available
MM14 Stirling Single No 1 • MM18 Furness Railway D5
MM23 Hull & Barnsley J28 • MM24 Maryport & Carlisle
Order kits & lists by phone 01246 863579
or by email pbarker265@btinternet.com

TRIDENT TRAINS
No10, The Craft Arcade
Dagfields Craft Centre,
Crewe Road, Walgherton, Nantwich,
Cheshire. CW5 7LG
www.tridenttrains.co.uk
HORNBY-BACHMANN-HELJAN-FARISH DAPOL-PECO-LENZ-TCS-GAUGEMASTER-METCALFE-RATIO+MUCH MORE
01270 842400

TUTBURY MODELS
COLLECTABLES 01283 814777 MODELS
UNIT 9, TUTBURY MILL MEWS, TUTBURY, Nr. BURTON-UPON-TRENT DE13 9LS
BASS/WORTHINGTON VENT VAN.................£12.50 (plus £2.80 p&p for either one or two)
6-WHEEL MILK TANK NESTLÉ 'OO' GAUGE......£17.50 (plus £2.80 p&p for either one or two)
BASS/WORTHINGTON GRAIN HOPPER..........£13.75 (plus £2.80 p&p for either one or two)

Visiting the Isle of Wight?
UPSTAIRS DOWNSTAIRS
Pier Street - Sandown
PO36 8JR
Two floors of locomotives, wagons, coaches, buildings, scenery, electrics, figures, cars and more!
ALL BRANDS N-OO9-HO OO-On30-G
01 983 406 616 - www.trainshop.co.uk

Waddell's Models
0141 552 8044
56 Bell Street, Merchant City,
Glasgow, Lanarkshire G1 1LQ
Open for Modelling Advice, Service & Repairs, DCC Decoder Fitting and Limited Edition Models selling all scales and gauges including 2mm, 4mm, N, OO
We stock: Bachmann * Dapol * Farish * Heljan * Hornby * Peco * and many more...

THE HOBBY BOX
121 High St, Uckfield TN22 1RN Tel: 01825 765296
www.thehobbybox.co.uk
Bachmann | Carrs | C&L | Cambrian | Cooper Craft | Dapol | Eckon | Evergreen | Expo | Farish Gaugemaster | Heljan | Hornby | K&M | Kadee | Kestrel | Knightwing | Lenz | P.D. Marsh | Metcalfe | Noch Parkside | Peco | Plastruct | Railmatch | Ratio | Romford | Seep | Slaters | Smiths | Springside | Southern Pride Superquick | SE Finecast | SMP | Tiny Signs | Wills | Woodland Scenics Etc.
Open: Tue-Fri 10am-5.30pm, Sat 9.30am-5pm

THE MODEL RAILWAY SHOP
• Unique and Generous Part-Exchange Service – Honest Prices Paid on your Exchange Goods
• Free Servicing – Only Parts Chargeable
• Stockists of New, Used, Hard to Find and Unusual Items
30 Station Lane, Featherstone,
Ponteract, West Yorkshire, WF7 5BE
01977 706730/07940 368316
modelrailwayshop@hotmail.com

Aspire Gifts & Models
OPENING TIMES: Mon 2pm-5pm Tues, Wed, Thurs 10am-5pm
Suppliers of all Major Railway Brands, We Chip, Service and Repair Engines.
Layouts built from Track to finished Item.
THOUSAND'S OF ITEMS AVAILABLE ON OUR WEBSITE   CREDIT CARDS WELCOME
Unit 4. Court Farm Business Park, Buckland Newton.Dorset. DT2 7BT Telephone: 01300 345355
email:edward.aspire@btinternet.com   Website:www.aspiregiftsandmodels.co.uk